General Richard Montgomery
and the American Revolution

The American Social Experience
SERIES

General Editor:
JAMES KIRBY MARTIN

Editors:
PAULA S. FASS, STEVEN H. MINTZ, CARL PRINCE,
JAMES W. REED & PETER N. STEARNS

1. The March to the Sea and Beyond: Sherman's Troops in
the Savannah and Carolinas Campaigns
JOSEPH T. GLATTHAAR

2. Childbearing in American Society: 1650–1850
CATHERINE M. SCHOLTEN

3. The Origins of Behaviorism: American Psychology, 1870–1920
JOHN M. O'DONNELL

4. New York City Cartmen, 1667–1850
GRAHAM RUSSELL HODGES

5. From Equal Suffrage to Equal Rights: Alice Paul and
the National Woman's Party, 1910–1928
CHRISTINE A. LUNARDINI

6. Mr. Jefferson's Army: Political and Social Reform
of the Military Establishment, 1801–1809
THEODORE J. CRACKEL

7. "A Peculiar People": Slave Religion and Community-
Culture among the Gullahs
MARGARET WASHINGTON CREEL

8. "A Mixed Multitude": The Struggle for Toleration
in Colonial Pennsylvania
SALLY SCHWARTZ

9. Women, Work, and Fertility, 1900–1986
SUSAN HOUSEHOLDER VAN HORN

10. Liberty, Virtue, and Progress: Northerners and
Their War for the Union
EARL J. HESS

11. Lewis M. Terman: Pioneer in Psychological Testing
HENRY L. MINTON

12. Schools as Sorters: Lewis M. Terman, Applied Psychology, and the Intelligence Testing Movement, 1890–1930
PAUL DAVIS CHAPMAN

13. Free Love: Marriage and Middle-Class Radicalism in America, 1825–1860
JOHN C. SPURLOCK

14. Jealousy: The Evolution of an Emotion in American History
PETER N. STEARNS

15. The Nurturing Neighborhood: The Brownsville Boys Club and Jewish Community in Urban America, 1940–1990
GERALD SORIN

16. War in America to 1775: Before Yankee Doodle
JOHN MORGAN DEDERER

17. An American Vision: Far Western Landscape and National Culture, 1820–1920
ANNE FARRAR HYDE

18. Frederick Law Olmsted: The Passion of a Public Artist
MELVIN KALFUS

19. Medical Malpractice in Nineteenth-Century America: Origins and Legacy
KENNETH ALLEN DE VILLE

20. Dancing in Chains: The Youth of William Dean Howells
RODNEY D. OLSEN

21. Breaking the Bonds: Marital Discord in Pennsylvania, 1730–1830
MERRIL D. SMITH

22. In the Web of Class: Delinquents and Reformers in Boston, 1810s–1830s
ERIC C. SCHNEIDER

23. Army of Manifest Destiny: The American Soldier in the Mexican War, 1846–1848
JAMES M. MCCAFFREY

24. The Dutch-American Farm
DAVID STEVEN COHEN

25. Independent Intellectuals in the United States, 1910–1945
STEVEN BIEL

26. The Modern Christmas in America: A Cultural History of Gift Giving
WILLIAM B. WAITS

27. The First Sexual Revolution: The Emergence of Male Heterosexuality in Modern America
KEVIN WHITE

*28. Bad Habits: Drinking, Smoking, Taking Drugs, Gambling,
Sexual Misbehavior, and Swearing in American History*
JOHN C. BURNHAM

*29. General Richard Montgomery and the American Revolution:
From Redcoat to Rebel*
HAL T. SHELTON

Richard Montgomery, portrait engraved by E. Mackenzie from the
original oil by C. W. Peale. Courtesy of the New-York Historical
Society, New York, N.Y.

General Richard Montgomery
and the American Revolution

From Redcoat to Rebel

HAL T. SHELTON

NEW YORK UNIVERSITY PRESS
New York and London

NEW YORK UNIVERSITY PRESS
New York and London

Library of Congress Cataloging-in-Publication Data
Shelton, Hal T. (Hal Terry), 1935-
    General Richard Montgomery and the American revolution : from
redcoat to rebel / Hal T. Shelton.
        p.   cm. -- (The American social experience series ; 29)
    Includes bibliographical references and index.
    ISBN 0-8147-7975-1
    1. Montgomery, Richard, 1738-1775.   2. Generals--United States-
-Biography.   3. United States.   Continental Army--Biography.
4. Canadian Invasion, 1775-1776.   I. Title.   II. Series.
E207.M7S48   1994
973.3'092--dc20
[B]   93-30767
              CIP

Manufactured in the United States of America

10   9   8   7   6   5   4   3   2

To the memory of my late father,
William Oble Shelton — my first mentor,
and one who serves as my continuing reference point.

Contents

	Acknowledgments	xiii
ONE	*Introduction*	1
TWO	*Ancestry and Early Life*	8
THREE	*Duty in the Seven Years' War*	17
FOUR	*Decision for the Patriot Cause*	35
FIVE	*Service in the Provincial Congress*	51
SIX	*The Patriot Call to Arms*	65
SEVEN	*The March to Canada*	79
EIGHT	*Struggle and Success against St. Johns*	97
NINE	*On to Quebec*	116
TEN	*Attack on Quebec*	133
ELEVEN	*Aftermath of Quebec*	151
TWELVE	*Epilogue*	172
	Appendixes	183
	Notes	189
	Bibliography	227
	Index	239

Acknowledgments

Like all authors, I amassed a tremendous debt of gratitude during the production of this volume. The many persons who contributed to the fulfillment of this work are too numerous to individually credit here. However, some deserve singular recognition.

This book grew out of my doctoral dissertation, completed at the University of Houston. All historians are products of their education and teachers. Thus, an acknowledgment of the most influential individuals who helped me mold my career is in order. First and foremost, I would like to thank my academic advisor and friend, James Kirby Martin, Professor of History, University of Houston, who gave unstintingly of his time and expertise to inspire and motivate me in this effort. While I was his student and graduate assistant, he demonstrated to me the attributes of a true scholar—devoted to teaching, research, and writing. I consider myself extremely fortunate to have become associated with him and reaped the benefits of his knowledge and guidance. He will always stand in my estimation as the epitome of an educator and someone whom I aspire to emulate. A special word of appreciation also goes to Joseph Glatthaar, Chair, Department of History, University of Houston, who materially contributed to my endeavor through his renowned scholarship in military history.

This work could not have been written without access to the document collections of various research institutions and archives. The David Library of the American Revolution serves as the only depository and facility dedicated exclusively to this period of American history. I am greatly indebted to its President and Director, Ezra Stone, and its Director of Research, David J. Fowler, for their personal and professional association and the use of their fine resource center. The archival staffs at the New York Public Library, New-York Historical Society, and Princeton University Library were extremely competent and helpful in making available pertinent materials in their possession.

Funding played a significant role in bringing this book to fruition. I would like to express my gratitude to the University of Houston for the Robert Giesberg Award for Outstanding Teaching Fellow (1988), the Murry A. Miller Graduate Student Scholarship (1988–89), and the Graduate Student Research and Activity Scholarship (1989); and to the David Library of the American Revolution for its research grant (1988).

New York University Press served as the midwife of the manuscript. The finished product is due to the outstanding skill of its highly professional staff: Colin Jones, Director; Niko Pfund, Editor-in-Chief; Despina Papazoglou Gimbel, Managing Editor; and Jennifer Hammer, Assistant Editor. All patiently worked with me to convert my rough drafts into a comprehensible and publishable work.

Finally, I wish to thank my family—Myrtle Lynn Shelton, mother; Sutthida (Toi) Shelton, wife; Shane Shelton, son; Scott and Darla Shelton, son and daughter-in-law; Sheila and Derek Matthys, daughter and son-in-law—for their understanding and support. A writer's task is sometimes a solitary one. These loved ones endured abandonment on many occasions in allowing me the time to complete my work.

General Richard Montgomery
and the American Revolution

Introduction

Brief, brave, and glorious was his young career,—
His mourners were two hosts—his friends and foes;
And fitly may the stranger, lingering here
Pray for his gallant spirit's bright repose;
For he was Freedom's champion, one of those,
The few in number, who had not o'erstept
The charter to chastise which she bestows
On such as wield her weapon; he had kept
The whiteness of his soul, and thus men o'er him wept[1]

A t 3 A.M. on December 31, 1775, a band of desperate men stumbled forward in the middle of a dark night and during the worst of a Canadian winter storm. In the midst of gale-driven snow and sleet, the men's labored breathing soon covered their faces with ice. The torturous weather caused physical pain and a numbness of the senses. They trudged along a narrow, jumbled path that followed the river lying below. A careless step could plunge a hapless individual onto the frozen stream that lay to one side of the slippery trail. Any rational being would have sought immediate relief from the hostile elements, but the leader to whom this group was committed exhorted them beyond individual concerns for comfort or safety.[2]

A mixture of New Yorkers and New Englanders, the members of this command joined the Continental army with short-term enlistments, many of which were due to expire in less than twenty-four hours. Although the military expedition had captured Fort Chambly, Fort St. Johns, and Montreal in recent encounters, rapid personnel turnover caused the unit to remain largely unseasoned. Most of the soldiers maintained a cavalier attitude toward military duty, disdaining martial discipline and regimen. They were also sectionalists, highly distrustful of anyone who came from outside their home region. This situation presented a great challenge to their leader. He most recently resided in New York but was an Irishman by birth and had served in the British Army. Through personal example on the battlefield, however, he was able to inspire this ragtag army and form it into an effective fighting force. The men respected his military experience and admired his brave and dauntless demeanor.

Therefore, these American patriots were grudgingly willing to endure the present hardship with the hope that the same storm that ravaged them would also provide a measure of protection. They trusted that the severe weather and darkness would conceal their presence from the enemy and thereby aid in their enterprise. Thus, there would be no turning back. The men covered the firing locks of their muskets with the lappets of their coats to protect them in firing order, leaned against the raging blizzard, and advanced toward the fortress-city of Quebec, where the British army awaited.[3]

After several more hours of struggle, the Continental soldiers reached the outskirts of Quebec and prepared to launch a planned, coordinated attack to seize the city. American military leaders considered Quebec a critical prize, since they believed it to be the key to the conquest of Canada. In September 1775, George Washington, the newly appointed commander in chief of the American army, expressed his thoughts on the significance of the capture of Quebec and the Canadian invasion when he stated that the operation was "of the utmost importance to the interest and liberties of America."[4]

By 5 A.M., the American force initiated its assault. The commander of the attacking troops positioned himself in the front of his men, as was his custom during battle. Raising his sword in the air, he spurred the cold, wearied soldiers forward to follow his lead. After surmounting two un-manned defensive barricades, the American troops encountered yet an-other obstacle. This time, the British were waiting in ambush. Cannon grapeshot and musket fire rained upon the attackers from well-concealed positions within a blockhouse. The patriot leader crumpled to the ground. Gen. Richard Montgomery was dead of three grapeshot wounds fired at point-blank range.[5]

A member of Montgomery's party reported that "the fatal stroke of losing our general, threw our troops into confusion."[6] The remaining Americans could not regain the offensive. Those attackers who survived the violent rebuff from the enemy retreated or were captured. Guy Carleton, the British commander of Quebec, summarized the operation by asserting that the attack "was soon repulsed with slaughter."[7] Without Montgomery's leadership, the American offensive against Quebec turned into a disastrous failure.

The British force did not ascertain Montgomery's death until the next day. The British sent out a party to survey the American dead at that time. With the cooperation of a captured Continental officer, the detail found and identified Montgomery's body where he fell the day before. About three feet of accumulated snow partially obscured the solidly frozen remains, but his raised arm remained visible above the snow. The party also discovered his sword lying beside the body. Violent death had reduced this imposing figure of a military leader in life—tall, straight, lean, vibrant—to a grotesque, distorted form with knees drawn up toward the head.[8]

The British were almost as regretful of Montgomery's death as the Americans. Gov. Guy Carleton and other British officers who defended Quebec against Montgomery's attack had served with him earlier during the Seven Years' War. Montgomery saw duty in the British army from 1756 to 1773, rising to the rank of captain before he sold his commission. He subsequently settled in New York, married Janet Livingston of the prominent Robert R. Livingston, Sr., family, and in 1775 took up arms against his former country when offered a brigadier general's commission in the Continental army. Even though Montgomery changed allegiances, his former military acquaintances still respected his personal character and military leadership ability.[9] Guy Carleton ordered Montgomery's body decently buried within Quebec.[10]

Soon after his death, Edmund Burke, an opposition statesman, delivered an eloquent and moving eulogy of Montgomery in the British Parliament. Prime Minister Lord Frederick North, however, became agitated by this discourse and replied: "I cannot join in lamenting the death of Montgomery as a public loss. A curse on his virtues! They've undone this country. He was brave, he was noble, he was humane, he was generous: but still he was only a brave, able, humane, and generous rebel." Charles James Fox, another liberal member of Parliament, retorted, "The term of rebel is no certain mark of disgrace. The great asserters of liberty, the saviors of their country, the benefactors of mankind in all ages, have all been called rebels."[11]

Americans were even more profuse in their praise of the fallen general. Benedict Arnold served under Montgomery at Quebec. Arnold, who could be a harsh critic, paid his superior officer sincere tribute and maintained that had not Montgomery "received the fatal shot . . . the town would have been ours."[12] Gen. Philip Schuyler, Montgomery's commanding officer during the Canadian operation, grieved: "My amiable and gallant General Montgomery is no more. . . . My feelings on this unhappy occasion are too poignant to admit of expression. May Heaven avert any further evils."[13]

Mourning Montgomery's untimely death was not confined to those closely associated with him. He was the first American general officer killed in the War for American Independence. Joseph Warren, whom the Continental Congress had appointed major general but had not yet confirmed his commission, died at Bunker Hill six months earlier. Montgomery's heroic deed eclipsed that of Warren, and the Americans quickly elevated him to martyrdom in their struggle for independence. During the critical time when the colonists debated the issue of armed revolt, revolutionary Americans touted Montgomery's sacrifice to evoke patriotic spirit toward continuing the war.

In 1776, a patriot pamphlet appeared in Philadelphia under the title *A Dialogue between the Ghost of General Montgomery and an American Delegate in a Wood Near Philadelphia*. This work is generally attributed to Thomas Paine, revolutionary America's most influential pamphleteer.[14] In 1777, Hugh Henry Brackenridge published a heroic tragedy, *The Death of General Montgomery*. It was a dramatic poem clearly intended to arouse colonial sentiments against the British.[15]

> The hapless fortune of the day is sunk!
> Montgomery slain, and wither'd every hope!
> Mysterious Providence, thy ways are just,
> And we submit in deep humility.
> But O let fire or pestilence from Heaven,
> Avenge the butchery; let Englishmen,
> The cause and agents in this horrid war,
> In tenfold amplitude, meet gloomy death.[16]

The Continental Congress played an important role in advancing Montgomery's contribution to the patriot cause. After learning of the general's death, Congress issued a proclamation stating "their grateful remembrance, respect, and high veneration; and desiring to transmit to future ages a truly worthy example of patriotism, conduct, boldness of enterprise, insuperable perseverance, and contempt of danger and death."[17]

On January 22, 1776, Congress appointed a committee, which included Benjamin Franklin, to "consider a proper method of paying a just tribute of gratitude to the memory of General Montgomery."[18] Three days later, the committee recommended that a memorial be obtained from Paris, "with an inscription, sacred to his [Montgomery's] memory, and expressive of his amiable character and heroick achievements."[19] Congress approved the recommendation, and Benjamin Franklin made the necessary arrangements for a stone marker to be made. In the following year, Franklin described the completed monument as "plain, but elegant, being done by one of the best artists in Paris."[20]

Finding a suitable location for the shrine was delayed until after the war. Eventually, New York City accepted the honor of receiving the nation's approbation to the American patriot. In 1787, with proper ceremony, authorities erected the marker at St. Paul's Church. It remains today as the first monument dedicated by the government to an American revolutionary hero. The memorial bears the following original inscription:

This Monument
is erected
By order of Congress, 25th January, 1776
To transmit to posterity
A Grateful Remembrance
of the
Patriotism, Conduct, Enterprize and Perseverance
of
Major General Richard Montgomery
who after a series of successes
Amidst the most discouraging difficulties,
Fell in the attack on Quebec,
31st December, 1775. Aged 37 years.[21]

In 1818, American officials reclaimed Montgomery's remains from Quebec and reinterred them appropriately within his chosen country. The final resting place was located next to the original monument at St. Paul's Church.

The Continental Congress also used Montgomery's death as a justification for expanding state commitments to the revolutionary effort. On September 24, 1776, Congress sent resolves to the states, raising quotas and increasing enlistment time for troops to be provided for the Continental army. In a letter enclosed with the resolves, John Hancock stated: "The fall of the late Genl. Montgomery before Quebec is undoubtedly to be ascribed to the limited time for which the troops were engaged; whose impatience to return home compelled him to make the attack contrary to the conviction of his own judgment. This fact alone furnishes a striking argument of the danger and impropriety of sending troops into the field under any restrictions as to the time of their enlistment. The noblest enterprize may be left unfinished by troops in such a predicament, or abandoned at the very moment success must have crowned the attempt."[22]

It is somewhat ironic that Richard Montgomery, who was so well regarded by his contemporaries and whose death was so highly instrumental in forming general opinion during the Revolution, should now occupy such an obscure place in the historiography of that period. Of the twenty-nine major generals who served in the American Revolution, all but six have been treated as subjects of book-length biographies. Richard Montgomery remains one of the neglected few. The brief sketches that have been produced on his life hardly do him justice.[23]

The paucity of biographical studies pertaining to Montgomery in the literature is even more perplexing, since Montgomery's fame has endured with the passage of time. The lasting permeation of Montgomery's life into the national consciousness is reflected by an examination of county-designation records within the nation. Traditionally, government officials select the name for a county from some well-known historical entity or personage. Excluding presidents and governors, Montgomery ranks fifth on the list of persons for whom the greatest number of counties have been named. Some sixteen counties throughout the nation were named after Montgomery.[24] One might expect that a county in New York would be designated for its adopted son and that some states on the East Coast where the Revolution predominantly raged would remember Montgomery; however, other far-flung counties across the country bear names to honor Montgomery's memory.[25]

Therefore, Montgomery not only had a significant impact on the American Revolution, but he remains an important historical figure. Although his life and military career were brief, Montgomery's association with the American revolutionary army was unique. He was a former

British officer who had settled in the colonies shortly before the Revolution. Subsequently, Congress called upon him to serve in the American patriot's cause. Unlike other former professional soldiers in this situation, Montgomery did not solicit military appointment and responded reluctantly when urged to join the Continental army. During this crucial initial period of the Revolution, the patriot leadership was struggling with establishing and organizing an army to compete with the world-renowned British armed forces. Montgomery's service in the fledgling Continental military offers an appreciation for the way these measures were undertaken. Montgomery was also well regarded by both the British and the Americans throughout the Revolution. How he reconciled his divided loyalties and fought against his former military comrades should add to the intellectual history of the time. How the British and Americans related to his experiences in the war should provide some critical insights into the revolutionary era. Thus, this study constitutes an effort to install Richard Montgomery in his rightful place in the scholarly conscience.

Ancestry and Early Life

If anything human could now reach his ear, nothing but
the great concerns of virtue, liberty, truth, and justice
would be tolerable to him; for to these was his life
devoted from his early years.[1]

Richard Montgomery was born on December 2, 1738, at his father's country estate, near Swords in County Dublin, Ireland.
Thus, he joined a respectable family of Irish gentry as the son
of Thomas Montgomery and Mary Franklin (Franklyn) Montgomery.
His father, who had inherited a title of baronet, was a former captain in
the army. He was serving as a member of the Irish Parliament for Lifford,
in County Donegal, at the time of Richard's birth.[2] Many of the traits
that Richard Montgomery would exhibit later in life may be explained by
his ancestry. Richard was directly descended from a family that had been
prominent in Ireland and Scotland for many generations. Some sources
even trace the early genealogy of the Montgomery family back to Normandy beyond A.D. 912.[3] This lineage is replete with military, moral,
and public-service references. Most of Richard's forebears functioned in
the armed forces and positions of civil duty. A few entered the private
sector, seeking careers in commercial pursuits. The evidence also indicates that many of the personal conflicts experienced by this kinship
involved ethical issues.

Richard's father provides an excellent point of entrée into the Montgomery ancestry. Thomas Montgomery, a headstrong individual, defied his

patriarchal father, Col. Alexander Montgomery (Montgomerie), in the matter of matrimony. Alexander opposed his son's marriage to Mary Franklin, an English lady of fortune, but Thomas was unrelenting in his devotion to Mary. Alexander never forgave his son's defiance of his wishes and designated Thomas's eldest son, Alexander John, as the benefactor of his will.[4]

The union of Thomas and Mary Montgomery produced four children. Richard was the third son of the family, which also included a younger daughter. Richard's oldest brother, Alexander John, served as a captain in the British 43d Regiment in America during the Seven Years' War. Subsequent to his military duty, he was a member of the Irish Parliament for Donegal for thirty-two years. He never married, and he died at the age of seventy-eight on September 29, 1800.[5] John Montgomery, the second son, was one of the exceptions to the Montgomery legacy of military and public service. He became a noted merchant in Portugal.[6] Sarah Montgomery, the daughter, married Charles Ranelagh, an impoverished Irish viscount, and raised a large family.[7]

Richard Montgomery himself chose to trace his origin from Count de Montgomery (Gabriel de Lorges), a French nobleman of Scottish extraction (c. 1530–1574).[8] Although Richard was not a direct descendant of the count, this selection is significant because it reveals what personal qualities Richard admired most in his ancestry. A biography of Count de Montgomery fairly bristles with military prowess and moral courage.

On June 28–30, 1559, King Henry II of France held a celebration in Paris on the occasion of the marriage of his daughter, Isabella, to King Philip II of Spain. The king had a penchant for sporting activities, so he ordered a tournament to be conducted throughout the three-day festival. On the last day of the games, Henry II personally entered into the jousting match. The queen, Catherine de' Medici (Catherine de Medicis), feared for her husband's safety and urged him to forego the dangerous pastime. However, chivalry dominated the attitudes of the gentry during this era, and Henry prided himself on such attributes. He enjoyed a reputation as an accomplished horseman and man-at-arms. Like other noblemen, Henry had learned martial skills at an early age as part of his preparation for manhood. During a jousting training session, his father, King Francis I, delivered such a blow to his face that it tore a large gash in the flesh.[9]

According to custom, jousters used wooden lances and attempted to strike their competitors in order to unhorse them or to break their lances.

After demonstrating his skill in several tilts, the king wished to challenge another opponent. He summoned Montgomery, his captain of the Royal Scottish Guard, to run against him. Montgomery tried to decline the perilous honor, but the king insisted. Although Henry and Montgomery broke their lances during this run, the count caused his monarch to lose his stirrup, nearly unseating him. Embarrassed by his unsteady performance during the first match, the king wanted to run another bout against Montgomery. Disregarding the protests of those concerned over the king placing himself in unnecessary danger, Henry demanded a rematch.[10]

During this encounter, both jousters broke their lances deftly; but Montgomery, in his anxiety, failed to release his broken lance immediately after impact. The severed shaft remaining in Montgomery's hand unintentionally struck and raised the king's visor, allowing the splintered end to be driven through the monarch's eye. Hastily summoned surgeons removed a four-inch-long wooden fragment and four smaller pieces from Henry's head. At first, the doctors believed that he would only lose his eye. On the third day, he was conscious and asked for Montgomery. When told that the count had fled Paris, he said: "He must be brought back at all costs. What has he to fear? This accident happened not through his fault but by an unlucky chance."[11]

In spite of this momentary rally, the king's condition continued to deteriorate. Blood poisoning set in and brain damage ensued. Medical treatment proved to be futile. He lingered for ten days before succumbing to the wound. Henry II died on July 10 at the age of forty. He had been the victim of a tragic accident—and apparently forgave Montgomery for his part in the mishap. However, Catherine, the royal court, and other horror-stricken spectators who had witnessed the disastrous event blamed the hapless Montgomery for the loss of their ruler.[12]

Because of his censure, Count Montgomery retired initially to Normandy, where he maintained several estates, and subsequently fled to England. Also during this period, he converted to Calvinist Protestantism. Returning to France in 1562, he distinguished himself as a leader of the Huguenots in the religious civil war against Charles IX, son and successor to Henry II. Montgomery served as one of several Huguenot generals who fought against the Catholics during the rebellion. The others included the Prince de Condé (Louis I de Bourbon) and Count Gaspard de Coligny.

Most of the Huguenot military leaders came from the lesser nobility of France. Because of their landlord social status, they were particularly vulnerable to the high inflation that occurred from time to time. This economic condition severely reduced the value of money while land rental rates remained fixed by governmental regulation. In addition, French law forbade the gentry from supplementing their income through commercial enterprises. On the other hand, social convention dictated that the nobility maintain a certain standard of living. The maintenance of their station required a large, continuous expenditure for the education of their children, accoutrements of rank, and other trappings befitting a member of the lavish social order. Appearances had to be upheld at all costs. Therefore, the effects of the economy weighed harshly on this segment of society. These circumstances and the fact that the peerage traditionally received martial-arts training understandably turned many in this class to military pursuits. For them, war was the only trade they knew or were allowed to practice.[13]

During the first half of the sixteenth century, France engaged in wars with Spain and the empire (Valois-Hapsburg Wars, 1495–1559). With the ensuing years of peace, many French noblemen-soldiers became unoccupied and restless. The social tensions that had built up in this privileged group help explain the nature of their participation in the French Wars of Religion (1560–1598). These men, who were accustomed to living by the sword, became the protectors of the repressed French Protestants during an intense period of religious reformation and confrontation. This is not to suggest that the Huguenot generals were military mercenaries, attempting to reap only personal gain and glory. All of them had an almost fanatical devotion to their faith and dedication to their cause. Rather, their background offers an insight into why this religious struggle assumed a particular form. By inclination, these leaders were men of action, not politicians or men of letters. Therefore, it was inevitable that this civil strife would be played out through military confrontation instead of using intellectual or diplomatic alternatives.

The death of Henry II left at the head of state Catherine de' Medici as regent and queen mother of two young, sickly kings. Francis II, the first in succession, died on December 5, 1560, at the age of eighteen. Charles IX succeeded his brother when only ten years old. This period of uncertainty in royal power provided yet another catalyst for the Religious Wars. Initially, Catherine, acting as regent, attempted to reconcile the two religious factions; however, her actions proved to be ineffectual. France experienced a protracted cycle of pacification followed by violent outbreaks of armed conflict between the two sets of antagonists. Historians have differentiated up to eight separate wars during this turbulent period of nearly four decades of domestic strife. Met with this series of rebuffs, Catherine then exercised her matriarchal influence with Charles to align the monarchy with the Catholics and the established church. The conflict turned into a civil war, pitting the royalists and Catholics against the Protestants or Huguenots.[14]

Montgomery soon established himself as the most successful Huguenot military commander. Condé and Coligny suffered frequent defeat by the Catholics, and Condé lost his life after being captured in March 1569. Although Montgomery's forces were usually outnumbered by the opposition, they raided extensively in western France. Montgomery had many narrow escapes as the Catholic army harried his troops, but he managed to elude the ponderous and disorganized adversary. Because of these victories, Montgomery increased the size of his force from the areas in which he campaigned. Many of his followers came from Normandy, where he was well known. He was also instrumental in causing mutiny in the ranks of the Scotch Royal Guard, thirty of whom deserted to their former commander. This necessitated a reorganization of the guard in which the monarchy replaced the rebellious Scotch troops with Swiss soldiers. The King's Swiss Guard remained until the French Revolution.[15]

On St. Bartholomew's Day, August 24, 1572, Catherine attempted to accomplish by assassination what the Catholics had failed to do by military action—the overthrow of the Huguenot movement. By this time, she was convinced that the Huguenots constituted a real threat to the throne and that their activities might result in foreign intervention. In what is commonly referred to as the St. Bartholomew Massacre, the monarchy and Catholic forces plotted the murder of all the principal Huguenot leaders in a mass killing.

Conciliation toward the Protestants in the previous year had allowed Coligny to return to court. He was the first victim slain in Paris. Montgomery, quartered across the Seine River in St. Germain, was also a primary target for assassination that day. However, by the time assassins reached his location outside of Paris, Montgomery had received warnings of the danger and managed to foil his attackers. He escaped to Normandy and thence to England. The selected massacre soon raged out of hand into a general slaughter, with mobs roaming throughout Paris streets killing suspected heretics. In the next several days the carnage spread from Paris to the provinces. Thousands of individuals lost their lives in this brutal event.[16]

Of the chief leaders of the Huguenot armies, only Montgomery survived. His dramatic avoidance of the St. Bartholomew Massacre frustrated the French monarchy's plan to undermine the Huguenot movement. Therefore, Catherine and Charles were most anxious to apprehend Montgomery. However, Queen Elizabeth I of England maintained an active interest in Montgomery and his cause. Fancying herself as the upholder of Protestantism, she gave aid and encouragement to the Huguenots. She also forced mediation several times during the Religious Wars by threatening English intervention. Elizabeth had offered sanctuary and a sympathetic ear before to Montgomery. Thus, when Montgomery arrived safely in England, Elizabeth offered him refuge.

In its frantic attempt to use every means to dispatch Montgomery, the French monarchy disregarded Elizabeth's previous compassion for the Huguenots and sought her cooperation. When Charles's ambassador delivered a message to her requesting assistance in the capture of Montgomery, Queen Elizabeth employed subterfuge by citing an instance when King Henry II refused to surrender some English fugitives upon the request of Queen Mary. Queen Elizabeth responded thus: "I would answer your master as his father answered my sister, Queen Mary, when he said, 'I will not consent to be the hangman of the Queen of England.' So his Majesty, the King of France, must excuse me if I can no more act as executioner of those of my religion than King Henry would discharge a similar office in the case of those that were not of his religion."[17]

Montgomery soon returned to France and continued the Huguenot crusade. He and his followers eventually mounted a stout resistance to the French crown. The Huguenots established control over the province of Normandy by holding the strategic towns of St. Lô and Domfront. At this time, Montgomery threatened to bring extensive French territory under the power of the Protestants. In 1574, Charles IX tried to negotiate an armistice with the count, promising him protection if he would lay down his arms. However, Montgomery replied that the memory of St. Bartholomew prevented him from doing so.[18]

Montgomery's remarkable military career was destined to be brief. The royalists and Catholics finally organized a strong suppressive force and launched a sustained attack on the Huguenot stronghold of St. Lô. Since he was outnumbered and besieged, with little hope of success or escape, Montgomery's situation became desperate. Although suffering tremendous losses, he evaded destruction. However, the loyalist forces overtook Montgomery a few days later at Domfront and forced him to surrender the remnants of his command. Montgomery's apprehension occurred three days before King Charles IX finally succumbed to a long illness.[19]

The capture of Count Montgomery was particularly gratifying to Catherine de' Medici, who had never forgiven the unfortunate knight for her husband's death. Montgomery's warring against her son who succeeded the late king further exasperated her feelings. Therefore, Catherine did not wait for her other son, Henry III, to assume the throne before venting her rage against Montgomery. Assuming the position of regent once again, she ordered an immediate trial in Paris. The court found Montgomery guilty of treason and sentenced him to death by decapitation.[20]

On June 26, 1574, Gabriel Montgomery died, facing death as courageously as he had lived. Proud and defiant until the end, he maintained silence under torture when his captors tried to extract a confession. He also remained constant to the faith that he embraced after his initial flight to England. To a friar who attempted to convince him that he had been deceived by his conversion, he replied: "If I have been deceived, it was by members of your own order; for the first person that ever gave me a bible in French, and bade me to read it, was a Franciscan like yourself. And therein I learned the religion that I now hold, which is the only true religion. Having lived in it ever since, I wish, by the grace of God, to die in it today."[21]

On the scaffold, Montgomery addressed the spectators, speaking movingly in support of his religious principles. He also requested "that they would tell his children, whom the judges had declared to be degraded to the rank of 'roturiers,' that, if they had not virtue of nobility enough to reassert their position, their father consented to the act."[22] Refusing a blindfold, he then offered his neck to the executioner's sword. Gabriel Montgomery thus entered martyrdom. His military exploits and the manner in which he conducted himself during his execution served as inspiration to the remaining Huguenots. Instead of destroying the Huguenot sect as Catherine had expected, Montgomery's death had just the opposite effect. It infused new life into the cause, which at that time was at its lowest ebb.

Gabriel Montgomery's legacy of loyal devotion to heartfelt convictions apparently served as an incentive for his family to regain their noble status. By 1583, in Normandy, young Count Montgomery had succeeded to the rank of his father and taken up arms in the Protestant cause.[23] The wars continued until 1598. At that time, Henry of Navarre, who gained decisive military victories as a Protestant leader, brought political as well as military unity and peace to France by embracing the Catholic religion as King Henry IV.

Another more direct Montgomery descendant, Sir Hugh Montgomery, went to England with William III of Orange in 1689 and commanded a regiment during the wars with Ireland (1690–1691). William rewarded him with vast land grants in Ireland. Many of his relations migrated to live on the Montgomery landholdings in Ireland, and this period gave rise to the Irish branch of the Montgomery family.[24]

Also during this era, the Montgomery kin devised the heraldic armorial insignia, which Richard Montgomery would later inherit. Some sources record that Gabriel Montgomery emblazoned on his shield a man impaled by a lance, in grim memory of the mortal wound that he delivered to Henry II. However, evidence indicates that this account was a fabrication, invented by the Catholics to rally loyalist hatred and opposition to Montgomery during the war. A reference to this incident was not included in the Montgomery coat of arms until the Irish Montgomerys redesigned it many years later, adding an arm clad in armor grasping a broken lance to the design. The designers also changed the motto inscribed below the shield at this time by substituting "Patriae Infelici Fidelis" (Loyalty but Misfortune in One's Native Land) for the Scottish "Garde Bien" (Protect Well).[25]

These past events and personalities, then, formed the lineage that Richard Montgomery inherited. His heritage helped to shape his value system and worldview throughout his life. Therefore, an understanding of the Montgomery ancestry facilitates perceptions of Richard's later decisions and conduct.

With this warlike family tradition, it was natural for Richard to be disposed toward a military career. Befitting a son of landed gentry, he acquired a liberal education as a youth. After receiving his initial education at St. Andrews School, Richard enrolled in Trinity College, Dublin, in 1754. He attended two years of college when, upon the advice and urging of his father and oldest brother, he made a final decision in favor of joining the army. Thomas probably influenced his son toward military service because he wanted Richard to follow in his footsteps and those of his forefathers in maintaining the Montgomery military tradition. Alexander had already established himself as an army officer, having received an appointment sometime before. His father purchased an ensign's commission for Richard, and he entered British military service on September 21, 1756, at the age of eighteen. He spent the next eight years of his early manhood in the 17th Regiment of Foot in the British army.[26]

The 17th Regiment had a long and honorable history. In 1688, King James II hurriedly expanded his army to meet the threat of William III to his throne. He added four thousand Englishmen to the army lists, together with three thousand men from both Ireland and Scotland. Raising the new regiments, which included the 17th, brought the total army strength to forty thousand men. King James felt confident that he could defend his crown with such a force. However, political conspiracy, not force of arms, caused the overthrow of James. Most of his high-ranking officials deserted him, and he fled into exile without a major military confrontation. The 17th Regiment survived the "Glorious Revolution" and several army reorganizations that followed. It later distinguished itself during the War of the Spanish Succession (1701–1714), fighting under the Duke of Marlborough throughout war-torn Europe.[27]

It is ironic that Richard Montgomery became a member of the same regiment that James II formed to oppose his ancestor, Sir Hugh Montgomhery, who was then in the service of William III. Nevertheless, the 17th Regiment was proud of its reputation as a time-honored Irish unit, loyal in its support to the British Empire. Richard must have shared this military tradition after joining the 17th as a young, inexperienced officer. The time of Richard's induction into the army was the eve of a momentous world event that would provide the 17th another opportunity to bravely serve the king—the Seven Years' War. It would also furnish Richard an opportunity to uphold the Montgomery family heritage and prove himself as a professional soldier.

Duty in the Seven Years' War

When first a soldier . . . I stood in arms. Then, in
Britannia's cause. I drew my sword, and charg'd the
rival Gaul.[1]

Having borne a share in all the labour of our American
wars, and the reduction of Canada. Little did he foresee
the scenes which that land had still in reserve for him!
Little did those generous Americans, who then stood by
his side, think they were assisting to subdue a country,
which would one day be held up over us a greater
scourge in the hands of friends, than ever it was in the
hands of enemies![2]

The nagging imperial rivalry between Great Britain and France in
the seventeenth and eighteenth centuries led ultimately to the
Seven Years' War between these two contending national powers
as they struggled for world supremacy. Although global in overall scope,
the part of the military conflict that occurred in North America became
known as the French and Indian wars. This belligerency represented a
series of protracted colonial wars between the British army, augmented
by provincial militia, and French troops, assisted by their Indian allies.

Competing British and French claims in the Ohio Valley on the colonial western frontier touched off the final confrontation for control of the
continent. In 1747, a group of prominent Virginians organized the Ohio
Company of Virginia for the purpose of land speculation and fur trading.

Two years later, the company was able to influence the British government to grant it some two hundred thousand acres in the Ohio Valley.

The French, viewing the British initiative as a direct challenge to their own claims and designs in the region, retaliated by building two forts on the upper Ohio River and increasing their presence in the disputed area. In 1753, Virginia Gov. Robert Dinwiddie sent a twenty-one-year-old militia officer, Maj. George Washington, to protest the French intrusion into territory that the British claimed as part of the Virginia colony. The French spurned Washington's diplomatic grievance when he presented it to the military authorities at Fort Le Boeuf (near the present-day site of Erie, Pennsylvania).

The British-French contention then focused on a strategic geographic area identified by the Forks of the Ohio (near present-day Pittsburgh). During January 1754, a Virginia militia company began work on a stronghold there. On April 17, 1754, a larger French force captured the half-completed stockade and then built Fort Duquesne on the site. The Virginia assembly countered by raising an independent regiment and sending a small expedition under Washington against the French. In May 1754, the young officer (now a militia lieutenant colonel) routed a French patrol and killed its commander. Expecting an attack from the main French military establishment at Fort Duquesne, Washington retreated and hastily constructed Fort Necessity while waiting for the rest of the regiment to join him. On July 3, 1754, a superior French and Indian force attacked Fort Necessity, forcing Washington to surrender his untenable position the next day. This action gave France temporary control of the entire Ohio region.

When news of Washington's defeat reached London, the British government sent Gen. Edward Braddock to America with the mission of defending Britain's claims. On July 9, 1755, Braddock was leading his army of some fourteen hundred British regulars and seven hundred colonial militiamen in an advance on Fort Duquesne when attacked by a nine-hundred-man force of French and Indians. Braddock's humiliating rout, which cost him his life, was one of the worst military disasters in British history and underscored the depths that English fortunes had plunged in the struggle against France in North America.[3]

In May 1756, the Seven Years' War formally began in Europe, with Britain and Prussia pitted against France, Austria, Sweden, and some German states. Spain would join the French alliance later. During this period, Britain suffered frustration and disappointment in its military strategy against France. After William Pitt became prime minister in 1758, British prospects in the conflict began to improve. Pitt, who recognized the value of Canada and the American western frontier to the British war effort, sent a well-organized military task force to the colonies to turn around the situation. Montgomery's 17th Regiment was included in this army upon which Britain pinned its hopes.

The orders for his regiment to be part of the invasion force must have been a welcome change for young Montgomery. Since he accounted for just one of nine ensigns (the lowest-ranking officer in the army) assigned to the unit, he was eager for an opportunity to distinguish himself. At this point in his life, Montgomery represented a loyal and proud member of His Majesty's armed forces, sworn to protect the British dominion. Advancement through the ranks measured success in his chosen profession of arms, and the aspiring officer knew that military recognition and promotion were attained much more rapidly in wartime. Like all junior officers, he trusted that enthusiasm and fortitude would overcome his lack of experience in the pending hostilities.[4]

Montgomery also regarded the mission as a grateful break in the tedium of routine garrison duty. Since joining the unit, his days had been filled with endless drill and practice as the regiment simulated battlefield tactics during peacetime. This was the opportunity to employ these skills for their intended purpose. Braddock's debacle had raised questions by some detractors over the British army's readiness to fight the French and Indians in America, but Montgomery and his comrades maintained confidence in their abilities. The British officer corps held no doubt about the effectiveness of its military doctrine and training against any enemy. After all, the renowned reputation of the British army had been established throughout the world as it helped to win an empire upon which the "sun never set." So, Montgomery received the news that his regiment would participate in the forthcoming operation with great expectation and even exhilaration.

On February 3, 1757, the British government issued orders for the 17th Regiment to march from its garrison at Galway to Cork in Ireland to prepare for overseas deployment. Brig. Gen. Edward Richbell commanded the regiment when Montgomery joined, but he died on February 24, 1757. Richbell's successor, Col. John Forbes, led the unit during its initial activity. Six other Irish regiments joined the 17th at Cork to await passage abroad.[5]

All of the units designated for the expedition were foot (infantry) regiments—the backbone of the British army organization. A number of companies made up each regiment, including a company of grenadiers and a light-infantry company. Grenadiers represented the tallest and strongest men in the army, originally selected because they could throw a grenade, or hand bomb, farther than ordinary troops. By this time, none of them actually carried grenades, but they stood out for their physical strength and endurance. The light-infantry troops possessed similar attributes. They could march faster and farther while carrying less supplies than common soldiers. Separate ranger troops, who were specially trained in raiding tactics, were also included in the organization. These three units, then, formed the elite contingent of the army.

The standard-issue individual weapon of foot soldiers was a flintlock musket that weighed twelve pounds and measured four feet nine inches in length. Its nickname, "Brown Bess," came from the color of the walnut stock. King George I introduced the weapon into the British army in the early 1700s. A thin-bodied triangular-shaped bayonet, fitted to the muzzle, added another fourteen inches and two pounds to the weapon, and might have been its most important component. The musket fired a lead ball three quarters of an inch in diameter (.75 caliber) and weighing one and a half ounces—considerable stopping power even by modern standards.

Yet, the range and accuracy of the musket presented a problem. Because the musket was designed to be loaded expeditiously by its muzzle using a ramrod, the clearance between the bore and the lead ball was not close. This caused much of the propelling power from the exploding powder charge to escape around the ball when the weapon discharged. The muzzle-loading characteristic of the musket limited its maximum effective range from fifty to one hundred yards. Because the musket had a smooth bore, it imparted very little guidance to the ball once it was shot out of the barrel. This unstable trajectory resulted in a relatively inaccurate weapon.

Consequently, the muzzle-loading, smooth-bore musket dictated the tactics that the soldiers armed with it used. Its inaccuracy was reflected in the British manual of arms. There was no command to "aim." Instead, men were ordered to "level muskets" before firing. To compensate for the lack of accuracy from individual weapons, battlefield maneuvers stressed compact formations from which a wall of massed musket fire could be presented to the enemy. Foot soldiers usually deployed into battle lines three ranks deep. The musket's restricted range also forced combat into an encounter at close quarters. Trained troops could perform the dozen steps involved in loading and shooting their weapons to lay down a steady two to four rounds per minute. This time-consuming reloading left soldiers vulnerable to return fire and promoted hand-to-hand combat. A volley from the muskets followed immediately by a bayonet charge was the logical battlefield tactic when forces converged in short-range engagements. The shock of cold steel was usually the moment of truth for opposing eighteenth-century field armies. Battles were won or lost by how well foot soldiers stood up to this physical and psychological trial.[6]

Artillery battalions were highly specialized units that employed cannons in an attempt to give depth to the battlefield by concentrating long-range firepower on enemy troop staging areas or dueling with opposing artillery positions. However, cannons lacked effectiveness during close infantry clashes because of their erratic accuracy and the possibility of inflicting friendly casualties. Supply and transportation difficulties persisted, because cannons consumed huge amounts of shot and powder and were ponderous to move. Thus, most cannonry was employed during more deliberate siege warfare.[7] Military planners left British cavalry regiments in the British Isles, where they engaged in ceremonial and internal security tasks. Heavily forested terrain in the North American theater of operations led British strategists to regard it as unsuitable for the use of cavalry tactics. Also, support demands of mounted troops were much more costly to a field command than those of foot soldiers. Maintenance of horses required extensive forage, which created a drain on supply efforts. To conserve shipboard space, higher headquarters even ordered the Irish foot regiments to dispose of their baggage horses before they set sail.[8]

The seven Irish regiments embarked upon transport vessels at Cork on May 5 for the convoy to North America. These troop ships arrived at Halifax, Nova Scotia, in early July 1757. The French stronghold at Louisbourg on Cape Breton in the Gulf of St. Lawrence emerged as the vital military objective of the British forces. Only after the capture of this fortress could a British offensive be safely sent further up the St. Lawrence River to strike at the heart of New France. The amphibious assault and seizure of Louisbourg, which had been hardened against attack by extensive defensive preparations, hinged on establishing a clear superiority in land and sea forces. By late 1757, this prerequisite military buildup had not yet taken place. The British fleet at Halifax remained inferior to the French naval squadrons that retained command of the sea around Louisbourg.[9]

Meanwhile, the 17th and other regiments, deployed from both Ireland and England, made use of the time to practice maneuvers that would be employed during the projected confrontation. The combined British force occupied winter quarters at Halifax that year. Command and staff personnel changes also occurred during this interim period. Colonel Forbes became adjutant general of the general staff, leaving Lt. Col. Arthur Morris as acting commander of the 17th Regiment.[10]

While allowing the Royal Navy to concentrate more of its fleet in North American waters, the British expeditionary force under Gen. James Abercromby finalized its invasion plans. The strategy to be undertaken in America contained three campaigns. First, Gen. Jeffery Amherst with fourteen thousand British regular troops and two thousand provincial soldiers would besiege Louisbourg. Concurrently, Abercromby, aided by Gen. George Howe with ten thousand regulars and twenty thousand provincials, would advance upon Ticonderoga and Crown Point and push forward if possible to Montreal and Quebec. Additionally, nineteen hundred regulars and five thousand provincials were to repair Braddock's loss and wrest Fort Duquesne from the French. Forbes, who received a promotion to brigadier general, led this last operation.[11]

By the spring of 1758, the British had amassed enough military resources to put their war plan into action. The French garrison at Louisbourg numbered three thousand regulars and some five hundred Swiss mercenaries, Canadians, and Indians. In addition, six ships of the line and five frigates in the harbor guarded the fortress. The British force at Halifax, consisting of eleven regular and two provincial regiments totaling 13,142 troops, was over three times greater than that of the French in Louisbourg. The Royal Navy component amounted to twenty-three ships of the line and thirteen frigates.[12]

An imposing fleet of 155 warships and troop transports put to sea from Halifax on the evening of May 28, 1758. By June 2, the British armada reached an anchorage about seven miles from Louisbourg, but five days of dense fog and stormy weather frustrated subsequent plans to land. Finally, at daybreak on June 8, the warships commenced firing on the French emplacements. Fifteen minutes later, landing craft filled with British soldiers rowed for shore. Selected landing areas lay from one to three miles from the fortified city. However, French troops had prepared defensive positions to cover these likely disembarking locations and were waiting for the British invasion. The defenders held their fire until the boats were well within range; then they opened up a withering fusillade as the invaders neared the beach.[13]

Although the soldiers accompanying Montgomery in the assault craft were anxious to return fire and ready bayonets in preparation for landing, he enforced the standing orders: "No man fire his piece from out of the boat . . . bayonets are fixed in a moment after the men are landed." A raging surf capsized some boats, drowning a number of soldiers before they could reach shore. Montgomery and his troops managed to land amid the pounding waves and incoming fire. As fast as the men got out of the boat, Montgomery deployed them into formation and marched forward to secure the landing area. Having failed to thwart the amphibious assault, the French outer defense fought a withdrawal action back to the safety of the Louisbourg fortress. Montgomery's unit and the rest of the British force pursued the retreating troops until they reached a point just outside the range of the fort's cannons. There, they prepared for a siege of the city.[14]

Because of continuing bad weather and heavy swells, it was June 16 before provisions for the besieging troops could be landed. Although it was possible to get some artillery ashore on June 18, intermittent bad weather continued for an extended period and hampered the siege buildup. As weather conditions improved, the British were able to bring up and emplace guns to bombard the fortress city. Under this fire cover, Montgomery urged his men on in the back-breaking task of digging trenches and building breastworks, as the British troops pushed forward a series of entrenchments in an ever-tightening ring around the city. At the same time, Montgomery had to keep his soldiers vigilant of French troops attempting to escape the encirclement.[15]

On July 9, a French force of about six hundred troops attempted a desperate breakout through the siege lines. The sortie struck at the grenadier company of the 17th Regiment, killing its captain and wounding a lieutenant. Raiders killed or wounded several other grenadiers before they were driven back to the city, leaving twenty French troops killed and about eighty wounded or captured. The enemy sent out a flag of truce so that they could claim their dead. After this was accomplished, the cannonading resumed. The vigor with which the British repulsed their bid for relief dampened any further plans by the French to force the siege. In addition, the British fleet stationed in the bay prevented any possibility of the besieged fortress receiving reinforcements from the sea. From the French point of view, the situation was hopeless. On July 26, 1758, the French governor agreed to an unconditional surrender of Louisbourg.[16]

Casualties during the entire campaign were small. Final British army losses amounted to three officers and forty-seven other ranks killed (all but twelve drowned), five lieutenants and fifty-five men wounded. Of these figures, the 17th Regiment had one captain, one corporal, and ten privates killed; one captain, one lieutenant, one sergeant, one drummer, and thirty-one privates wounded. British navy losses added eleven men killed, four officers and forty-eight men wounded. The French claimed their total casualties to be 114 killed or wounded.[17]

Although annalists would record the assault and siege as a relatively limited affair in terms of casualty statistics, it had a more personal meaning to the participants. The conflict presented a life or death struggle for the soldiers who suffered through it, whatever its scope. Montgomery's first taste of combat was a gut-wrenching experience. He witnessed the sickening sight of men being maimed and slaughtered. He felt the cold fear of his own life being placed in imminent peril. Yet, he sensed that he had been entrusted with a noble mission of serving king and country, and he carried out his duties in the midst of danger.

Montgomery also learned that soldiers would normally carry out their orders and perform functions for which they had been trained, even under fire and exposure to injury or death, if properly motivated. An officer on the battlefield had to lead the troops, not merely direct them, to earn their confidence and willingness to follow. As a junior officer, he personally influenced a small number of men that represented only a fraction of the overall operation. Still, he understood that if he accomplished his assignment well, this segment combined with other integral parts of the whole effort completed in like manner could ultimately add up to a total success.

The effectiveness with which Montgomery discharged his duties at Louisbourg caught the attention of General Amherst. Rather than resorting to showy battlefield heroics to call attention to his actions, the young ensign demonstrated a quiet but unmistakable competence during combat. Thus, he proved himself to be a solid officer who could be depended upon to carry out his assigned tasks. As a result, Montgomery received a promotion to lieutenant, effective July 10, 1758.

The protracted siege of Louisbourg had occupied too much time for the expedition to continue against Quebec that summer. Nevertheless,

Montgomery and his fellow British soldiers had gained some valuable combat experience. Montgomery also acquired some practical knowledge of conducting siege warfare that he would draw upon at a later date.

While the British army enjoyed a successful investment of Louisbourg, Abercromby's campaign met with dashed hopes. Gen. George Howe was killed on July 6, 1758, in a preliminary skirmish near Fort Ticonderoga (called Fort Carillon by the French who occupied it). Two days later, Abercromby with fifteen thousand men mounted his main attack on the fort defended by Gen. Louis Montcalm and thirty-six hundred troops. The ill-planned frontal assault resulted in the British soldiers being cut to pieces before they could breach the fort's perimeter. Abercromby lost 1,944 men while inflicting only 377 casualties on the French.[18]

In August 1758, the 17th and several other regiments embarked from Louisbourg and sailed to Boston. After arriving there, the regiment marched to join and bolster Abercromby's expeditionary force in upper New York. The soldiers, awaiting deployment the next year, occupied winter quarters near Lake George. Morale of the surviving troops that fought under Abercromby had plummeted. This feeling of bitter disappointment, however, mingled with the optimistic outlook of the 17th Regiment fresh from victory, and overall esprit improved.[19]

On November 9, 1758, the British government recalled Abercromby and replaced him with Amherst as commander in chief. The capture of Fort Duquesne by Forbes's expedition on November 25, 1758, dissipated some of the disgrace inflicted on the British army by Abercromby's ineptitude. British authorities renamed this strategic location Pittsburgh in honor of the prime minister, William Pitt. Forbes, who had been ill for some time, died in the spring of 1759.[20]

Military authorities now devised a three-pronged offensive to force a French capitulation in Canada. Gen. James Wolfe, who had distinguished himself at Louisbourg and assumed command of that expedition upon the departure of Amherst, would take Quebec by leading nine thousand soldiers up the St. Lawrence River; a second column of two thousand British regulars would seal off a French retreat westward by a thrust through Niagara; and Amherst with seven thousand men would capture Ticonderoga and Crown Point.[21]

Montgomery and the 17th Regiment were attached to Amherst's expedition under the reorganization. On May 6, 1759, the regiment combined with the other expeditionary units then assembling near Albany. After extensive preparations, the troops advanced up the Hudson River toward Ticonderoga. Montgomery exhorted his troops to be watchful for an ambush during the treacherous march through the New York wilderness. His concern was confirmed three days after their departure when a band of thirty Indians surprised a hapless party of twelve men of the 17th, killing one lieutenant, one sergeant, and two men, and wounding three others. Arriving at Lake George, the soldiers erected a fort and procured boats to convey them through the waterway. When the British approached Ticonderoga on July 24, they were met by initial stiff resistance from the French. Yet a short time later, the enemy withdrew its main body of twenty-five hundred men to concentrate its defense at Crown Point, leaving a four-hundred-troop rear garrison. After reaching Ticonderoga, the British expedition laid siege to the fort.[22]

While conducting normal siege operations, Montgomery noticed an uneasiness in his men that all soldiers in combat experience from time to time, particularly at night when diminished visibility stimulates the imagination. So, he took precautions to ensure that his men followed the general order specifying no firing at night, but receiving any enemy with the bayonet. The significance of this practice became evident one evening when a false alarm occurred and a British company of light-infantry began indiscriminate firing into the dark. Other soldiers in the siege line joined the errant shooting, resulting in the death of an officer and the wounding of several men from the 17th Regiment.[23]

On July 26, the French garrison at Ticonderoga blew up the fort and retreated to Crown Point. The total British loss at the taking of Ticonderoga was one colonel, one lieutenant, and fifteen privates killed, and about fifty wounded. Of this number, the 17th had two killed and eight wounded. The expedition resumed its advancement northward. However, the French destroyed and abandoned Crown Point before the British could reach it. Montgomery and other members of the expedition spent the next two months reconstructing the works at Crown Point, establishing control of Lake Champlain, and building a road to the Connecticut River. The next objective was Isle aux Noix, some 120 miles down the lake where the French had retired, but the late season interrupted this operation. When cold weather arrived in October, the troops at Crown Point went into winter quarters. Gen. Robert Monckton assumed command of the 17th Regiment in October 1759, officially replacing the deceased Forbes.[24]

In the meantime, the other two expeditions were progressing as planned. Fort Niagara surrendered to the British on July 24, 1759. Troops under Wolfe were closing on the French stronghold at Quebec. Montgomery's oldest brother, Capt. Alexander Montgomery, served in the 43d Regiment, which was included in Wolfe's expedition. Unfortunately, some researchers have confused Richard Montgomery with Alexander Montgomery in an incident during the Quebec campaign. Lt. Malcolm Fraser of the 78th Regiment asserted that on August 23, 1759, his detachment was brought under the command of Captain Montgomery for an attack on a village in the vicinity of St. Joachim. In his journal, Fraser stated: "There were several of the enemy killed and wounded, and a few prisoners taken, all of whom the barbarous Captain Montgomery, who commanded us, ordered to be butchered in a most inhuman and cruel manner . . . one shot and the other knocked down with a tomahawk and both scalped in my absence."[25]

Fraser's outrage over the event is curious in one respect: scalping was not an uncommon practice during the war. One of the earlier instances of its usage was when Col. George Washington sent the scalp of a French officer taken by Indians to Virginia's Governor Dinwiddie in March or April 1756. Because the French had greater Indian allies, they probably were more involved in this practice than the British. However, both sides condoned this savage behavior and encouraged their Indian confederates in the brutality by offering them scalp bounties. The guerrilla or irregular nature of the war contributed to the general acceptance of this atrocious form of combat. Wolfe addressed the issue by signing an order on July 27, 1759, stating that "the general strictly forbids the inhuman practice of scalping, except when the enemy are Indians or Canadians dressed like Indians." Warranted or not, Montgomery's brother gained the name of "Black" Montgomery because of the wartime affair.[26]

Wolfe's force continued to descend upon Quebec and on September 18, 1759, overcame the French defenders there. Both Wolfe and Montcalm, who was in command at the fortress-like city, lost their lives during the contest.

Montgomery continued to rise steadily through the officer ranks. On May 15, 1760, the commanding officer appointed him regimental adjutant, an assignment reserved for the most promising lieutenant in the unit.

Success of the British offensive triad cleared the way for the final stage in the conquest of Canada. The major French opposition that persisted was concentrated in Montreal, which subsequently became the target for a climactic strike by the three British expeditions poised at Quebec, Lake Ontario, and Lake Champlain. The 17th Regiment formed part of the

Lake Champlain division. It set out from Crown Point on August 11, 1760, and captured the intermediate objectives of Isle aux Noix and Fort Chambly before arriving at Montreal. There it merged with the other two divisions in a fine example of strategic concentration to threaten the last French bastion of resistance. As the British troops enveloped the vicinity, refugees crowded into the city, Canadian militiamen deserted, and the twenty-four hundred French regulars found themselves greatly outnumbered. The French commander, realizing that he was unable to withstand the opposing forces, unconditionally surrendered Montreal on September 8, 1760. With this capitulation, all of Canada passed to the British.[27]

From Montreal, Montgomery and his regiment marched to New York during the summer of 1761, and encamped on Staten Island. After conquering Canada, the British government formulated a plan to subdue the French in the West Indies. Plans called for an expedition to be assembled in Barbados and placed under the command of Monckton, who had received a promotion to major general on February 20, 1761. Having been designated as part of the operation, the 17th Regiment, mustering 488 men, sailed from New York on November 19, 1761. After arriving at Barbados on December 24, the regiment joined other units from North America and different garrisons in the West Indies. The combined army numbered thirteen thousand troops accompanied by a large naval flotilla, including transports, frigates, and sixteen ships of the line. This invasion force departed Barbados on January 5, 1762, proceeding toward the initial objective of the campaign—Martinique, an island colonized by the French in 1635.[28]

Even though the British strove to maintain secrecy with their planning and mobilization, the French in Martinique received warning of an intended attack on that island, and took measures to strongly oppose any attempted assault. The French command readied a defense in depth, augmenting natural barriers of steep and rugged terrain with fortified outposts and redoubts that extended over the entire island. In the middle of January 1762, the British forces, including Lieutenant Montgomery and the 17th Regiment, landed on Martinique and established a beachhead. At daybreak on January 24, they opened the main offensive against stout resistance. The enemy's outlying works were eventually stormed one by one, and survivors fled to the citadel at Fort Royal, the island's capital. Losses of British troops in these actions amounted to 33 officers and 350 men killed or wounded. Included in these figures, the 17th

Regiment had one captain wounded; three rank and file killed and sixteen wounded.

By the first of February, the British had closed around and were ready to launch an onslaught on Fort Royal itself. Reduction of several batteries on the heights overlooking the fortress cost the British another 150 casualties, but only one man from the 17th Regiment. On February 3, the French commander, observing the extensive preparations by His Majesty's troops to force the city, now judged it prudent to surrender the fort. It consisted of about 800 regulars and militia, as 150 men were killed or wounded during the siege.

Nine days more sufficed to consolidate the British hold on the rest of the island. On February 12, after suffering over a thousand casualties, the French governor-general agreed to surrender Martinique to the British. General Monckton summed up the conduct of his troops during the campaign in one of his dispatches: "The difficulties they had to encounter, in the attack of an enemy, possessed of every advantage of art and nature, were great, and their perseverance in surmounting these obstacles furnishes a noble example of British spirit." After the capture of Martinique, threatened garrisons on the other main islands of the French West Indies—Grenada, St. Lucia, and St. Vincent—submitted to the British without hostilities.[29]

Fearing that a British victory in the global conflict would jeopardize its New World possessions, Spain belatedly entered the contest in 1761, allied with France. Now that Britain had overcome France in North America and the West Indies, the British ministry decided to avail itself of the large amassment of troops then in the Caribbean area by attacking the Spaniards, as they had the French, in some of their principal settlements. Havana, Cuba, was an important Spanish seaport at this time. Since all Spanish commerce in Mexico and South America funneled through there, to take Havana would sever the lifeline between Spain and its great colonial empire. Therefore, the British resolved to start their Spanish West Indies campaign with Havana. General Monckton returned to New York, to which the British government had appointed him governor before the Martinique campaign. Gen. George Keppel, Earl of Albemarle, assumed command of the new expedition. Once again, the 17th Regiment would see combat—this time as a component of Keppel's eleven-thousand-troop expedition.

On May 6, 1762, the military command rewarded Montgomery's exceptional service by promoting him to captain and giving him one of the ten companies in the 17th Regiment to lead. As company commander, the new captain would be accountable for the activities and welfare of some seventy-five men assigned to his unit. During the upcoming battles, the lives of these men would depend on the correctness and timeliness of his decisions. Although Montgomery realized the heavy responsibility, he was self-assured in his abilities and welcomed the opportunity to live up to the confidence his superiors had placed in him.

The expedition, accompanied by 24 ships of the line, 22 frigates, and 150 transports, set sail from Martinique on May 6, 1762. Shortly after the armada dropped anchor off Havana on June 6, twelve ships of the line raced to the mouth of Havana Harbor to bottle up the Spanish fleet. The city was strongly fortified and garrisoned. Occupation troops numbered seventeen thousand regulars and militiamen. In addition, nine thousand armed sailors and marines were stationed on the twelve warships in the harbor. The Spanish deliberately sank three of these ships when the British squadron arrived to block their entrance into the harbor. On June 7, the British army landed unopposed approximately seven miles from Havana.

Shortly thereafter, the army divided into five brigades. The 17th Regiment, including Montgomery's company, would take part in the siege and capture of Moro Fort. This fortress was the key position of the extensive works that protected the city and was considered by the Spanish to be impregnable. On July 4, the British batteries opened fire with forty-seven guns that had been dragged across a rough, rocky shoreline. Battleships outside the harbor, with a total of 220 cannons, kept up a continuous bombardment. The Spanish answered with their own artillery, driving away the British ships. Nevertheless, the British land batteries eventually managed to silence all the Spanish guns but two. On July 30, Montgomery and his men, together with the other troops of the brigade, captured Moro Fort by storm. The British force could now bear down on the last defenses of the city. At this point, the Spanish governor-general saw that further resistance would be useless and surrendered. On August 13, 1762, the Cross of St. George flew over the Governor's Palace —the British had seized Havana and Cuba.[30]

The successful struggle of more than two months against a superior force defending fortifications that they deemed invincible was a glorious campaign for the British army. The triumph, however, exacted a heavy toll. British troop casualties totaled 520 men killed or dead from wounds received in battle, including the 17th Regiment figures of one sergeant and five men killed, two officers and two men wounded. However, the appalling statistic was the multitude of British soldiers who perished from disease—forty-seven hundred, or almost half of the expedition. The 17th Regiment fared much better, which might be attributed to its leaders— only losing four sergeants and twenty-two men to sickness.[31]

The tropical Cuban climate in the middle of summer took a deadly toll on the unacclimated British troops. The expedition executed its campaign under a relentlessly burning sun when there had been no rain for fourteen days. A scarcity of water compounded the problem. Because there was no fresh water source in the area of operations, drinking water had to be brought from a great distance, resulting in a precarious supply for the troops. One participant described how "excessive thirst soon caused the tongue to swell, extend itself outside the lips, and become black as in a state of mortification; then the whole frame became prey to the most excruciating agonies, til death at length intervened, and gave the unhappy sufferer relief."[32]

On August 20, 1762, Montgomery and his regiment left Cuba in three transports and arrived at New York four days later. However, the debilitating effects of the rigorous campaign lingered. A chaplain who served in the operation reflected that "perhaps those were happiest who died and left their bones around Havana, for those who returned home, took with them broken strength, and a languor which lasted to their life's end."[33] A surgeon examined members of the regiment after they landed at New York and rendered a medical report to General Amherst: "I have visited the above regiments, and am sorry to inform you of the deplorable situation they are in, . . . with dangerous fevers and fluxes, many of the men are past recovery and the rest so weak, that I fear a long time will elapse before they are again fit for service, . . . nor are the officers in a better condition; several cannot recover, and the greater number of the remainder will, for a long time, be weakly, and unfit to undergo much fatigue."[34]

The 17th Regiment and other units that had been involved in the West Indies campaign entered an extensive program of rehabilitation and reorganization while in New York. On February 10, 1763, Britain, France, and Spain signed the Treaty of Paris, officially ending the Seven Years' War. Britain had established its world supremacy with the territorial concessions that it won resulting from the conflict. Except for a few islands off Newfoundland and in the West Indies, France relinquished its New World empire by ceding Britain all of its lands east of the Mississippi, and transferring its claims west of that river and New Orleans to Spain. In return for Cuba, Spain gave Florida to Britain. Thus, Britain prevailed over its rivals for colonial power.

Months of grueling combat exacted a toll on Montgomery. Years later, Janet Montgomery recalled her husband telling her of the campaign that "the duty was so severe, and he complained that by the heat and severity he lost a fine head of hair."[35] Although his ordeal left him with no permanent health impairment, Montgomery's outstanding service during the Seven Years' War sapped much of his vigor. In 1764, his family became concerned about his weakened condition and requested the British government to grant him a leave to return home: "The Relations of Captain Richard Montgomery, of the 17th Regiment of Foot, . . . having represented to me, that the bad State of Health, to which he is reduced by Seven Years Service in America, makes it necessary for him to return to this Kingdom, where His private Affairs also require his Presence."[36] However, Montgomery felt that he could not curtail his duties with the regiment. Several months later, British Army Headquarters in North America replied to the ministry: "Captain Richard Montgomery's Regiment Being ordered upon Service, he will decline accepting any permission, to absent himself from his Duty at present, but as soon as the Service, for which his Regiment is intended, is over he will have leave to return to England."[37]

The service to which the dispatch referred involved hostilities with the Indians, known as Pontiac's Rebellion. This Ottawa chief had been France's staunchest ally during the French and Indian War. Angered by the French surrender, Pontiac organized a general uprising of eighteen Indian tribes against the British. In 1763, he denounced the Treaty of Paris and instigated attacks on British outposts throughout the northwestern frontier, overwhelming eight of twelve scattered forts and forcing the evacuation of two more. After an initial surprise assault failed, the British stronghold at Detroit continued as a prime target for subsequent attacks by Indians. On May 12, 1764, the military command placed the 17th Regiment into a newly formed expedition under Col. John Bradstreet with a mission of reinforcing the beleaguered Detroit garrison. After arriving there, Montgomery and his regiment were instrumental in preventing Indians from taking the important location. As a result, the rebellious tribes became discouraged and eventually forced Pontiac to sign a peace treaty in 1766.[38] After the crisis at Detroit had passed, Montgomery finally took his leave to return home in 1765. Two years later in July 1777, the 17th Regiment concluded its North American tour of duty and redeployed back to England.

While in Britain, Montgomery gradually recovered his health. He also had time to step back and reflect on the larger meaning of the war. On the one hand, he was justly proud of his military accomplishments and advancement within his chosen field of endeavor. On the other, he encountered the disillusionment that many feel when weighing the consequences of a horrific conflict in its aftermath. After all, Montgomery had beheld at close range the carnage and ruin that empire-building engendered. Thus, he was left torn between these two powerful emotions.

A precipitous impediment to the rate of promotion within the officer corps added to Montgomery's growing discontent. During wartime, military expansion and personnel casualties allowed rapid battlefield promotions for deserving soldiers. With the onset of peacetime and demobilization, advancement in the British army became bogged down in political and bureaucratic maneuvering. Patronage, once again, reigned over merit as a basis for military preferment. Montgomery had risen from ensign to captain in less than six years. Ten more years would pass while he languished at the rank of captain. Nearing twenty years of total time in service and lacking an influential benefactor, Montgomery considered his prospects for attaining a personally rewarding culmination to the brilliant earlier part of his career.

During the late 1760s, Montgomery became friends with such prominent Whigs as Isaac Barré, Edmund Burke, and Charles James Fox. These political opposition leaders were becoming progressively more outspoken in their criticism of the British ministry. Barré shared a similar experience with Montgomery. He had entered the British army as an ensign in 1746 and later served with great distinction in North America during the Seven Years' War. Although he rose ultimately to the rank of lieutenant colonel and commanded a regiment, Pitt turned down his next promotion, ending his interest in a military career. Montgomery, Barré, and Burke also were fellow alumni. All three received a liberal education at Trinity College in Dublin, although Barré and Burke had graduated some years before Montgomery. All these factors served to strengthen the intellectual bond among these individuals. They spent many hours together discussing politics while Montgomery was stationed in England. However, Montgomery's association with Barré, Burke, and Fox garnered him little favor with the politicians who dominated the British government.[39]

So, Montgomery concluded his remarkable military service in the Seven Years' War—and beyond. Yet, he remained concerned about his future in the British army and began to question the validity of governmental political policies. This period of fallow service, based on stagnation in rank, would position the unfulfilled, restless war veteran at the crossroads of a major life change.

When a chance to purchase a major's commission presented itself in 1771, Montgomery eagerly lodged his money. However, a political favorite of Lord North's ministry procured the majority to which Montgomery felt his services entitled him. Because of his lack of influential political patronage, Montgomery found himself shut out from continued advancement in the British military establishment. On April 6, 1772, the disappointed captain sold his own commission in revulsion to what he regarded as the deprivation of his rightful military promotion.[40]

Now, Montgomery had resentfully quit the British army that he faithfully and ably served for so long. Still a relatively young man at the age of thirty-three, he began looking for new horizons where he could find the opportunities that had eluded him since the end of the Seven Years' War.

CHAPTER FOUR

Decision for the Patriot Cause

In this most eligible of all situations,
the life of a country gentleman . . .
he devoted his time to sweet domestic intercourse . . .
Nor from that happy spot did he wish to stray . . .
But when the hand of power was stretched forth
against the land of his residence,
he had a heart too noble not to sympathize
in its distress . . .
Although his liberal spirit placed him
above local prejudices,
and he considered himself as a member
of the empire at large;
yet America, struggling in the cause of Liberty,
henceforth became his peculiar country,
and that country took full possession of his soul,
lifting him above this earthy dross, and every
private affection . . . [1]

In late 1772 or early 1773, Richard Montgomery migrated to America. Before making this major change in his life, he explained his reasons for leaving England in a letter to his cousin, John Montgomery: "As a man with little money cuts but a bad figure in this country among peers, nabobs, etc., I have cast my eye on America, where my pride and poverty will be much more at their ease." Montgomery obviously understated his financial situation. Although lacking a title or influential patronage, he was far from impoverishment. He received a middling inheritance when his father's will divided the family resources among him and two other siblings. Proceeds from the sale of his captain's commission further augmented his total assets.[2]

Because of his disappointment in promotion and future advancement possibilities in the British army, Montgomery became disgusted with military service. He decided upon a course of retreat and solitude removed from the vexations of politics and public service, vowing never to marry or take up arms again. Montgomery sought solace and a new beginning in the colonies, where both of his vows would be relinquished within three years. As a repose from his previous turbulent military career, he intended to establish an idyllic lifestyle for himself as a gentleman-farmer. During Montgomery's wartime service in America, the vastness of the country and the unlimited opportunities it offered impressed him. An enterprising gentleman of modest means, he reasoned, could readily accumulate land and eventually amass an estate. Shortly after his arrival, Montgomery bought a sixty-seven-acre farmstead at King's Bridge, located in the out ward, some thirteen miles north of New York City.[3]

While Montgomery settled into his new surroundings during the first winter and spring, he became reacquainted with Janet Livingston. They had met eight years before when he was an ambitious young officer in the British 17th Foot and she was passing into womanhood. During the French and Indian War, Montgomery's unit traversed up the Hudson River en route to its station at Michilimackinac in Michigan territory. When the soldiers disembarked from their boats near Clermont, the grand Livingston manor, Janet's father graciously invited the officers to visit. Richard and Janet experienced their first meeting during this occasion. It probably amounted to no more than a formal introduction and polite discourse, and left little impression on either.[4]

By the time of their second encounter, thirty-year-old Janet had developed into a most eligible lady for courtship and marriage. The eldest daughter in the large family of Judge Robert R. Livingston, one of the most affluent and influential men in New York, she personified a privileged, accomplished, and attractive woman of the time. Montgomery must have been immediately taken with her, as he wasted no time in vying for her affections. Since Janet held the social status of a Livingston, the selection process for her husband was deliberate and discriminating. In her memoirs, she claimed a long succession of suitors before Montgomery, but none had been successful in winning her hand. She rejected the advances of those who displeased her for one reason or another. Janet also wrote of a romantic notion that portended doom for men who sought her affection: "There was a fatality attending most of those who offered themselves." She related how two suitors broke their necks after falling from their horses and another was lost at sea after establishing a romantic relationship with her.[5]

Janet's family withheld approval of other suitors whom they deemed socially unacceptable: "I nearly fell in love with an officer who had only his beauty and his regimentals to boast of—he had neither education nor talents. I saw these defects and yet in despite of all gave him a preference. I would have been his wife could my parents have consented. They detested redcoats and had my happiness too much at heart." The Livingstons' estimation of the British soldiers obviously had deteriorated from the French and Indian War, when they cordially welcomed them into their home.[6]

During that war, colonists generally appreciated the security benefits that British troops brought by pushing French authority out of North America and subduing the Indians. After the conflict, however, numerous colonists came to resent a continued large British military presence. They suspected that the soldiers were an instrument of the ministerial government for coercing provincial submission to increasingly stringent imperial political measures. By the time of Janet's courtship, many colonists regarded so-called "redcoats," "lobsterbacks," or "bloodybacks" with disdain. This dramatic transformation of the Livingston family attitudes toward British troops in the colonies was indicative of the evolution of patriot attitudes concerning British authority in America.

During their unusually brief engagement, Janet still retained her anxiety over foreboding misfortune that she felt could befall a potential husband. Richard lightly dismissed her fears, however, and her sisters offered supportive counsel. After receiving favorable consideration from Janet, Richard followed convention by formally requesting permission for marriage from the parents of the intended bride. In late May 1773, Montgomery wrote to Judge Livingston: "I have been extremely anxious to solicit your approbation, together with Mrs. Livingston's, in an affair which nearly concerns my happiness and no less affects your daughter. . . . I have ventured at last to request, sir, that you and Mrs. Livingston will consent to a union which to me has the most promising appearance of happiness, from the lady's uncommon merit and amiable worth." He concluded with a polite compliment regarding how he would be honored to join the Livingston family: "Nor will it be an inconsiderable addition to be favored by such respectable characters with the title of son, should I be so fortunate as to deserve it."[7]

While his prospective father-in-law deliberated over the request for marriage, Montgomery's social status and former service in the British army were probably areas of some concern. When the patriarch of the Livingston dynasty, Robert Livingston, died in 1728, he divided his vast estate between two of his sons. The elder son, Philip Livingston, received the bulk of the property (about 141,000 acres), known as Livingston Manor. The younger son, Robert Livingston, Jr. (Janet's grandfather), inherited the adjacent Clermont estate of 13,000 acres. Consequently, the two Livingston branches at Livingston Manor and Clermont constituted one of the largest land-owning families in New York.[8]

Influence accompanied the affluence of this family, which cooperated in achieving political ascendancy of the province. Judge Robert R. Livingston (of Clermont), Janet's father, took an active part in colonial affairs. He served as a colonel in the militia, functioned for a time as high sheriff of New York, and represented Dutchess County in the General Assembly from 1757 to 1768. He attained appointment as Judge of the King's Bench in 1763, which operated as the New York supreme court of those times. In 1765, he attended the Stamp Act Congress as a delegate from Dutchess County. During 1772, he acted as chairman of the New York Committee of Correspondence, part of a network to coordinate colonial vigilance against the British. When New Yorkers divided over the question of remaining loyal to the king, Judge Livingston emerged as a recognized leader of the whig or patriot faction.[9]

The fact that he had earlier resigned his commission and elected to live in the colonies probably exonerated Montgomery from his British affiliation in Judge Livingston's mind. Montgomery's prior association with Whig leaders in Parliament—Edmund Burke, Isaac Barré, Charles James Fox, and other opposition politicians sympathetic with the American colonists—must have enhanced his acceptability with the Livingstons. After family consultations and investigation into Montgomery's character and reputation, Judge Livingston replied to his future son-in-law on June 21, 1773: "Since we heard of your intentions, solicitous for our daughter's happiness, we have made such inquiries as have given a great deal of satisfaction. We both approve of your proposal and heartily wish your union may yield you all the happiness you seem to expect, to which we shall always be ready to contribute all in our power."[10]

With the formalities completed for his marriage, Montgomery became concerned over how the local press would announce the event. Anti-imperialist fervor of that time disdained any trappings of royalty. Montgomery's sister, Sarah, had married an Irish viscount, Charles, Lord Ranelagh. The peerage was the only inheritance that befell Ranelagh, as he became strapped to support his large family. This was probably all the more reason for the despoiled lord to cling to his nobility, trying to bolster his familial pride and honor. Montgomery had no desire to be linked publicly to his titled relatives in Ireland during his present circumstances. He felt that it would only subject him to possible embarrassment. Just before his wedding day, Montgomery expressed a hope that the journalists would "let me down easy" by not advertising the royal inference. To his chagrin, a New York City newspaper pronounced: "Last Thursday evening was married at the Manor of Livingston, Richard Montgomery, Esq., brother to the Right Hon. the Countess of Ranelagh, to Miss. Livingston, eldest daughter of the Hon. Robert R. Livingston, Esq.; one of the Judges of the supreme court of judicature, a lady of fine understanding, and very amiable accomplishments."[11]

The wedding announcement became a subject of some good-natured humor directed at Montgomery by the Livingstons. Like most of the privileged social group in the colonies, the Livingston family embraced the idea of a natural elite, but they were careful not to portray themselves as aristocrats or noblemen. The colonies were evolving toward a culture that fancied the concept of the self-made person, apart from the European tradition of relying on bloodlines to determine social status. Although adhering to deferential values, the prosperous and influential segment of the population had no wish to become a catalyst for class struggle by callously flaunting its social position.[12]

Thus, on July 24, 1773, Richard Montgomery and Janet Livingston married at Clermont with most of the Livingston family present for the ceremony. Richard leased his farm at King's Bridge to a tenant, and the Montgomerys established their residence in a small house at Rhinebeck where Janet owned property. With most of his remaining funds, Richard purchased more land adjoining Janet's tract. He then set to work fencing the pasture, plowing the fields, building a small grain mill, and laying the foundation for a larger home. Janet's sister, Catharine, formed a favorable opinion of Richard during this time, but she also noted his bouts of melancholy brought on by fears that his contentment was too good to last: "Mrs. [Catharine Livingston] Garretson, who sometimes came to stay with her eldest sister at the cottage, had ample opportunity of knowing this brother. She spoke of the influence of his manly character upon the villagers, of his grave rebuke of idleness and vice and of his many amiable domestic virtues. . . . He was so happy in his domestic relations that forebodings would sometimes arise and he would exclaim, 'I never was so happy in all my life; everything conspires to make it so,' then shaking his head sadly he would say, 'This cannot last; it cannot last.' "[13]

Janet told of a strange and frightening dream that she had three months after their marriage. In it, Montgomery and his brother engaged in a fierce duel, and Richard sustained a mortal wound. Upon awakening and relating the vision to her husband, he said, "I have always told you that my happiness is not lasting. . . . Let us enjoy it as long as we may and leave the rest to God."[14]

Although both were basically fatalists, the personal philosophies of the Montgomerys differed somewhat. While Richard seemed to accept fate with little reservation, Janet tended to agonize more over their destiny and turned to her husband for reassurance. Although Richard had forsaken his army career, the lingering mental attitudes formed by years of service were not as easily shed. His military background probably conditioned him for a direct, confrontational approach to life's problems. This professional soldier's mindset prevented him from dwelling upon matters that he deemed beyond human control. On the other hand, Janet's thinking reflected the cultural role of privileged women of that era. Society accustomed women of leisure to a seemingly gentle, passive existence in which demure ladies attained their goals through indirect means. With this feeling of being limited in personally directing their lives, many of these women tended to brooding reflection of their perplexities.

Ominous perceptions, however, could not spoil the marital bliss that the Montgomery newlyweds enjoyed. The Livingstons welcomed Richard into their family, and he emerged as an industrious and faithful husband who cherished his quiet, rural life. Janet readily accepted her position as a devoted and dutiful wife.

Still, the couple experienced some areas of contention. Janet, for instance, wanted to have a child, particularly a son, as soon as possible. However, Richard did not share her enthusiasm. He chided her by saying, "Be contented, Janet. Suppose we had a son, and he was a fool. Think of that!" As in most other matters, Janet deferred to her husband's judgment.[15]

In a letter written in late 1774 to Perkins Magra—friend of both

Richard and Janet, and an officer who had served with Montgomery in his previous British regiment—Montgomery admitted to nostalgia about his former comrades: "There are some in the corps [17th Regiment] for whom I entertain a more cordial regard than I shall probably ever feel again for any of my fellow creatures." The newly established country squire then turned to a description of his present life, writing with zeal and pride about the improvements he had initiated on his small estate: " 'Tis a pity you can't come help me plan a house which I shall lay the foundation of this fall. My mill is almost finished." He also confirmed his contentment in his current existence: "Your suspicions touching my hobby horse are not well founded. I rode a skittish nag for fifteen years. A country life is the only recourse of disappointed ambition, to have something to do the surest means of procuring good spirits and comfortable feelings." The retired soldier closed his letter with a fateful remark: "I begin to think I shan't die by a pistol."[16]

By 1775, emerging events surrounding increasingly antagonistic relations between the colonies and England interrupted the tranquil life of the Montgomerys. The practice of maintaining unwanted British soldiers in the colonies under the Quartering Acts had resulted in the Boston Massacre, and the protracted series of restrictive trade and taxation acts culminated with the Boston Tea Party in late 1773 and the Intolerable or Coercive Acts of 1774. These last measures brought the closing of the port of Boston and the declaration of martial law in that colony. All of these points of contention contributed to unraveling the bonds of the parent British state with the American colonies. When colonial leaders gathered at the First Continental Congress in September 1774, the situation had reached crisis proportions. With the open hostilities between British troops and colonial militia at Lexington and Concord in April 1775, and the convening of the Second Continental Congress in May 1775, American patriots decided to secure a full redress of their grievances with Britain by armed rebellion.

The most publicized events that received the bulk of British reaction erupted in Massachusetts, which Parliament considered to be the seedbed of the revolt. Similar incidents, however, occurred throughout the colonies. New York produced its share of extralegal activities directed against British authority. Yet, avid patriots in other colonies occasionally faulted their fellow colony for demonstrating an apathetic zeal toward their cause. After returning home from a visit to New England in the summer of 1773, a Philadelphia enthusiast wrote to his friend in Boston that patriotism "seemed to have taken but shallow root in some places, particularly New York, where political principles are truly as unfixed as the wind. One year sees the New Yorkers champions for liberty, and the next hugging their chains."[17]

The reputation thus acquired by New York was mostly unfair. The slow maturation of the patriot infrastructure in this province largely resulted because New York City functionally served as the capital of the British government in the colonies. Many New Yorkers, probably more than anywhere else, owed their livelihoods to the English bureaucracy. This widespread affiliation took some time to erode and generated a deceptive image of the colony. New York was slow in its revolutionary efforts only in contrast to the New England colonies, the crucible of the Revolution. The tortuous path of New York's patriot movement concealed the depth of its commitment only to an unwary observer.

Six weeks before the Boston Massacre, New York City residents rioted against British troops. On January 19, 1770, strained civil-military relations in Manhattan led to two days of street fighting, referred to as the Battle of Golden Hill. Built-up animosity between royal military forces stationed in the city and the populace precipitated open fighting between British soldiers and New Yorkers in the Golden Hill area on John Street. Hostilities between the two factions resumed the next day with a second riot on Nassau Street before order returned.

A disturbance involving a felled liberty pole served as the provocation for this incident. In March 1766, New Yorkers joined most of the other colonies in erecting so-called liberty poles to celebrate the repeal of the unpopular Stamp Act, a major political victory over Parliament. These structures usually occupied a prominent location in the town. They functioned as patriotic symbols and rallying points for speeches and demonstrations espousing opposition to British policies in the colonies.

British troops, who considered themselves faithful agents of the Crown, regarded the liberty poles as a flagrant insult to imperial authority. Usually acting without specific orders while off duty, soldiers felt honor bound to cut the liberty poles down as quickly as they reappeared. The destruction of the fifth successive liberty pole in New York City resulted in the Golden Hill and Nassau Street riots, involving some sixty harassed troops and hundreds of angry civilians. During these brief but intense clashes, soldiers used bayonets against threatening crowds armed with weapons of opportunity. Although the participants suffered no fatalities and most casualties amounted to only cuts and bruises, the encounters underscored the combustibility of anti-British sentiment in New York.[18]

The reported case of Michael Smith glorified the individual action supposedly taken by some New York citizens in this affair. When word of the confrontation reached Smith, a Broadstreet chairmaker's apprentice, he grabbed a leg of an unassembled chair and ran toward the commotion. Using the chair leg as a club, he attacked a British grenadier and captured the soldier's weapon. Smith triumphantly returned to his shop after the fray with the musket and bayonet. He regarded the appropriated firearm as a trophy of his personal triumph over the British, and proudly displayed it while relating the circumstances of its acquisition on any occasion that presented itself. The New York Sons of Liberty seized upon these particular acts by New Yorkers to build the participants into folk heroes and strengthen the patriot rhetoric against ministerial government.

Some partisan commentators erroneously reported later that the troops killed one citizen during the New York riots and touted the skirmish as the "first blood shed" in the American Revolution. The Boston Massacre on March 5, 1770, however, with its confirmed fatalities, overshadowed the Battle of Golden Hill in the contemporary patriot mind.[19]

New York also participated in its own tea party. In May 1773, Parliament passed the Tea Act to rescue the floundering British East India Company. Since the company represented the largest business establishment in the British Empire, this commercial enterprise was so vast that it influenced the national economy. Unfortunately, the tea trade had fallen into desperate economic straits that threatened the British financial climate. Colonial boycotts over previous British government revenue measures were responsible, in large part, for a large stockpile of unsold tea in England and the company's possible bankruptcy. In passing the act, the government intended to give the East India Company a monopoly on tea sales in the colonies. Parliament hoped that this marketing concession would relieve the company's warehouses, which were burdened with 18 million pounds of surplus tea.

Even though the Tea Act would actually lower the price of tea for the consumer, it would eliminate colonial middlemen and errant tea-smuggling operations that especially flourished in the provinces of New York, Pennsylvania, and Rhode Island. Thus, powerful colonists engaged in this lucrative business stood to lose a part of their commercial domain, and they joined with popular patriot leaders to turn public opinion against the bill. The issue that emerged from these circumstances was that Parliament had devised yet another devious scheme to tax the colonies without representation, requiring the colonists to continue their vigilance against imperial slavery by resisting East India tea. When the tea ships arrived from England at the principal ports of Boston, New York, Philadelphia, and Charleston, hostile crowds awaited them. Boston Harbor became the site of the first encounter, resulting in the Boston Tea Party on December 16, 1773, where a well-organized crowd destroyed the tea by dumping it into the water before it could be unloaded.

By the fall of 1773, the people of New York had become concerned over the tea tax as well. Constant public attention focused by local media and frequent rumors that the tea ships were approaching kept the populace agitated. The Sons of Liberty circulated an "association" pledge not to buy, sell, or use East India tea, and a wide cross section of New Yorkers signed. A clandestine patriot body, calling itself the "Mohawks," published a notice in Rivington's *Gazetteer* on December 2, 1773, that they were "prepared to pay an unwelcome visit" to any ship that arrived with the boycotted tea. News of the celebrated Boston Tea Party reached New York by December 21, 1773, to heighten dissension further.

Finally, on April 18, 1774, a tea ship anchored outside New York Harbor. After several days of heated negotiations with the patriot "committee of inspection," the captain prudently decided not to risk the wrath of New Yorkers by trying to unload his consignment of tea, and he began to make preparations for a return to England. The master of another tea ship that arrived on April 22, 1774, was not as accommodating. He docked his vessel at a New York pier and attempted to conceal its cargo of tea while he devised a way to off-load it. The patriots suspected his plot, and their intelligence network soon confirmed their skepticism. Facing mounting animosity, the unnerved captain eventually broke down and admitted his cargo included East India tea.

Patriot activists immediately started to plan operations to prevent unloading of the tea. That night, a large crowd, under the influence of the Sons of Liberty, assembled at the wharf where the tea ship was docked. The "Mohawks" were expecting to do their duty by disposing of the tea at a prearranged time. However, the dockside crowd became so aroused and impatient by about eight o'clock that some of them took matters into their own hands. They boarded the ship and destroyed seventeen chests of tea, valued at £2,000, by opening and throwing them

into the harbor. This premature activity by the crowd took the "Mohawks" by surprise, as they were donning Indian disguises in a nearby
tavern at the time, and preempted their planned event. The next morning, festive celebrants watched the two tea ships set sail for England—
one with all of its tea plundered and ruined, and the other with a hold of
undelivered tea. This was New York's "Tea Party," which approximated
and reinforced that of Boston.[20]

All of these events formed the backdrop to Montgomery's studied
detachment from politics. Although he favored a simple existence of
noninvolvement, his lifestyle was not reclusive. Montgomery must have
confronted reports of these happenings on a regular basis as he went
about the daily routine of managing his estate. Information concerning
aggravated British-colonial relations dominated newspapers, broadsides,
pamphlets, rumors, and conversation of the time. In addition, Montgomery no doubt had firsthand knowledge of some of these incidents. He
possessed an educated and inquiring mind, and these events begged
analysis. The jarring conditions of the times were not conducive to
prolonged stoicism. Compelling external forces intruded upon and altered
the lives of the colonists. Like the rest of his contemporaries, Montgomery eventually felt the pressure to choose sides in the growing controversy. All alternatives had to be considered to resolve the dilemma in his
own mind and arrive at a personal decision. Then, there was the Livingston connection.

The Livingston dynasty projected the family into a position of power
in New York provincial politics. Yet, it did not enjoy absolute primacy
in this respect. The De Lanceys paralleled the Livingstons in their evolution into prominent and influential families. As these two houses built
ambitious and competitive commercial enterprises, it was natural that this
contention be extended to the political front. Also, most of the socioeco-
nomically advantaged colonists felt that it was an obligation of their social
station to serve the community as political leaders. So, these two families
were not the only members of the ruling elite involved in New York
politics, but they were undoubtedly the most active. After a visit in early
1774, John Adams noted, "The two great families in this province, upon
whose motions all their politics turn, are the De Lanceys and Livingstons."[21]

The predominance of the Livingstons and De Lanceys in politics dated
from the 1740s, and they competed on generally equal terms, with control of the provincial assembly alternating between the two for several

decades. Additionally, the Livingston–De Lancey rivalry was not limited to kinship. Political activists of all sorts broadened the partisan system by lining up behind one family standard or the other. In opposing each other, the two factions amended their agendas as political expediency dictated. The Livingstons and De Lanceys engaged in a balancing act between currying favor from the governor and the Crown, and seeking cooperation with an emerging popular movement hostile to ministerial rule. Thus, if changes in the political system were inevitable, each side maneuvered to be well positioned in the new order that would follow. The prerevolutionary period would finally resolve this longstanding family and political rivalry. The Stamp Act crisis opened a crucial period in which the De Lanceys almost delivered a death blow to Livingston political prospects. Both factions supported the Stamp Act Congress held in New York City to voice disapproval of such imperial measures. Judge Livingston served as a delegate to the congress and authored the petition that was sent to King George III, respectfully protesting the stamp legislation. But, the Livingstons suffered from the measured, reasoned manner by which they fashioned their moderate opposition to the British in the general emotional storm that ensued. The De Lanceys fared much better because of the strong ties they forged with the more radical, popularly supported Sons of Liberty.[22]

In the aftermath of the Stamp Act protests, a widespread tenant or land riot broke out in the rural districts north of New York City. This general disorder consisted of five hundred to two thousand participants, as disgruntled tenants roamed the countryside in armed bands during 1766 and clashed with the Hudson Valley landlords. During these disturbances, the "levelers," as they sometimes called themselves, killed and wounded a number of men, burned houses, and destroyed crops. This activity centered on the large Livingston estates and threatened New York City before local law enforcement units and British soldiers subdued the outbreak.[23]

A rebellious spirit that challenged established civil authority provided the atmosphere for the tenant riots, although these hostilities were not an integral part of the coming Revolution. The New York Sons of Liberty, for example, regarded the riots as a separate issue and did not support them. A British officer who participated in apprehending the offending tenants snidely remarked in his journal that the Sons of Liberty were "great opposers to these rioters as they were of the opinion no one is entitled to riot but themselves."[24]

Judge Livingston's propensity for law and order in protecting manorial property was revealed when his cousin, the lord of Livingston Manor adjacent to Clermont, wrote to him for advice on dealing with riotous tenants. The judge responded, "I would let the mob go on their own way and as soon as they had separated get a warrant and take up those that are most dangerous and guilty, and carry them to Albany Gaol. . . . If they should chance kill any person in the Fray every man of them is guilty of murder and the Government must interpose even if they should be obliged to raise men for the purpose."[25]

The Quartering or Mutiny Act matter heated up after authorities quelled the tenant uprising. This legislation required colonial assemblies to provide quarters and supplies for British soldiers stationed in their province. Parliament had annually passed temporary acts for quartering troops in America during the French and Indian War. Many Americans came to regard the acts as strictly wartime emergency measures. After the conclusion of hostilities, therefore, the colonies proved less willing to support the British military establishment in their midst. Yet at the time of its passage in 1765, the latest act stirred little controversy in the New York Assembly. Its members were too occupied with adopting resolutions against the Stamp Act to give the Quartering Act much of their attention.

Parliament persisted in seeking adherence to its decree. Now reeling from recent events, the Livingstons embraced the quartering statute in the hope that British troops could safeguard the colony from such domestic law-breaking and attacks on property as experienced during the land riots. Since they were the principal plaintiff in the riots, the Livingstons' self-interest in the bill was all too obvious. As a result, they appeared to be willing to jeopardize the common good—because the same British soldiers could also be used to enforce the Stamp Act and other objectionable ministerial measures—for selfish considerations.

The Livingston-led New York assembly pushed through quartering-enabling legislation in July 1766. Even so, the measure did not fully conform with the Quartering Act. It did not acknowledge Parliament's authority to pass such a law and treated the requirement as a mere requisition, with the final decision resting with the New York assembly. Mounting tensions over the measure led to a clash between citizens and soldiers on August 11, 1766. Subsequent action by the New York assembly led to continued reluctance for unconditionally implementing provisions of the bill. On July 2, 1767, a frustrated Parliament declared the province in rebellion and passed the New York Restraining Act, which ordered the assembly suspended effective October 1, 1767, as punishment for noncompliance. Meanwhile, New York assemblymen voted for a more liberal interpretation of the Quartering Act, but it still fell significantly short of complete conformity. Fearing that a prolonged confrontation with New York over the issue might unite the colonies in opposition and defeat its original intent, Parliament decided not to invoke the suspension.

The damage had already been done. The Restraining Act, even though it had not been enforced, provided a cause célèbre to kindle colonial resistance. Richard Henry Lee, the ardent Virginia patriot, referred to the act as a "flaming sword over our heads."[26] New York's recalcitrance toward the Quartering Act also provided an example for other colonies to emulate. Of the seven continental colonies (New York, New Jersey, Massachusetts, Georgia, South Carolina, Connecticut, and Pennsylvania) specifically affected by the Quartering Act, all but two (Connecticut and Pennsylvania) followed New York by refusing full compliance at one time or another.[27]

As a result of the Livingstons' conspicuous advocacy of the Quartering Act, public opinion increasingly regarded the family leaders as self-serving patricians who had lost touch with the general cause. The De Lanceys took good advantage of the situation to discredit and displace the Livingston political machine. After 1769, most members of the Livingston family grew dispirited and withdrew from New York politics. William Livingston, the cousin of Judge Robert R. Livingston, actually left New York in 1772 and settled at his country retreat, Liberty Hall, near Morristown, New Jersey. He quickly adapted to politics in that colony and became its first revolutionary governor. Judge Livingston remained as the only member of the former dynasty with an important political office after 1769. Never since the first Livingston entered public life in the seventeenth century had the family political fortunes sunk so low.[28]

The continuing revolutionary crisis brought a remarkable turnaround in the Livingston–De Lancey rivalry. By 1773, the De Lanceys joined the movement in support of the British and became the senior loyalist faction in America. This unfortunate decision wrecked their provincial interests and political influence. Their property in the colony suffered sacking and confiscation as members of the De Lancey family eventually emigrated to England. The Livingstons, on the other hand, managed to shed their previous stigma and became imbued with intensified patriot commitment. Their revived association with the revolutionary element propelled the family once more into a political leadership position in New York.

Shortly after Montgomery became a member of the Livingston clan, the family engaged in a political discussion. Janet, in her memoirs, described how her grandfather turned to her father and said, "You and I will never live to see this country independent. Montgomery, you may, but (speaking to his grandson) Robert, you will!" Janet continued her remembrance of her grandfather's passion for American independence: "On the breaking out of war he was in raptures. In beginning with the Bostonians he said 'They have taken the bull by the horns.' His sanguine temper made him expect with confidence our independence." Janet, however, surmised that the turbulent atmosphere of 1775 hastened the end for this aged patriot, who was then in his eighty-seventh year: "I verily believe the Battle of Bunker Hill (of which such a false and disastrous report was made) was his death. He took to his bed immediately, lay a week without pain, and died. The last words he muttered were 'What news from Boston?' " His son, Judge Robert R. Livingston, followed him in death six months later.[29]

The Livingston family's stature as ardent supporters of the patriot cause may be gauged by the level of criticism they received from the royalist opposition faction. Thomas Jones, a fervent New York loyalist who vigorously denounced the Revolution as nothing more than widespread lawlessness, singled out the Livingstons for particularly venomous treatment in his history of the Revolution. Jones alleged that a Livingston instigated an atrocity against a British officer in December 1776. The related incident involved the assassination of Capt. Erasmus Phillips as he passed through Princeton to join his regiment: "One of the party who committed the murder, his name shall be mentioned, was a John Livingston, one of the sons of Robert R. Livingston, late one of the Judges of the Supreme Court of the province of New York. This barbarian, in a public company at Middletown, in Connecticut, boasted of this horrid murder as an act of heroism, a noble achievement; and so little remorse had he for this cruel act in which he had taken a principal part, that he declared, 'That Captain Phillips made one of the handsomest corpses he had ever beheld.' " Jones continued quoting remarks that he attributed to John Livingston: " 'We stripped him,' says he, 'of all his clothes and left him naked in the street.' 'I thought,' added he, 'that I should be obliged to have cut his head off, to get at his diamond stock buckle, but I effected

my purpose by breaking his neck and turning his head topsy turvy.' "
Jones concluded this lurid account with a provocative condemnation: "Let
the public judge whether a more barbarous, cruel, unchristianlike act was
ever committed among civilized nations. But it was done by rebels. It
was an act of rebellion, and done by people who bragged of their humanity."[30]

After 1773, the Livingston family embraced the patriot movement en
masse. All of Judge Livingston's sons who were old enough became
involved in the Revolution in some capacity. Even all his sons-in-law
actively participated in the conflict against Britain. So, the persuasion of
the Livingstons must have fallen heavily on Montgomery. Yet, the former
British officer was a strong-willed person, quite capable of independent
thinking. He reached his individual decision after considering all the
realities as he perceived them at the time. Like many other provincial
inhabitants, of which he was now one, Montgomery grew to regard
himself less as an Englishman and more as a self-determining American.
Increasingly, he viewed England in antagonistic terms as an unneeded,
oppressive, and even tyrannical parent-state. Montgomery perceived little
benefit to be derived from the British government and resented its dicta-
torial interference in his life. Montgomery's lingering bitterness over his
rejected commission in the British army certainly conditioned his attitude. In time, he became estranged from his former allegiance to England. Thus, the influence of the Livingston family ties and his own
intellectual convictions combined to draw Montgomery inexorably into
the patriot cause.

Service in the Provincial Congress

> Having a heart distended with benevolence, and panting
> to do good, he soon acquired, without courting it from
> his neighbors, that authority which an opinion of su-
> perior talents and inflexible integrity never fail to
> create. . . .[1]

aving swayed him to the patriot cause, prevalent events coaxed
Montgomery's entrance into politics to serve in the New York
Provincial Congress. This extralegal body had evolved from
several precedent assemblies that New Yorkers called to consider the
mounting crisis with England. Long before the Revolution, New Yorkers
became accustomed to creating unauthorized political pressure groups to
protest against and win concessions from the constituted government.
Through the years, the process evolved as a means of redress against any
autocratic governor. As the conflict between the colonists and the British
government became more acute, New Yorkers formed committees, corresponding with those of other colonies, to devise ways of opposing
perceived oppressive measures by the British government. The Navigation Laws revived in the 1760s, the Sugar Act of 1764, and the Stamp
Act of 1765 engendered such reactions. Although these organizations
initially included members who were moderate in their views toward
King and Parliament, their voices were progressively drowned out by
more extreme rhetoric. Thus, the patriot faction increasingly dominated
the ad hoc governmental entities.

Following the royal colony pattern, New York's official government before 1775 consisted of a Crown-appointed governor and council and a locally elected general assembly. By 1774, a power play began in the colonies to wrest political authority from royalist control and place it in the hands of patriot bodies. The First Continental Congress recommended that the various colonies establish a network of committees in order to mount a unified opposition to unwanted British policies. On January 20, 1774, even before the First Continental Congress met, this movement started in New York with the creation of a Committee of Correspondence, also known as the Committee of Thirteen, to keep watch on the ministerial government and to coordinate with like committees in other colonies.

Since the duly constituted General Assembly authorized its establishment, the Committee of Correspondence was an officially sanctioned organization. However, on May 16, 1774, the Committee of Thirteen spawned the Committee of Fifty, which had no legitimate basis for its existence. Three days later, the group admitted an additional representative, becoming the Committee of Fifty-One. The New York committee system flourished with the apparent inability of royal officials to counter it effectively and reaped increased popular support.[2]

The colony was without its chief royal official during this critical period. In April 1774, Gov. William Tryon had sailed for England to discuss deteriorating conditions within his province with the British government. Lt. Gov. Cadwallader Colden, the acting governor, displayed an attitude of forbearance in dealing with the licentious situation. In a July 1774 report to the colonial secretary in Parliament, Colden described the current committee's political transgressions as "dangerous and illegal transactions," but questioned "by what means shall Government prevent them?" He then agonized, "An Attempt by the Power of the Civil Magistrate, would only shew their weakness. . . . It is thought much more prudent to avoid; and to shun all Extreams. . . . Things may take a favourable turn."[3]

The heady atmosphere caused by the success of these extralegal activities encouraged more individuals to risk being singled out under charges of sedition. Expanded committee representation reflected this boldness. On November 22, 1774, a Committee of Sixty succeeded the Committee of Fifty-One. On May 1, 1775, a Committee of One Hundred replaced the Committee of Sixty. In addition to enlarging their membership, the committees assumed an increased range of functions, including enforcing the nonimportation of British goods, harassment of loyal colonists, and designation of even more radical groups.[4]

Controlled by the loyalist faction in February 1775, the New York General Assembly refused to approve the proceedings of the First Continental Congress and to appoint delegates to the Second Continental Congress. The patriot faction soon retaliated. On March 1, 1775, the Committee of Sixty advised county committees to send representatives to a Provincial Convention that would meet in New York City to elect delegates to the Second Continental Congress. Although four or five of the fourteen counties failed to respond, approximately one hundred representatives from widespread regions of the province reported to the convention when it met on April 20, 1775. Two days later, the convention appointed twelve delegates to represent New York at Philadelphia, including Montgomery's brother-in-law, Robert R. Livingston. Having accomplished its work, the convention then dissolved.[5]

The startling news of the Massachusetts militia and British army skirmish at Lexington and Concord reached New York by an express rider from Connecticut on the Sunday afternoon of April 23, 1775, the day after the convention concluded. The feelings of betrayal and outrage with which many New Yorkers received the report aroused general sentiment against the British government and inflamed patriot ardor. For several days, New York City disintegrated into mob rule, while a large number of residents, led by Sons of Liberty radicals, vigorously demonstrated against British authority. Crowd activity focused on confiscating public stores. Isaac Sears, John Lamb, and Marinus Willett organized a gang to force open the arsenal at City Hall and distribute about six hundred weapons among the "most active citizens." Armed groups paraded in the streets. The customs house closed, and business came to a standstill. British troops, reduced to a garrison of about one hundred soldiers because of reinforcements sent to Boston, confined themselves to their barracks. All regular government disappeared, and the municipal committee could not cope with the situation.[6]

The General Assembly had adjourned for one month on April 3, 1775. Now on April 24, Acting Governor Colden and his councilors met to assess the disturbing turn of events. The council considered strong measures but concluded that they lacked the means to enforce them. In their opinion, the local royal government was "entirely prostrated." Feeling helpless and vulnerable to escalated hostility if their authority became too conspicuous or intrusive, they decided to maintain a low profile. William

Smith, one of the councilors, recorded the outcome of the meeting in his memoirs: "We were thus unanimously of Opinion that we had no power to do anything and the best mode of proceeding for private Safety and general Peace was to use Diswasion from Violence." With civil power eluding his grasp, Colden prorogued the assembly to June 7, 1775.[7]

Meanwhile, patriot leaders scrambled to assert full control over the extreme reactionaries and their followers during this state of upheaval. Patriots had already formed provincial congresses in several other colonies, from Massachusetts to South Carolina. Now, it was New York's turn. To meet the crisis, the patriot faction determined upon the extension of its jurisdiction and reorganization. While Colden and his councilors were conferring, the Committee of Sixty called for a public rally. An estimated eight thousand people responded and approved proposals to authorize the committee with "full and unlimited power" for the protection of the city and its citizens. On April 26, 1775, the Committee of Sixty made provisions through a general election for expanding into a Committee of One Hundred, which convened on May 1, 1775. Concurrently, the Committee of Sixty sent a proposal to the counties for the establishment of a provincial congress to function in concert with the Continental Congress. This represented a significant change in the scope of the patriot movement in New York. Before, the patriots largely confined their activities to the provincial capital; now, they began taking a larger view of their operations.[8]

During this time, Montgomery continued building and improving his country estate removed from the political storm center at the seat of government. Thus, he remained only an interested and sympathetic bystander during the patriot committee system accession to civil authority. However, with the advent of the New York Congress, Montgomery would be swept into the political maelstrom.

To secure an effective sanction for the proposed infrastructure, the Committee of Sixty published a General Association on April 29, 1775. This declaration pledged support for "whatever measures may be recommended by the Continental Congress or resolved upon by our Provincial Congress." More than one thousand persons signed the affidavit when it was first presented. Later, committee agents posted copies in various public places so that other citizens could affix their signatures. Although signatories abated somewhat as a few passions sobered, this instrument helped patriots coerce many reluctant individuals into choosing sides in the escalating political confrontation. The committee ordered its agents to report the names of those persons refusing to sign, although such persons were not to be designated enemies to their country "but by the determination of the Continental or Provincial Congress, or by this Committee." In effect, a person either made a public commitment for the patriot cause or became readily identified as a loyalist sympathizer.[9]

The Provincial Congress thereupon emerged as New York's de facto government, supplanting the General Assembly. The assembly, after its adjournment on April 3, 1775, was never able to resume its normal functions because of patriot disruption. The patriot faction in New York took advantage of the chaotic times by moving swiftly to fill the vacuum vacated by the irresolute colonial government, securing support from a large segment of the population and usurping legal authority. The Committee of One Hundred would act as the city government and become subordinate to the Provincial Congress in this extralegal hierarchical political system. The New York Congress, in turn, would cooperate with the Continental Congress.

By May 1775, the eighty-seven-year-old lieutenant governor, Cadwallader Colden, was weary of the political disputation and retired in disgust to Spring Hill, his country estate near Flushing on Long Island. He explained: "When Congresses and Committees had taken the entire direction of government it was extremely disagreeable to me to remain as a spectator of the proceedings and confusions in town which I had not in my power to prevent."[10]

The repressive measures inflicted recently by British authorities against Boston and Massachusetts alarmed many New Yorkers. An impending threat of similar actions directed against their province seemed very real to them. As the patriots waited for the Provincial Congress to assemble, the Committee of One Hundred met practically every day to organize the city's defenses. A subcommittee considered how additional supplies of arms and ammunition could be obtained. The committee ordered each ward to organize militia companies and established a military night watch. It also undertook the suppression of loyalists by confiscating and forbidding the sale of arms to tories and thwarting their efforts to mount an effective opposition. When convened, the Provincial Congress continued these measures.[11]

On May 16, 1775, Dutchess County officials met at Poughkeepsie and elected Montgomery as one of the ten deputies to represent the county in the New York Provincial Congress. Although he had been in the colony only two years and had not sought political involvement, Montgomery was well known and respected throughout the area. Consequently, with this draft into public service, he felt obligated to answer the call. Reluctantly, Montgomery put his personal affairs in order, bid goodbye to his wife, and departed for New York City, some eighty miles away.[12]

Upon arriving, Montgomery threw himself unrelentingly into his work. From the initial session on May 22 to its adjournment on July 8, 1775, the First New York Congress increased its work load until it met twice daily Monday through Saturday, with an occasional session on Sunday. Montgomery served on eleven committees. Only Gouverneur Morris and Alexander McDougall undertook more assignments, with sixteen committees each. Most other deputies, including those from New York City, participated in six or seven congressional committees.[13]

One of the first orders of business for the New York Congress was to legitimize its authority. Therefore, on May 26, 1775, Montgomery and the other ninety-seven delegates signed a resolution:

We the Deputies of the different Counties of the Colony of New York in Provincial Congress convened being greatly alarmed at the avowed design of the Ministry, to raise a revenue in America, and shocked by the bloody scene now acting in the Massachusetts Bay, do in the most solemn manner resolve never to become slaves, and do associate under all the ties of Religion, Honour, and Love to our Country, to adopt and endeavour to carry into execution whatever measures may be recommended by the Continental Congress or resolved upon by this Provincial Congress for the purpose of preserving our Constitution, and opposing the execution of the several arbitrary and oppressive acts of the British Parliament, until a reconciliation between Great Britain and America, on constitutional principles, which we most ardently desire, can be obtained.[14]

Although this political body eventually became the provincial bastion of dissent against English rule, some of its initially elected members, representing a sizable segment of New York society, still harbored loyalist sentiments. In addition, its membership included individuals from a wide spectrum of patriot persuasions, including conservatives, moderates, and radicals. As the resolution indicated, reconciliation remained a desirable course of action.

Montgomery's whig sentiments fell between the conservatives, who would carry their opposition to the British government only to a point short of armed rebellion, and the radicals, who would settle for nothing less than complete independence from Britain. Montgomery essentially held the views of a moderate patriot. He felt that the British government had wronged the colonists but hoped for an honorable reconciliation. If this were not possible, he would advocate rebellion as a last resort in lieu of submission. When writing to his brother-in-law, Robert R. Livingston, in the Continental Congress, Montgomery expressed his feelings: "I most heartily wish your endeavor at an accommodation may be successful." However, he concluded his thoughts by stating: "The minister has fallen a victim to the just resentment of an injured people." Janet Montgomery noted her husband's conversion in her memoirs: "It was not until all our petitions were rejected and Boston was declared out of the Kings's protection that my hero would listen to any argument contrary to his loyalty." [15]

As the situation progressed, the faction that maintained allegiance to the Crown lost its influence in the New York Congress. A survey of the congressional attendance record indicates that those who afterward became avowed loyalists failed to participate on a regular basis. In fact, some of them refused to take their seats after they were elected. The most active members came from the patriot faction, and they soon dominated the proceedings. When general attendance eroded, the patriots lowered the requirement for a quorum and continued meeting. Montgomery diligently attended congressional sessions, only absenting himself to conduct activities in conjunction with assigned committee functions. [16]

Many pressing matters competed for the attention of the New York Congress. However, shortly after the New York Congress convened, the delegates confronted a request from the Continental Congress for assistance with Fort Ticonderoga. The Ticonderoga situation would prove to be a catalyst to strengthen the patriot movement in New York.

Three separately conceived but coincidently executed patriot military missions against Fort Ticonderoga plunged New York into direct confrontation with the British army. Some two hundred men, including the Green Mountain Boys under Col. Ethan Allen and Massachusetts militia headed by Col. James Easton and Maj. John Brown, converged by chance during their advance on Ticonderoga. Although independently organized, the various units decided to join forces in executing their common mission, and they elected Ethan Allen as their joint force commander. Benedict Arnold, a captain in the Connecticut militia, had similar military designs. He went to Boston where the Massachusetts Committee of Safety issued him a colonel's commission and orders to proceed against Ticonderoga. Leaving the recruiting of his authorized force to his officers, he rushed forward to reconnoiter accompanied only by an aide. When

Arnold encountered the united group headed by Allen, he presented his commission and orders. Then, he demanded command of the expedition. The soldiers refused to follow anyone except their own leaders, and the officers were loath to relinquish authority to a brash outsider and newcomer. Arnold, a commander without troops at this time, exchanged heated words with Allen, Easton, and Brown. Finally, they agreed to Arnold and Allen sharing command, but the ill feelings remained. Just before dawn on May 10, 1775, this combined force surprised the British army garrison of the strategically located but isolated military outpost. Awakened by his second in command and confronted by the attackers as he exited his quarters, the British officer in charge of the fort quickly capitulated without resistance.[17]

Massachusetts authorized the Easton and Brown expedition and conferred Arnold's commission, whereas Connecticut sponsored the operation involving the Green Mountain Boys. Since Ticonderoga lay within the province of New York, the two New England colonies had disregarded diplomacy by carrying out the operation without first consulting the New York provincial authorities. Apparently, the expediency of the situation overrode considerations of protocol. The fort's cannons were sorely needed to reinforce the critically meager presence of artillery in eastern Massachusetts, where Americans had besieged the British troops that had withdrawn onto the Boston peninsula after Lexington and Concord. In addition, only a small garrison of about fifty British troops was defending Ticonderoga, making it an opportune target for attack.

On May 26, 1775, the Massachusetts Congress explained its actions in a message sent to the New York Congress: "Perhaps this may appear to you extraordinary, but we trust that you will candidly overlook such a mistake (if it is one) being made in the hurry and confusion of war; and we most solemnly declare to you, that this Congress, and the inhabitants of this Colony, are at the utmost remove from any disposition or design to make any the least infraction upon, or usurpation of the jurisdiction of any of our sister Colonies." The next day, the Massachusetts Congress sent a similar message of explanation to the Continental Congress saying that if they "had considered the proposal in a calmer season, perhaps . . . it would have been proper previously to have consulted our brethren of the Colony of New York." Then, the Massachusetts patriots offered their assurances "that nothing can be more abhorrent to . . . this Congress . . . than any attempt to usurp on the jurisdiction of any of our sister Colonies, which, upon a superficial consideration of this step, there may seem to be some appearance of." [18]

The language of the Massachusetts Congress and the participation of the Green Mountain Boys in the operation contained deeper meanings. Ticonderoga was located near an area that had been under contention for a number of years. The New Hampshire Grants were claimed after 1724 by the colonies of New Hampshire, Massachusetts, and New York. Authorities had set New Hampshire's borders with Massachusetts by 1741. The most stubborn dispute, however, remained between New Hampshire and New York. New Hampshire contended its boundary stretched westward from the Connecticut River, and New York maintained it possessed all territory reaching eastward to the same river. Thus, both colonial governments attempted to assert jurisdiction over the New Hampshire Grants, or what is now Vermont. In 1764, King George III decided in favor of New York. However, a grass-roots movement sprang up among the grantees living there to attain political autonomy for this area. The Green Mountain Boys emerged as the military arm of this movement and opposed New York governmental authority within the Grants. Several armed skirmishes had taken place between these antagonists prior to the Ticonderoga expedition. Although regional differences remained, the more immediate, mutual problem with the British government, as manifested in the attack on Ticonderoga, transcended these old territorial disputes—an example of how the colonies banded together for the common cause. [19]

Two days after the capture of Fort Ticonderoga, a contingent of the Green Mountain Boys led by Seth Warner seized Crown Point, located twelve miles north, without opposition. Then, the zealous colonial forces under Allen and Arnold exceeded their authority by conducting raids against the British outpost of St. Johns in Canada. At that time, the colonial provisional government had to face the implications of these hastily conceived and executed maneuvers. The two New England colonies referred the problem to the Continental Congress for resolution. Initially, Congress considered the action too radical and leaned toward relinquishing the fort back to the British. However, reports from Arnold and other expedition leaders emphasized the danger of Britain's army presence in Canada to the future welfare of the colonies. The perceived threat of attack by these British troops against the rebellious colonies eventually persuaded the Congress that Fort Ticonderoga was too valuable as a strategic military location and source of war matériel to give up.[20]

Fort Ticonderoga, guarding the portage between Lake Champlain and Lake George, lay astride a traditional invasion route that extended by natural waterway from the St. Lawrence River on the Canadian border, via the Richelieu River and lakes Champlain and George, toward New York City. The Hudson River, flowing through its readily defensible highlands, formed the lower segment of this approach. The Hudson Highlands referred to the hilly terrain through which the river coursed some forty miles above New York City. This region also lent its name to the well-known strategy that involved the overall invasion route. The so-called Hudson Highlands strategy, as a plan for a British army invasion from the north in response to colonial resistance, seemed to be a distinct possibility to the patriots. In addition, reports that British agents were enlisting Indians to assist in this punitive action added to heightened patriot apprehension.[21]

As a former army officer, Montgomery certainly appreciated the military importance of the Hudson Highlands and retaining Fort Ticonderoga. In a letter concerning his evaluation of a prospective troop commander, he indicated his attitude toward maintaining Ticonderoga: "I was exceedingly pleased with the idea of Davis having a command. . . . [However] I have since heard a anecdote that has cooled my inclinations to trust him. . . . He made a proposal . . . of garrisoning Ticonderoga with New York troops and then delivering it up to Mr. Carleton. I will endeavor to be better informed on his head."[22]

During the last of May, the Continental Congress recommended to the New York Congress that two locations be fortified and defended against possible British military incursion: King's Bridge, which linked New York City and Manhattan to the mainland in the north, and the Hudson Highlands. The Continental Congress also recommended that the New York militia be brought to a state of military readiness and raised to a level of three thousand troops. In the meantime, the Continental Congress requested Connecticut, whose militia was already mobilized, to man Fort Ticonderoga and aid in the safeguarding of New York City. New York, in comparison to its neighboring colonies, responded rather sluggishly in supporting the patriot cause. Consequently, before the taking of Ticonderoga, it was far behind the New England colonies in preparing for contingencies against the British government. Massachusetts, Connecticut, New Hampshire, and Rhode Island exceeded New York in the mobilization of militia and the securing of weapons.[23]

The New York Provincial Congress, responding quickly to the appeal by the Continental Congress for mutual action, began military preparations. However, these initial defense arrangements probably contributed to the reputation that New Yorkers acquired of being reluctant patriots. A Connecticut officer sent to Ticonderoga observed: "I am much unesy at the dead coldness of the People in this Province. Their whole Dependence is on Connecticut for to Do their Drugery for them, but I hope that him who sees all things will open their eyes and make them Patient in So Just a Cause."[24]

During this time, the attention of the New York Liberty Boys concentrated on one of the few remaining prominent symbols of ministerial authority in the city—the British garrison, manned by about one hundred men of the Royal Irish Regiment. They launched a vigorous campaign to encourage the soldiers to desert, utilizing the press and propagandistic broadsides thrown over the barracks walls. Although only four men defected from May 1 to May 23, 1775, in the next three days four more deserted. On May 26, 1775, the garrison commandant, Maj. Isaac Hamilton, expressed to Colden his concern over the desertion rate. Ten days later, Hamilton wrote to Colden that his occupation of the garrison was becoming untenable: "The loss of our men by Desertion is so great. . . . I therefore think it is necessary for the good of the service to retreat on Board his Majesty's Ship the Asia."[25]

The British warship had arrived from Boston a few days before and was lying in the East River. Its captain, George Vandeput, drew up plans with Major Hamilton for the troops to embark as soon as possible. Before starting, Hamilton requested and received assurances from the Committee of One Hundred that the soldiers could depart peaceably. On June 6, 1775, the troops emerged from their barracks to march down Broad Street to the harbor where the *Asia* awaited at anchor. A large crowd assembled to jeer them and urge further desertions, of which there were a few. When Marinus Willett learned that the soldiers were taking with them "sundry carts loaded with chests filled with arms," he decided to capture "these spare arms." As the weapon and ammunition carts at the rear of the procession reached Broad and Beaver streets, Willett and his followers stepped out from the crowd and seized them. A brief altercation ensued with the military escort, but Willett insisted that the committee had not given its consent to remove any arms except those individual weapons that the soldiers carried on their person. The column continued along its route without the weapons as the crowd prevailed. A short time later, the troops rowed out to the *Asia* to take up their duties there.[26]

"Yesterday the troops stationed in the town embarked on board the man-of-war," Montgomery wrote. "Their baggage was stopped on account of some spare arms." "We thought we had sufficiently secured the troops by a resolve from any insult," he explained, and "many of us were exceedingly angry—but the people say that they did not understand that our resolve extended to supernumary arms."[27]

After the Provincial Congress became informed of the incident, it voiced disapproval over the seizure of the weapons and issued instructions to have them replaced. The next night, a party of men made a raid on a royal magazine at Turtle Bay on the outskirts of the city. The keeper, Francis Stephens, notified the Provincial Congress, which sent eight of its deputies to intervene personally in the plundering of the stores. While pursuing measures of opposition, the generally moderate patriot Congress continued to maintain a delicate policy of also attempting to avoid a complete break with New York loyalists and the British government. Thus, it strove to control the radical wing of the patriot movement. It tried to discourage unofficial acts by popular leaders, fearing that they would discredit congressional authority. This aspiring governmental body wanted to guarantee its own control of events. Despite its efforts, sporadic incidents emerged. One reason for the inability of the Provincial Congress to curtail undirected activity was that a few firebrands like Willett, Sears, Lamb, and McDougall were popularly elected to sit on the committees or in the Congress itself.[28]

Meanwhile, the Provincial Congress became engaged in a multitude of functions: continuation of military preparations, issuance of passes and passports, diplomatic moves to foster goodwill with the Canadians and Indians, provisions for punishing British army enlistment by imprisonment, and control of inoculation for smallpox. Because of his previous professional military experience, the Congress leaned heavily on Montgomery in related matters. Thus, he served on various defense-related committees. Two days after the Congress convened, it appointed Montgomery to a committee to consider what action should be taken regarding Fort Ticonderoga. As a result, the New York Congress decided to participate in the dismantling of cannons and holding of the former British fort. A few days later, Congress named Montgomery to serve in a site selection committee to determine the placement of local military defensive positions. Accordingly, the committee designated Montgomery's farm at King's Bridge as a location for a fortified post—a concession for which he would receive no compensation. In the first part of June 1775, the Congress began a comprehensive survey to ascertain what supplies were available in the city that might be employed in the province's defense. It assigned Montgomery to a committee to survey "such parts of the Goods retained by the Merchants of this City . . . as may be necessary to be retained at the expense of the Colony." When the New York Congress authorized a three-thousand-man provincial militia, Montgomery became involved with the raising and organization of these units and securing military equipment to issue their troops.[29]

Through the endless, tedious hours that Montgomery devoted to serving in the Provincial Congress, he never lost his keen sense of humor. When grappling with matters of grave consequences, he seemed able to relieve some of the tension by occasionally making light of the situation. "I have heard nothing from the powder maker," he wrote to his brother-in-law while on a committee to procure gun powder. "I hope that he is not blown up."[30]

While Montgomery labored with concerns of the New York Congress, his wife managed their personal affairs at Rhinebeck. Janet Montgomery felt proud of her husband's election to the Provincial Congress, but she also lamented the personal turmoil that the separation caused. New York City was too far removed from Rhinebeck to allow any but infrequent visits from her husband. Therefore, she was left to her own resources. The activities of several hired hands and slaves had to be supervised in order to continue agricultural production and attend to the myriad tasks associated with the proper maintenance of a farmstead. Although she proved to be quite capable of taking charge of the Montgomery estate, it was a function that she did not covet. Janet Montgomery adhered to her socially prescribed subordinate status to her husband. Heading a country estate was typically a man's work. While rising to the occasion, she nevertheless felt that it was an aberration of the normal scheme. Thus, Janet Montgomery joined many other privileged women who were thrust into nontraditional roles by the upheaval of revolutionary events.[31]

On May 25, Janet Montgomery wrote another letter to their friend, Perkins Magra. In it, she composed a verse which related to her husband's new enterprise:

And your friend too, at Rhine Beck from town far removed,
Who wished but to enjoy there the quiet he loved,
So content & so pleased with his own private Station
Thought politics nothing but noise and vexation.
So as all must assist in these days of distress,
So our country have chosen him one of the Congress,
And here has left his two Sisters and Spouse
To write Stupid verses and govern the house,
While himself is engaged in some learned debate
And in Senate is settling our matters of State.
But to Shorten the matter, behold as a Summary
That as Member for Du[t]chess, came Mr. Montgomery.[32]

The Montgomery family tradition of patrician political and military service in Ireland had imbued Richard with the principle of noblesse oblige. He had an ingrained susceptibility to public duty. In his mind, to refuse a common trust that the community had conferred upon him would bring dishonor to himself and his wife. Although he retained a personal attachment to many Englishmen, he had come to question the value of British political institutions. The seeds were planted when his association with Burke, Barré, and Fox in England opened his mind to the liberal view of British politics. The opposition political faction challenged many traditional aspects of British government that the loyalists defended. Montgomery's disillusionment with the British military promotion system helped crystallize this attitude, and newly found associations and interests in his adopted land confirmed these feelings of antipathy toward his native commonwealth. In the spirit of self-sacrifice, Montgomery reluctantly relinquished his desire to live a quiet, retiring life to answer the call for public service to the patriot cause.[33]

The Patriot Call to Arms

Come Soldiers all in chorus join,
To pay the tribute at the shrine
Of brave Montgomery,
Which to the memory is due
Of him who fought and died that you
Might live and yet be free . . .
With cheerful and undaunted mind,
Domestic happiness resigned,
He with a chosen band
Through deserts wild, with fixed intent,
Canada for to conquer went,
Or perish sword in hand.[1]

After choosing George Washington to head the Continental army on June 15, 1775, the Continental Congress turned next to selecting the senior military commanders to serve under the new commander in chief. The delegates found it necessary to represent all sections of the country in this high command to assure as much support for the common cause as possible. The province of New York posed an important consideration because of its strategic location, connecting New England with the remaining colonies. Without New York committed to the Revolution, coordination between north and south would be difficult. During the selection process, the New York delegates to the Continental Congress requested that their Provincial Congress recommend two individuals for command in the Continental Army. One would hold the rank of major general, the other would serve as a brigadier general. This touched off a lengthy debate in the New York Congress over who would be most qualified for these appointments.

The assembly favored Philip Schuyler for the first position. However, Montgomery expressed concern over Schuyler's fortitude for the task. He wrote to his brother-in-law, Robert Livingston, "Phil Schuyler was mentioned to me. . . . His consequence in the province makes him a fit subject for an important trust—but has he *strong nerves?* I could wish to have that point well ascertained with respect to any man so employed." Since Schuyler's previous wartime service had involved the supply and support of militia, Montgomery was probably referring to Schuyler's lack of demonstrated combat-troop-leading experience. Whatever his military qualifications, political considerations facilitated Schuyler's nomination. The apparent reluctance of New York to support the patriot cause occupied the thoughts of the delegates. Awarding the position to someone of broad influence such as Schuyler would help to "sweeten and keep up the spirit in that province." [2]

Montgomery became aware that he was under consideration for the second position, but he did not solicit the appointment. Remaining aloof from the proceedings, he did not try to curry support for the nomination. Like many others, the former British officer had initially questioned the colonist's strength of resolve for open hostilities with Britain. In addition, he probably harbored a low opinion of the provincial soldier that prevailed among British regulars during their association in the French and Indian War. When news of the Bunker Hill battle arrived, however, Montgomery remarked: "What I feared has not happened. The Americans will fight." Yet, he was content to leave this enterprise to noisier and more ambitious individuals. [3]

Montgomery's background as an experienced professional soldier certainly recommended him for the Continental army assignment. Actually, the patriots held a paradoxical attitude toward the British army. On one hand, they deeply resented the British soldier as a brutish instrument of an enslaving home government; on the other, they grudgingly respected his professionalism and combat experience. The Continental Congress commissioned other former British officers, including Charles Lee and Horatio Gates, as general officers in the Continental army; but unlike Montgomery, they had actively sought their appointments. The delegates must have sensed the military leadership potential that lay within this latent warrior. Once again, his adopted colony asked for Montgomery's service, and he dutifully responded. The Provincial Congress "unanimously resolved and agreed that Colonel Philip Schuyler is the most proper person in this Colony to be recommended as a Major General, and Richard Montgomery, Esq., as a Brigadier General."[4]

Montgomery never regarded himself as an adroit politician. He worked hard in the New York Congress, but he did not feel completely at ease in that arena. Because of his previous training and experience, he understood that military service was his forte. If continued public service was inevitable and could not be avoided honorably, he held no reservations concerning his capacity to perform as a senior army commander. Still, he exhibited the modesty that was a part of his nature. When writing to his brother-in-law, Montgomery stated that he "would most willingly decline any military command from a consciousness of want of talents." "Nevertheless I shall sacrifice my own inclinations to the service of the public, if our Congress should be of the opinion they cannot find a more capable servant." In a later letter, he reiterated his reluctance to serve, but expressed compulsion to answer a civic calling. "The Continental Congress have done me the melancholy honour of appointing me a brigadier. I am most truly at the public service, but could have wished to have served in a private capacity."[5]

Writing again to his friend, Perkins Magra, on July 2, 1775, Montgomery expressed his adherence to the American cause and his perceived destiny: "You left me callous in politics, suspicious of both sides from the very bad opinion I have of my fellow creatures. I now yield to a generous impulse which will not permit me to withhold my little assistance in support of rights, without which life is a burden. Hard fate to be obliged to oppose a power I had been ever taught to reverence!" Montgomery then addressed the possibility of having to oppose his old regiment in battle: "I have just heard six reg[imen]ts more are under orders from Ireland for this country. . . . It is with the deepest concern I hear the 17th is one of them! My warmest and affectionate wishes attend my old friends of that corps. How sorry shou'd I be to meet them on such a business! Forbid it, fortune! or whatever regulates human affairs."[6]

Montgomery kept the news of his recommendation and impending appointment from Janet while he turned it over in his mind. He knew how his wife would react to the prospect of her husband going to war, but he wanted her concurrence before finally accepting the commission. He obliquely broached the subject to Janet with a half smile by asking her to make a black ribbon into a cockade, which was customarily worn on a military hat. Her reaction, as Richard had anticipated, was one of panic: "What is it you ask of me—my God, you are not engaged to fight." Richard gently responded, "No, not engaged, but this depends on you alone." Janet exclaimed, "Oh, if on me never will I consent." Taking her hand, Richard spoke his mind: "When I entered your family I was a stranger in your country. I have hardly been two years in it, yet without my wish or knowledge they appoint me to the committy [committee] from Dutchess. The times were such I could not refuse however reluctant. . . . But a soldier from my youth what could I do as a statesman? Now without consulting me they have made me a general. In this capacity I may be of service for just cause. Can I refuse?" Richard concluded with his thoughts regarding his obligation as a gentleman and responsible member of society: "Honour calls on me. And surely my honour is dear to you yet, with you I leave this point—say you will prefer to see your husband disgraced and I submit to go home to retirement." Janet realized she could not protest such an appeal. She tearfully took the ribbon and made the cockade.[7]

The week after officially designating George Washington as commander in chief of the army, the Continental Congress appointed four major generals, including Philip Schuyler. On June 22, it named eight brigadier generals. Selection of these generals for the Continental army resulted from considerable political maneuvering as congressional delegates patronized their favorite sons. Congress allotted brigadier appointments for each colony in proportion to the number of troops raised by those provinces, and followed the recommendations of the colonies in the actual selection.[8]

However, Congress created problems in the commissioning process by a haphazard method of determining seniority and status among the appointed generals. Consideration of previous troop-leading experience and an objective evaluation of military leadership potential gave way too often to more subjective means of ranking the general officers by popularity. Additionally, some appointments depended more on the lobbying skills of the candidate's patrons in Congress than the aspirant's competence. This resulted in several instances where individuals with mediocre credentials were selected over better-qualified candidates. Consequently, some officers felt slighted by the treatment they received by the selection process.

Massachusetts provided an excellent example of this problem in consequence of the first general-officer appointments in June 1775. Congress initially designated the Massachusetts contingent of Seth Pomeroy, William Heath, and John Thomas as the first, fourth, and sixth brigadier generals, respectively. Most people regarded Thomas, a combat veteran of the French and Indian War, as the logical choice for the ranking Massachusetts general because of Pomeroy's advanced age of sixty-nine years and Heath's lack of combat experience. Moreover, Thomas outranked Heath in the Massachusetts militia. When Congress announced its determination, Thomas took it as a personal rebuff. The situation was resolved when Pomeroy declined his appointment, citing his age. This opened the way for Congress to fill Pomeroy's vacancy with Thomas as the first brigadier general.[9]

Although Montgomery was clearly the best qualified of all the brigadier candidates, Congress retained him as the second in rank of the brigadier generals during the shuffle. However, the record does not reflect any ill feeling on the part of Montgomery toward the ranking process. The prospects of a general officer's appointment far exceeded the thwarted major's commission that he sought earlier in the British army. Nevertheless, James Duane, a New York delegate to the Continental Congress, sent a letter of explanation to Montgomery:

> I am directed by the Congress to acquaint you of an arrangement in the Massachusetts Department and the reason which led to it least by misunderstanding it you might think yourself neglected. When Brigds. General were to be appointed it was agreed that the first in nomination shoud be one of the Massachusetts generals. The gentlemen from that province recommended General Pomeroy who was accordingly fixed upon but before his commission arrived at the camp he had retired from the army. Under these circumstances the Congress thought it just to fill up the commission designated for Mr. Pomeroy with the name of General Thomas as first Brigadier; you consequently hold the rank to which you were elected. I sincerely hope this may not give you any displeasure as I am confident no disrespect was intended.[10]

The lack of uniformity concerning officer ranking and promotion would plague the Continental army throughout the Revolution. A few years later, the practice contributed to Gen. Benedict Arnold's defection from the American army to join the British forces. Arnold was passed over for advancement and promotion in the American army by officers lacking his seniority and ability. His disgust with a system that he deemed flawed and unfair helped him to consider the more professional British army as a supplanter for his unrequited service.

The Pomeroy-Thomas controversy pointed out another weakness in the Continental army. Pomeroy had served as an officer in the Massachusetts militia since 1743, when he received an ensign's commission. Experiencing combat with the militia during the French and Indian War, he had risen to a major general in the Massachusetts militia before being offered a commission by Congress. His record reflected a strong attachment to his home province. When he participated in the Bunker Hill battle, he chose to serve not as a general in a leadership role, but as an individual rifleman in the redoubt among the Massachusetts militiamen. After ostensibly rejecting appointment in the Continental army because of age, he continued his involvement in the Revolution as a Massachusetts militia major general for almost two years. On February 19, 1777, he died of pleurisy while in provincial military service.

Pomeroy epitomized the provincial attitude of some officers during the Revolution. The notion of sectionalism acted as a deterrent to the unification of colonial military units into a truly continental army capable of opposing British forces. This feeling was even more prominent in the enlisted ranks, where the combat effectiveness of militiamen could often be measured by the geographical proximity of the conflict to their homes and whether they were under the leadership of local officers.

It is to the credit of George Washington and his Continental army generals—whose sense of nationalism surmounted sectional differences —that a united front was eventually established sufficient for continuing the Revolution. Foreign roots and worldly experience conditioned Montgomery to a broad perspective. Although he had earlier shown loyalty to his home province of New York, he quickly seized upon the continental view during his service. In his mind, the overall cause took precedence over localism. Later, as the field commander of the Canadian expedition, he would sharply criticize New York troops as well as soldiers from other colonies when their service fell short of his standards.

By June 23, 1775, the New York Congress learned that Washington would pass through New York City while en route from Philadelphia to Boston to take charge of the militia units besieging that city and adopting these forces into the Continental army. Schuyler, who had been appointed commander of the New York troops, accompanied Washington. Both Schuyler and Montgomery personally received their commissions from Washington as part of the general celebration that ensued during the commander's brief visit. Although Montgomery would have preferred to serve with Washington at the immediate point of confrontation near

Boston, Washington assigned him duty as deputy commander under Schuyler.[11]

Washington's visit to New York City also illustrated the duality of public sentiment prevalent in the province at that time. The arrival of the new commander in chief on Sunday, June 25, coincided, by chance, with the return of William Tryon, the royal governor. Tryon had just completed a trip to England for consultation with Parliament, a trip that had stretched into fourteen months. Washington's stopover in New York City would be transitory. Tryon, however, expected to stay indefinitely by resuming official residence in the city and presiding over the province much as before. The governor had built a political power base during his tenure that included support from many wealthy and influential New Yorkers.

The convergent events of this day presented a dilemma to the New York Provincial Congress, which had been formed during Tryon's absence. The delegates wanted to impress their new military commander, but they also did not wish to flagrantly offend the governor; they were acutely aware of the personal jeopardy in which the extralegal status of their assembly placed them.

British authority in New York government, which had been challenged by the patriots before, was effectively suspended after Tryon's departure. Yet, a disquieting British military presence in New York continued very much in evidence. Most of the British troops were destined to Boston when they vacated garrisons in New York City. However on June 6, 1775, the approximately one hundred remaining soldiers evacuated their barracks and took up station aboard several British warships, including the sixty-four-gun battleship *Asia* and the sloop *Kingfisher*, which lay menacingly in the harbor south of Manhattan.

Moreover, the New York Congress had not yet solidified its popular support to the extent that it had enough confidence to challenge the authority of the royal governor. Loyalist sentiment remained strong in many parts of the city. In trying to avoid alienating a segment of the populace—those who were still loyal British subjects but might be persuaded to condone the patriot cause if not provoked—the Provincial Congress struggled to find a diplomatic solution to the precarious situation.

The British warships positioned in the New York City harbor were also on the mind of Washington as he neared that location. When his traveling party reached New Brunswick, New Jersey, on June 24, Schuyler wrote to the president of the New York Congress: "General Washington . . . proposes to be in Newark by nine tomorrow morning. The situation of the men-of-war at New York (we are informed) is such as may make it necessary that some precaution should be taken in crossing Hudson's River; and he would take it as a favor if some gentlemen of your body would meet him tomorrow, at Newark, as the advice you may give him, will determine whether he will continue his proposed route, or not." [12]

This request for routing instructions gave New Yorkers an opportunity to solve their problem concerning officially receiving both Washington and Tryon on the same day. The Provincial Congress worked out a plan by which both dignitaries might be properly welcomed, but the two resulting celebrations would be widely separated. The city had only one militia unit, Col. John Lasher's independent battalion, available for ceremonial duty. Congress ordered Colonel Lasher to post one of his companies at the pier on the southern tip of Manhattan where Tryon's ship was expected to dock. A second company accompanied a four-man congressional committee, which included Montgomery, across the Hudson to Newark. They were to meet Washington and lead his party northward on a detour to the Hoboken ferry landing, located in the far northwest side of the city. The two locations were as far removed from each other as possible while remaining in the city. The bulk of Lasher's battalion was stationed about halfway between the two landing sites, with orders to proceed on the double to greet whichever official arrived first. [13]

The scheme to partition the two public celebrations in order to tactfully accommodate all popular political sentiments was a tenuous arrangement. However, Tryon's considerateness facilitated its success. While the governor waited aboard his ship in the bay for his official reception to be prepared, some of his friends and associates sailed out to visit him. When they briefed him on the situation in the city, Tryon decided to delay his landing time, originally scheduled for 4 P.M., by four hours.

Washington and his entourage, including generals Philip Schuyler and Charles Lee, military aides and staff officers, a troop of Philadelphia light horse acting as an honorary escort, and members of the congressional committee, arrived at the Hoboken ferry landing on Long Island at 4 P.M. The party repaired to the nearby home of a member of the Provincial Congress, Leonard Lispenard, for refreshment and a rest. This was a welcome respite for Washington and his men after one hundred miles of riding in less than three days. They were met there by the rest of the

New York Congress. Lasher's reserve companies were also able to catch up with them. All participated in a parade that commenced an hour later. An impressive crowd of spectators, in a holiday spirit, warmly welcomed Washington and joined in the parade.

The celebration for Washington continued until 8 P.M., the time for Tryon's postponed arrival. A respectably large gathering greeted the governor upon his landing. Although his reception was much less noisy and festive than Washington's ceremony, Tryon was apparently satisfied by the turnout. The governor, however, appeared to be in a somber mood. He issued some brief remarks to the crowd and then walked a few blocks to the townhouse of Hugh Wallace, a member of the governor's council. Here, he spent the night conferring with his aides and associates, and receiving callers. Only three blocks away, Washington engaged in similar activities at Robert Hull's Tavern.[14]

Some residents chose to boycott one or the other of the celebrations. Many other townspeople enthusiastically participated in both civic events by walking a few blocks from where Washington's parade ended to the pier where Tryon disembarked. To these New Yorkers, this was not an act of hypocrisy, but merely a practical reaction to the dichotomous politics of the times.

When Washington arrived at Lispenard's house earlier in the day, the New York Congress had presented him with a dispatch from the Massachusetts provincial council addressed to John Hancock, the president of the Continental Congress at Philadelphia. Agents of the New York Congress obtained the letter by intercepting the transient express rider. The chagrined New Yorkers urged Washington to open the packet and endorse it to its intended recipient. The message contained the first reliable report of the Battle of Bunker Hill. News of the extensive open hostilities between colonial militia and the British army, which occurred near Boston on June 17, placed more urgency on Washington's journey to assume command of the army.

Still, Washington delayed his departure from New York City until the afternoon of the next day. The Provincial Congress persuaded him to attend further official functions before he left. In addition, Washington wanted to draw up a suitable plan for the administration of the New York Department. If that area could be entrusted to a semi-independent command under Schuyler and Montgomery, then Washington would be free to devote his attention to military affairs around Boston.

After lengthy consultations with Schuyler and Montgomery, Washington issued general instructions that made them accountable to both civil and military superiors. They were to execute any orders that they received from the Continental Congress, and to keep Washington informed as to the situation of their command. He specifically requested that they "delay no time in occupying the several posts recommended by the Provincial Congress of this colony, and putting them in a fit posture." Washington also charged them with maintaining surveillance over loyalist activities in their area: "Keep a watchful eye upon Governor Tryon, and if you find him directly or indirectly attempting any measures inimical to the common cause, use every means in your power to frustrate his designs. . . . In like manner watch the movements of the Indian agent, Colonel Guy Johnson, and prevent, as far as you can, the effect of his influence to our prejudice with the Indians." Then, Washington concluded by stating: "Your own good sense must govern you in all matters not particularly pointed out, as I do not wish to circumscribe you within narrow limits." [15]

Washington's belated departure from New York City allowed him only to reach King's Bridge on the outskirts of town by the evening of June 26. Schuyler accompanied him during this time. Resuming their trip the next morning, they encountered David Wooster and his approximately eighteen hundred Connecticut soldiers at New Rochelle, New York. Wooster and his men had marched from Greenwich, Connecticut, to assist in the defense of New York. The three generals coordinated their plans and parted company the next morning. Washington continued on to Boston to assume command of the Continental army. Wooster remained near New York City or on Long Island throughout the summer. Schuyler returned to the city to join Montgomery and begin his new duties. [16]

Meanwhile, Tryon confirmed the reports that he had received during his absence. He realized that the "general revolt," as he called it, had usurped his political power. Although many New Yorkers respected him because of his personal popularity, they criticized his official office. Consequently, he discovered that he was governor in name only. The numbers of citizens who remained loyal to British authority were not well organized. As a result, the loyalists had remained ineffectual in countering the growing patriot surge.

Lacking the means to ensure compliance, Tryon saw no reason to try to forcibly reassert his authority with little expectation that it would be widely accepted. Instead, he quietly began to try rebuilding the loyalist infrastructure and regaining public confidence for his official position, while tacitly functioning with the Provincial Congress. He felt that, in time, the patriot movement would expose itself to be the lawless element that the loyalists already considered it to be. Like many moderate British authorities, Tryon believed that judiciousness and patience on his part would eventually outlast the arrogators. Unprovoked excesses and radicalism, in due course, would turn the masses against the ill-advised opposition front and restore the government to its original form.

Initially, Montgomery attached little danger to Tryon's activities. Writing to Robert Livingston, his brother-in-law in the Continental Congress, Montgomery stated, "I believe Mr. Tryon means to conduct himself with prudence. He will, however, be well watched." Although the governor never directly challenged the command of Schuyler and Montgomery, he remained a threat and source of suspicion and intrigue. In a later letter to Livingston, Montgomery mentioned his concerns that Tryon was "carrying on some secret designs" and wished that the governor be conducted to Hartford, Connecticut, where he would be "out of the way of mischief." But, when Isaac Sears, the most radical New York revolutionary, approached both congresses and the northern department with a plan to abduct Tryon to Hartford and hold him for political ransom, each authority rejected his scheme as too extreme.[17]

Rapidly developing events ultimately shifted the attention of Montgomery and Schuyler to the northern reaches of their department and patriot activities in New York City were left to the Provincial Congress. On the night of June 29, 1775, Schuyler received the first of a series of orders pertaining to Canada that would come from the Continental Congress. This message contained directives for the invasion of Canada, a reversal of previously established policy. On June 1, the day after Congress decided to retain Ticonderoga and Crown Point, it enjoined any military operation "by any colony, or body of colonists, against or into Canada." This was a reaction to the brief, impulsive incursions into Canada by Arnold and the Green Mountain Boys after seizing Ticonderoga and Crown Point. Congress did not want to jeopardize relations with the Canadians—whom it desired to unite with the thirteen colonies in the resistance against Britain—with such seemingly belligerent and expansionist actions.[18]

Earlier political reaction had seriously weakened Congress's attempts to win Canadian support for colonial resistance to Britain. Indications of American intolerance planted a seed of skepticism in the minds of many Canadians.

Parliament passed the Quebec Act in May 1774, which provided for a military style of territorial government in Canada, consisting of a royal governor and an appointed advisory council with no popularly elected representation. As a concession to the predominately French-Canadian populace, the act made provisions for retaining a French-based legal system and recognizing Roman Catholicism as the established religion. This legislation served to reinforce the beliefs of American patriot leaders that the British government intended to deny local representative government for all of its colonies. A provision of the act that extended Canada's boundaries southward to the Ohio River and preempted territory that American colonies expected to acquire further alarmed the patriot leadership.

The First Continental Congress reflected these provincial concerns when it responded strongly to the passage of the Quebec Act. Congress tried to garner support for the patriot cause by issuing a conciliatory message to the Canadians that emphasized Britain's heavy-handed governmental authority and the advisability of mutual resistance to these measures. At the same time, Congress dispatched a protest to England that denounced the Quebec Act. Foremost among the enclosed grievances was the provision of the act that favored the Roman Catholic religion. When the contents of the second communication became known in Canada, prominent French-Canadians noted the duplicity of Congress's diplomacy. Suspicion that the Protestant colonies to their south were fostering anti-Catholicism clouded a Canadian decision to enter a joint venture and complicated the efforts of Congress to forge an alliance against the British government.

Still, Congress continued debating the Canadian question, gradually leaning toward "making an impression into Canada." Fear of a successful British-Indian coalition and the arguments of Arnold and Ethan Allen concerning the vulnerability of British forces in the region heavily influenced the deliberations. Reports indicated that the efforts of Guy Johnson had been joined by Guy Carleton, the royal governor of Canada, in persuading the Indians, as well as the Canadians, to side with the British in any conflict against the colonists. Gen. Thomas Gage, the British commander in Boston, wrote a letter to Lord Dartmouth in the British Parliament that stated he had information that "the Rebels after Surprizing Ticonderoga, made Incursions and committed Hostilities upon the Frontiers of the Province of Quebec; which will Justify General Carleton to raise both Canadians and Indians to attack them in his turn, and we need not be tender of calling upon the Savages, as the Rebels have shewn us the Example by bringing as many Indians down against us here as they could collect."[19]

The accounts of Arnold and Allen, by comparison, emphasized that the British forces along the St. Lawrence numbered only about one thousand. In addition, they advised Congress that most Canadians—many of French extraction and smarting under English rule since the French and Indian War—were disposed toward the patriot cause against the British should they be given a choice. John Adams summed up the congressional dilemma on June 7: "Whether we should march into Canada with an army sufficient to break the power of Governor Carleton, to overawe the Indians, and to protect the French has been a great question. It seems to be the general conclusion that it is best to go, if we can be assured that the Canadians will be pleased with it, and join."[20]

In the end, Congress felt an offensive, which was conducted with diplomacy so as not to provoke the Canadians, would be the prudent way to defend against the standing threat of the Indians and British military in that area against the colonies. The strategic timing of such a venture also seemed favorable. Upon receipt of orders from the Congress directing the New York Department to undertake a Canadian expedition, this militarily important and politically sensitive initiative fell to Schuyler and Montgomery.

The two commanders plunged immediately into the myriad details necessitated by the operation. They had to raise, equip, train, and supply an army before an effective invasion into Canada could be expected. Schuyler and Montgomery urged the Provincial Congress to expedite the organization of New York regiments for the campaign. The Continental Congress directed that the Connecticut and Massachusetts troops scattered in outposts along the Hudson River from Lake George to New York City and at Ticonderoga would be assigned to the New York Department. By the first of July, the initial department troop return indicated that a force of almost three thousand men had been hastily accrued. Concurrently, the department commanders scoured the province and requested assistance from the Continental Congress in procuring weapons, gun powder, and provisions to equip and supply their army.[21]

While organizing and outfitting their force, Schuyler and Montgomery began formulating a military plan for the assigned operation. The strategy for the invasion of Canada was to reverse the ominous British scheme that the Americans were attempting to thwart. The New York Department would adopt a south-to-north variation of the traditional invasion route to conduct a preemptive strike into Canada. The operation called for utilizing the Hudson River and lake system in northern New York as a supply line and patriot-held Fort Ticonderoga as a staging area. Troops and supplies would be pushed up this passageway into Canada.

On July 1, Congress resolved that General Wooster and his Connecticut forces in the vicinity of New York City should remain there to provide local security. To compensate for this loss of manpower to the invasion force, Congress allocated the Green Mountain Boys to the New York Department. Schuyler was anxious to determine the state of preparedness of the varied, far-flung troops that had been assigned to the department, and to obtain first-hand intelligence pertaining to the offensive. On July 4, Schuyler departed for Fort Ticonderoga, leaving Montgomery to supervise final arrangements for advancing the operation northward.

A few weeks later, Montgomery felt that he had accomplished all he could at his location, and he prepared to move up the chain of outposts to join Schuyler at Fort Ticonderoga. On his departure, Montgomery bade farewell to the Livingston family. Judge Livingston cautioned Richard to "take care of your life." Montgomery respectfully answered, "Of my honour, you would say, sir." Janet, her sister Catharine, and their youngest brother, Edward, accompanied Richard as far as Saratoga. Years later, Edward recalled a poignant scene that occurred during this time: "It was just before General Montgomery left. . . . We were only three in her room: he, my sister, and myself. He was sitting in a musing attitude, between his wife, who, sad and silent, seemed to be reading the future, and myself, whose childish admiration was divided between the glittering uniform and the martial bearing of him who wore it, when, all of a sudden, the silence was broken by Montgomery's deep voice, repeating the following line, as one who speaks in a dream: ' 'Tis a mad world, my masters, I once thought so, now I know it.' . . . Perhaps he might have been contrasting the quiet and sweets of the life he held in his grasp, with the tumults and perils of the camp which he had resolved to seek without a glance at what he was leaving behind. Those were the last words I heard from his lips, and I never saw him more." Richard's last words to his wife were: "You shall never have cause to blush for your Montgomery." He then departed to join his troops.[22]

The March to Canada

Then through the lakes Montgomery takes,
I wat he was na slaw, man.[1]

Our incampment is so swampy, I feel, says he exceedingly for the
troops; and provisions so scarce, it will require not only dispatch,
but good fortune, to keep us from distress.[2]

O n his way northward, Schuyler wrote George Washington from
Saratoga revealing his thoughts about shaping his new corps
into an efficient military force: "Be assured my general that I
shall use my best endeavors to establish order and discipline in the troops
under my command. I wish I could add that I had a prospect of much
success in that way. It is extremely difficult to introduce a proper subordination amongst a people where so little distinction is kept up."[3]

A number of American troops were garrisoning Ticonderoga when
Schuyler arrived there on July 18. The soldiers under Col. Benjamin
Hinman, who had taken command of the fort subsequent to its capture
on May 10, 1775, numbered only about twelve hundred. They consisted
mainly of fresh Connecticut volunteers, unaccustomed to military service. Most of them were insubordinate and undisciplined. The conditions
that Schuyler found at the garrison highly annoyed the authoritative
disciplinarian.

After his arrival, he wrote another letter to George Washington: "You
will expect that I should say something about this place and the troops

79

here. Not one earthly thing for offense or defense has been done."
Schuyler then related the results of his unannounced nighttime inspection
of two outposts manned by negligent sentinels and a guard force that was
sound asleep: "With a pen-knife only I could have cut off both guards,
and then set fire to the blockhouse, destroyed the stores, and starved the
people here." He concluded his report with a hope "to get the better of
this inattention." "The officers and men are all good looking people, and
decent in their deportment, and I really believe will make good soldiers,
as soon as I can get the better of this nonchalance of theirs. Bravery, I
believe, they are far from wanting."[4]

Schuyler's concern about the training and discipline of colonial troops
would be shared by every American commander throughout the war.
These recruits chafed under the regimentation and conformity that their
leaders tried to impose on them in order to emulate the highly reputed
European model of soldiery. The nature of the Continental army's initial
composition may be seen during the raising of the New York regiments.

Some patricians viewed military organization during the Revolution as
an opportunity to retain a social status quo after the conflict. James Duane
wrote his fellow New York delegate in the Continental Congress, Robert
R. Livingston, that he was "pleased that young Mr. Livingston is raising
a company in the Manor . . . which will render landed property secure."
"We must think in time of the means of assuring the reins of government
when these commotions shall subside. Licentiousness is the natural object
of civil discord and it can only be guarded against by placing the command of the troops in the hands of property and rank who . . . will
preserve the same authority over the minds of the people which they
enjoyed in the time of tranquility."[5]

However, Duane and people of his ilk could not realize the full measure of their expectations for several reasons. Some men of property and
social status declined military command, with its concomitant personal
hardships and sacrifices, when it was offered to them. With the prospect
of a physically demanding, rough existence, the state of an individual's
health and age certainly played a role in this decision. A few of the
privileged class simply chose not to be inconvenienced and let others who
they deemed more suited to that type of work serve in the military. Most
realized that there was quite a difference from acting as the nominal
commander of a militia unit during peacetime, with its innocuous musters
and drills, to leading soldiers into actual combat. Into this military lead-

ership void stepped myriad personalities, each with his own motive in answering the call to arms—be it civic responsibility, ambition, adventuresomeness, or any number of other influences. Although most officers tended to be economically advantaged in civilian life before joining the army, many of them represented the upwardly mobile merchant or middle class of colonial society. Therefore, control of the military by the landed interest remained tenuous at best.

As a newly established country squire and member of the gentry, Montgomery subscribed to the notions that there existed a "natural elite" and that ownership of land bestowed one's prestige. But, he also felt that the privileged had a responsibility to society that should be discharged during periods of crisis as well as times of peace. He had no sympathy for aloof aristocrats when he sought volunteers to fill the officer positions in the New York regiments. Janet Montgomery recalled her husband's reaction to the general reluctance of most New York elite leaders to answer the martial call. "No gentlemen offered to take commissions in the army. The mechanics alone offered, and he [Montgomery] accepted them without demur. When the brigade was filled several gentlemen came forward, but he refused them the places, telling them they should have been first, and were too late."[6]

One incidental consequence in the establishment of the officer corps concerned the Sons of Liberty and other patriot radicals who had accumulated in New York City. Popular rabble-rousers such as John Lamb and Marinus Willett joined the newly formed New York regiments as junior officers, which effectively removed the extreme political element from the local scene. This alleviated much of the civil disturbance in the city and allowed the Provincial Congress to conduct its business in a more orderly fashion. Once in the army, however, the confrontational nature of these crowd leaders who had turned officers became a source of vexation to their military superiors. Following their example, subordinates frequently questioned and challenged the decisions of their commanders. Thus, this organizational dynamic contributed to the relatively egalitarian character of the American forces, which was unprecedented in eighteenth-century armies.

If the officers of the Continental army were indeterminate, the men were even more so. Mostly poor, nondescript people who had no better chance of earning a livelihood represented those who were willing to become common soldiers. The military command hoped that the virtual

xperience and regimentation of these recruits would be
their bravery and fortitude.

rk Congress directed that three thousand Continentals be
e province. Military organization formed these troops into
giments or battalions (terms used interchangeably) and an
a... any. A colonel (commander), lieutenant colonel (deputy
commander), major, adjutant (administrative officer), quartermaster (logistics officer), chaplain, and surgeon formed a regimental headquarters.
Each regiment, totaling approximately 750 individuals, consisted of ten
companies of seventy-five men. A captain and two lieutenants led every
company. All such units also had three sergeants, three corporals, a fifer,
a drummer, and sixty-four privates. This would be New York's contribution to the Continental army, sometimes called the New York Line.[7]

The 1st (or New York) Regiment, under the command of Col. Alexander McDougall, recruited its men largely in New York City and the
surrounding area. The 2nd (or Albany) Regiment, led by Col. Goose
Van Schaick, drew its members primarily from Albany, Tryon, Charlotte, and Cumberland counties. The 3rd (or Ulster) Regiment, commanded by Col. James Clinton, enlisted its contingent mainly in Ulster,
Orange, and Suffolk counties. The 4th (or Dutchess) Regiment, headed
by Col. James Holmes, recruited its men chiefly in Dutchess, Kings,
Queens, Richmond, and Westchester counties. Capt. John Lamb commanded the artillery company and enlisted his cannoneers from the New
York City area. Recruits for the 1st New York and New York Artillery
Company were generally laborers and seamen, while farmers and tradesmen, with a larger proportion of married men, filled the ranks of the
other three regiments. About one out of six soldiers was not yet twenty
years old.[8]

The recruiting process started when the Provincial Congress sent warrants to aspiring captains authorizing them to enlist men for a company.
If the warrant holder was successful in filling the unit-manning requirements, a commission would be forthcoming appointing him as commander of the company. Authorities also published advertisements and
broadsides encouraging people to volunteer for military service. Recruiting activities usually took place at a designated local inn or tavern. Recruiters promised inducements of pay, uniforms, weapons, and equipment to the prospective soldiers. Although the basic allowance for a
private of one shilling and eleven pence per day was modest by all
standards, the opportunity for regular pay, no matter how minimal, had

an appeal to the poorer segment of the populace. The Continental Congress limited the term of military service to the remainder of the year as a further incentive to volunteer.[9] The use of enlistment bounties was widespread: "Ten shillings shall be allowed to every Soldier, that shall enlist in the Continental Congress in this Colony, for the present Campaign, who shall furnish himself with a good musket."[10] As an additional stimulus to recruiting, the New York Congress resolved that "every officer, who has already enlisted or who shall hereafter enlist a soldier in the Regiments now raising in this Colony, shall be entitled to a dollar for each such soldier."[11]

Even with this vigorous recruiting activity, some companies were hard pressed to muster a full-strength complement. As in the other colonies, the vast majority of New Yorkers elected not to support the Revolution in a military status. The decision to join the army was not taken lightly by the general population. It meant separation from friends and family, and risking one's life. Compensation for this personal obligation offered by the recruiters amounted to nothing but promises at this point. So individuals who became emotionally involved in the revolutionary spirit, or indigents who hoped military service would improve their lives made up the bulk of the inductees. Only about 2,075 men enlisted in the New York regiments in 1775.[12]

These were the troops that Montgomery would endeavor to mold into an effective fighting force to assault Canada. He held no illusions regarding the quality of troops being recruited, suspecting that many "have entered into the Service from mercenary views [rather] than from a generous Zeal for the Glorious Cause of America." "Good soldiers," he announced, would be "cherished with the fond attention of an indulgent parent," but "the vicious, the disorderly and the disobedient would in due course be visited with deserved punishment."[13]

Montgomery preceded the New York forces on the way north and anxiously awaited their advance at Albany. However, complications with mobilization and supply of the regiments delayed their departure. Shortages of weapons and basic equipment prevented the troops from becoming ready for field duty. Inadequate time for training the raw recruits compounded the problems. In the middle of July, the Provincial Congress responded to the pleas of Schuyler and Montgomery to expedite the dispatch of the regiments by conceding: "Our troops can be of no service to you; they have no arms, clothes, blankets, or ammunition; the officers no commissions; our treasury no money; ourselves in debt. . . . We will remove difficulties as fast as we can, and send you the soldiers, whenever the men we have raised are entitled to that name."[14]

Regiments were outfitted in numerical order. By August 8, six weeks after recruiting was completed, four companies of the 1st New York were well enough armed and provisioned to be sent to Albany, under the command of Lt. Col. Rudolphus Ritzema. McDougall remained behind to supervise the preparations of the remainder of his regiment. Two days later, Ritzema's force encamped at Half Moon, a staging area established just north of Albany for the troops mobilizing for the Canadian campaign.[15] Schuyler and Montgomery were not impressed with many of the soldiers that had joined their expedition. "Fourteen of Col. Ritzema's men have already deserted since his arrival at Half Moon," Schuyler observed, "and I believe he will lose many more before he reaches Ticonderoga." "If those gone are like some that remain, we have gained by their going off."[16]

With the vanguard of the 1st Regiment finally on the move, Montgomery turned his attention to the 2nd Regiment. "The troops are to be forwarded to Ticonderoga as fast as they may arrive or as soon as those under your immediate command can be furnished with such articles as are absolutely necessary to enable them to take to the field," he instructed Colonel Van Schaick. Troop discipline during the march and the soldier's responsibility to society were also on Montgomery's mind. "I intreat you to enforce good order, that individuals may not suffer in their property," he ordered Colonel Van Schaick. "Impress the men with just notions of our duty to society and how infamous it is in us who have arms in our hands for the protection of our fellow citizens to betray that trust by any violation of their rights."[17]

Schuyler and Montgomery slowly gathered a conglomerate force at Ticonderoga to mount the campaign. This feat required forwarding and converging troop units over land and water some one hundred miles north from Albany between Lake George and Lake Champlain. When the British fleet standing off Manhattan weighted anchor to sail for Boston in the middle of July, the Continental Congress also ordered some of the Connecticut troops stationed around New York City to march for Ticonderoga. This force, commanded by Col. David Waterbury, joined Hinman's Connecticut contingent previously positioned at Ticonderoga. In addition, Massachusetts soldiers under Col. James Easton had arrived at Ticonderoga. Five companies of the 2nd New York combined with the four companies of the 1st New York to form the Yorker complement.

(Six companies of the 3rd New York and five companies of the 4th New York had only reached Albany by this time.) Three companies of New Hampshire Rangers commanded by Col. Timothy Bedel and a Green Mountain Boys Regiment from Vermont headed by Lt. Col. Seth Warner later joined the campaign en route to St. Johns. Two artillery companies —Capt. Samuel Mott's Connecticut gunners stationed at Ticonderoga and Lamb's New York unit, which would arrive shortly—lent fire support. Together, these recruits from Massachusetts, Connecticut, New Hampshire, Vermont, and New York comprised the troop force of the expedition by the last part of August. Drawn from different colonies, inadequately trained, unaccustomed to serving together, suspicious of outsiders, the soldiers of this makeshift rebel assemblage presented a challenge to anyone attempting to lead them.[18]

During the collection of their modest army, Schuyler and Montgomery also engaged in an industrious boat-building program on Lake George. A sizable fleet was needed to ferry the soldiers down Lake Champlain into Canada. Most of the craft were bateaux, which were boats about thirty feet long with a cargo capacity of three to seven tons. They could be rigged with sail but were usually paddled by an eight-man crew. By August, workers had completed enough of these boats to carry thirteen hundred men with a three-week supply of provisions. They also constructed several larger vessels capable of containing about three hundred individuals and suitable for naval warfare. These ships, combined with those that were built or seized during the capture of Ticonderoga, constituted a flotilla for the operation, which was only able to transport approximately half of the total force.[19]

All these preparations to invade Quebec Province did not escape the attention of the British military establishment in Canada. Guy Carleton, the royal governor at Quebec who also commanded the military forces, moved to Montreal shortly after receiving news that the Americans had captured Ticonderoga and Crown Point. There, he received intelligence regarding the concentration of field units by the Americans at Ticonderoga with the intent of driving northward into Canada.

The inhabitants of Canada did not generally rally to counter the Americans as Carleton had hoped. Although the clergy supported the British government—because the Quebec Act allowed Roman Catholicism to remain as the state religion—there was scant outpouring of active support from the French Canadians. Most of them took a watch-and-wait stance to determine which side would gain the upper hand in the contest over their homeland before they committed themselves. A large number of Indians seemed willing to fight alongside the British forces in Canada, but Carleton issued orders that restrained their participation. He requested the tribes to remain neutral, except for limited scouting activities. Based on his experience in the French and Indian War, Carleton simply did not feel that the native warriors could be trustworthy or reliable. With inadequate military forces—only two regiments of regulars and a few hundred Canadian volunteers, or fewer than one thousand men for the defense of the whole province—Carleton's situation at this point was not encouraging. However, he would prove himself an excellent strategist and resourceful field commander.

Carleton adopted an advanced defensive posture with the few troop resources that he had at his disposal to fend off the American invasion. He planned to confront the intruders shortly before or after they crossed the border. Carleton knew that he would have to fight his initial battle as close to the frontier as possible to keep the enemy at arms' length from the key cities of Montreal and Quebec. Therefore, he selected St. Johns (St. Jean), a prominent location east of Montreal on the Richelieu River guarding the traditional Canadian invasion route, as the place to make a stand. St. Johns suited his purposes well. It stood as an obstacle that could not be easily bypassed by a force intent upon capturing Montreal, and it provided a base from which vessels could sail to intercept any invaders while they were still on Lake Champlain. Nearby, Chambly would serve as an easily accessible supply depot for the British defensive network. So, Carleton began reinforcing St. Johns with as many forces as he could scrape together, and he launched a major naval building effort of his own.

Meanwhile, General Washington decided to expand the Canadian campaign. A second invasion route would be pursued, culminating in a two-pronged attack, with two armies entering Canada at different points and then combining to capture Quebec, the province's capital city. Washington selected Col. Benedict Arnold to lead this additional effort. While Schuyler and Montgomery continued their approach to Quebec along the St. Lawrence River, Arnold would lead an expedition through the Maine wilderness to meet them outside the city. Schuyler retained overall command of the enlarged Canadian campaign. Washington reasoned that his plan would place added pressure on Carleton's defensive measures. Writing to Schuyler, Washington explained that Carleton "must either break up and follow this [Arnold's] party to Quebec, by which he will leave you free passage, or he must suffer that important place [Quebec] to fall into our hands."[20]

On August 17, Schuyler returned to Albany to attend a conference with representatives from the Iroquois Indian tribe (Six Nations) aimed at keeping them neutral, leaving Montgomery in command at Ticonderoga. During Schuyler's absence, Montgomery received a message from Maj. John Brown, who had been sent out to conduct a reconnaissance into Canada. Brown's report confirmed other intelligence that two gunboats being built at St. Johns were nearing completion. Their entrance into service threatened to give the British control of Lake Champlain, thereby placing the American campaign in jeopardy. Without waiting to secure approval from his superior, Montgomery boldly decided to move north immediately to deny naval superiority of the lake by the enemy. His military training had taught him that timing could sometimes be more determinative than strength. By sunset of August 28, Montgomery embarked the greater part of Waterbury's Connecticut Regiment, four companies of Ritzema's 1st New York, and a small section of Mott's artillery company with several cannons—some twelve hundred men in all—aboard the schooner *Liberty*, the sloop *Enterprise*, and a number of bateaux. He left a like number of soldiers behind.[21]

Just prior to leaving, Montgomery sent a hasty letter to Schuyler explaining his actions. "I am so much of Brown's opinion," he wrote, "that I think it absolutely necessary to move down the lake with the utmost dispatch. Should the enemy get their vessels into the lake, 'tis over with us this summer." He clarified the reason that he made the decision on his own volition. "The moving without your orders I don't like; but, . . . the prevention of the enemy is of the utmost consequence." He urged Schuyler "to follow us in a whale-boat," saying, "It will give the men great confidence in your spirit and activity." "How necessary this confidence is to a general, I need not tell you." Montgomery then concluded: "I most heartily wish this may meet with your approbation, . . . all my ambition is to do my duty in a subordinate capacity, without the least ungenerous intention of lessening that merit so justly your due."[22]

The letter reflects the close personal and professional relationship that had developed between the two men in the short time they had served together. Although Schuyler and Montgomery contrasted sharply in their demeanor and deportment, they had established a mutual trust and respect. Schuyler, a punctilious, careful, and deliberate officer, was best suited for the functions of a behind-the-lines commander. His forte lay in organization and coordination. Ill health also plagued him throughout the campaign. Consequently, Schuyler entrusted the field command of the expedition to his energetic and dauntless second in command, allowing him wide latitude to discharge his duties. Montgomery fit the role of troop leader superbly while respecting the authority of his senior officer.

Most of the unhardened troops reacted to the precipitous order to advance toward St. Johns, some 120 miles to the north, with little enthusiasm. They felt unprepared and hesitant to close with the enemy. However, their dynamic general goaded them into motion. Montgomery felt that he had no time to spare for further preparations. The moment had come for decisive action; his soldiers would have to be tempered by combat. A Connecticut company commander hurriedly writing to his wife scrawled, "I have but one monet [moment] to rite as our orders are Suden for Marching and all in Confusion. . . . I think we are not Ready for Such an Important Task, But I Pray God may be with us, as the Battle is not to the strong." In a second letter on the next day, he wrote: "I must confess that it appears to me that we go on (in my openion) full as fast as we are Ready, but hope for the Best."[23]

Hampered by rain and unfavorable winds, Montgomery's force worked its way down the lake by navigating during the day and going ashore to bivouac at night. Montgomery felt relief that the campaign was underway at last. Weeks of frustration over the organization and supply of the mission caused him to grow impatient with its progress. Now with inertia of the mission finally overcome, the general developed an optimistic outlook. The soldiers' morale also improved markedly while actively engaged in a concerted effort under their positive and confident leader.

With the troops on the move and regaining their spirit, Montgomery had a few moments for some private considerations. Soldiers usually fall into an age-old ritual on the eve of combat—finding or deepening religious convictions, writing letters professing affection to loved ones, and attempting to put their personal affairs in order. For Montgomery, it was time to direct his attention to these kinds of thoughts and contemplate his own mortality. On August 30 while at Crown Point, he drew up his will. In it, he bequeathed his "personal fortune" and the farmstead at King's Bridge to his sister, Lady Ranelagh. To his wife, he left the Rhinebeck estate and his property there. He explained the provisions of the document by stating that "the ample fortune that my wife will succeed to [her share of the Livingston estate] makes it unnecessary to provide for her in a manner suitable to her situation in life and adequate to the warm affection I bear her. My dear sister's large family wants all I can share." He also recommended one or two of his sister's younger children to his wife's protection.[24]

On August 30, Schuyler returned to Ticonderoga from the Albany council meeting. He was suffering from his latest bout with fever and rheumatic pains. Some of the news that he received concerning the Green Mountain Boys offered no balm to his malaise. The irregular troop unit had been undergoing severe reorganization since the Continental Congress assigned it to the Northern Department. At that time, Congress authorized the Vermont region volunteers to elect their own officers, including the lieutenant colonel who would command them. This engendered a heated rivalry among several aspiring commanders, all of whom hindered mobilization efforts of the organization. As a result, the Green Mountain Boys as a distinct battalion did not join the campaign until much later than expected. In the interim, Schuyler and Montgomery employed individuals from the Green Mountain Boys as scouts and intelligence agents in Canada. The cavalier attitude of these soldiers and the autonomous nature of their missions made them difficult to control, resulting in several counterproductive incidents.

Capt. Remember Baker, a Green Mountain Boy on independent assignment, was the subject of this most recent matter of concern that Schuyler encountered upon his arrival at Ticonderoga. Schuyler reported to Washington that the disposition of the Canadians and Indians toward his campaign might have been undermined by the "imprudence of a Capt. Baker, who without my leave and contrary to the most pointed and express orders," precipitated a firefight with a group of Indians that had commandeered some canoes of his scouting party operating in the Canadian wilderness. Both sides in the skirmish received several casualties, and Baker died in the affair. "This event, my Canadian correspondent informs me has induced some of the Indians of that tribe to join the regular forces at St. John's," Schuyler wrote in a letter to two of the Northern Department Indian commissioners.[25]

The surviving troops, which had been driven away by the Indians, later returned to claim the body of their captain. They found Baker with his head and hands cut off and missing. Returning to their base, the scouts informed Ethan Allen of their experiences. Allen, the former commander of the Green Mountain Boys until displaced by Seth Warner, had offered his services to the campaign in an individual capacity. A subsequent patrol captured some prisoners who divulged that Baker's head was mounted on a pole standing in the parade ground at St. Johns. Allen called for volunteers and led them in a surreptitious sortie inside the walls of the stronghold. There, they recovered the severed head so that it could be properly buried with the body.[26]

On the next day after his arrival at Ticonderoga, Schuyler ordered forward five hundred of Hinman's regiment, three hundred of Van Schaick's 2nd New York Regiment, and some artillery. Then, in spite of his physical condition, he set out to catch up with Montgomery. On the morning of September 4, Schuyler rejoined Montgomery awaiting him at Isle La Motte, situated in the northern reaches of Lake Champlain. A fifth company of the 1st New York also was able to combine with the force at this point.

Assuming command, Schuyler issued orders to resume the advance to Isle aux Noix, located near the entrance of the Sorel or Richelieu River, where an attack against St. Johns would be launched. That evening, the invaders pitched camp at Isle aux Noix and spent their first night on Canadian soil. By the next day Schuyler's condition had worsened, but he drafted a proclamation to the Canadians, designed to curry their favor and support. Addressed to "Friends and Countrymen," the message explained that the "Grand Congress" in Philadelphia had ordered his army to expel the British troops acting under a "despotic Ministry" to enslave them. He pledged to "cherish every Canadian . . . and sacredly guard their property" during the campaign. Schuyler instructed Ethan Allen and John Brown to deliver the document to James Livingston at Chambly, with whom he had been in correspondence. A Chambly merchant sympathetic to the Americans' cause in Canada, Livingston was a likely contact to disseminate this patriot gesture of goodwill.[27]

On September 6, the Americans made their first attempt upon Fort St. Johns, which lay only twelve miles north of Isle aux Noix. Schuyler and Montgomery intended the initial operation, conducted without a clear superiority of forces and firepower, as an exploratory probe to test the British defenses. The assault force of approximately one thousand troops approached to within a mile of the fortified town when its battery opened a harmless cannonade upon their boats. Pushing forward half a mile nearer the post, they landed in a broad swamp that extended almost to St. Johns. Since Schuyler was incapacitated, he remained at the landing site with a few men to guard the bateaux. Montgomery started the main body of troops through marshy and heavily wooded terrain toward their objective.

Maj. Thomas Hobby and Capt. Matthew Mead of Waterbury's 5th Connecticut led a flanking party on the left and a little ahead of the others. After slogging a quarter of a mile through the wetlands, the flankers were crossing a deep, muddy stream when a hundred Indians led by Capt. Gilbert Tice ambushed them. Several of the Americans fell during the initial volley, but the rest returned fire and maneuvered smartly into a dense thicket to engage the hidden enemy. The ensuing firefight lasted for about half an hour before the Indians retreated back to the fort. Eight of the Americans were killed or fatally wounded; and eight, including Hobby and Mead, were injured less severely. The enemy suffered similar losses, including Tice, who received a slight wound. This was the first blood shed in the Canadian invasion.[28]

The skirmish, short as it was, disrupted the Americans' advance. In the almost impenetrable forest, it was difficult to ascertain the strength and disposition of the enemy spoiling force. Montgomery did not wish to expose his soldiers to an adversary whose numbers and location had not been determined. With nightfall not far off, he decided to suspend operations for the day. As dusk fell, his troops began preparing their position to provide local security. However, gunners at St. Johns located their encampment and began disruptive fire on the invaders, forcing Montgomery to withdraw his position to a point three quarters of a mile away and out of reach of the British cannons.[29]

As the force bivouacked that night, an intelligence agent came to brief Schuyler. The information that he imparted presented gloomy prospects for the quick capture of St. Johns. The informant stated that although a single regiment of British regulars was present in all of Canada, all but fifty of these were positioned with about a hundred Indians at St. Johns and Chambly. There, he claimed, the fortifications "were compleat and strong and plentifully furnished with cannon," and a well-armed schooner was nearly ready to be placed in action against the Americans. He also maintained that the Americans could expect no overt assistance from the Canadians, who preferred to remain neutral. Therefore, he advised the general that it would not be prudent to attack St. Johns under the present circumstances.[30]

Schuyler was discouraged from continuing the assault by the information available to him. The next morning, he called a council of war in which he reviewed the current situation with his senior officers. The Americans, with only two cannons, knew that "the weak state of our artillery" prevented them from laying siege to the fort. Furthermore, they could not hope to sink the sixteen-gun British warship while it remained within the protective cover of the fort's battery. They also understood that the "great forwardness" of the vessel posed a considerable threat, and they had to prevent it from breaking out into Lake Champlain. If it did, the line of communication with Ticonderoga might be severed and the campaign aborted. Therefore, the council of officers resolved to return to Isle aux Noix, where an already prepared boom could be thrown across the channel to block the enemy's ship from entering the lake. Then, depending upon more encouraging news from St. Johns and the arrival of additional reinforcements, an advance might again be mounted against the British stronghold.[31]

Once back at Isle aux Noix, the Americans installed the boom across the river and fortified the island into an excellent defensive position. However, Schuyler's health had deteriorated to the point that it was becoming a liability to the mission. Ritzema, one of the regimental commanders, observed that the general was "in a dangerous Situation." "This is very detrimental to us." The bedridden Schuyler informed the Continental Congress and General Washington of his disabled state and commended Montgomery for assuming the functions of command that he could no longer perform. "I cannot estimate the obligations I lie under to General Montgomery, for the many important services he has done and daily does, in which he has had little assistance from me, as I have not enjoyed a moment's health since I left Fort George, and am now so low as not to be able to hold the pen."[32]

Schuyler then received a reply to the message that he had sent earlier to James Livingston. The well-affected Chambly merchant reported that Canadians had responded positively to Schuyler's manifesto. He proposed that the Americans should establish a position near St. Johns to prevent the British vessel with its sixteen mounted guns, christened the *Royal Savage*, from escaping. Livingston promised the support of "a considerable party of Canadians" in the operation, which he suggested might even capture the ship. Reinforcements had arrived by that time—three hundred of Hinman's Connecticut troops, four hundred of the 2nd New York, and several pieces of artillery. The forward invasion force now numbered seventeen hundred men and had five cannons and three mortars. Schuyler enthusiastically adopted Livingston's scheme and made elaborate plans to carry it out. Two row-galleys, each carrying a twelve-pounder, the sloop, the schooner, and ten bateaux with 350 men were to lie in the river to prevent the *Royal Savage* from going south to the lake; and 800 men were to invest St. Johns, 300 of them to act as a covering party while 500 circumvented the fort and established a "corps of observation" to interdict communications between St. Johns and Chambly and control the waterway.[33]

On September 10, Montgomery put the plan into action. The expedition set out and at approximately 9 P.M. landed about three miles south of St. Johns. The covering party under Montgomery held that position, while Lieutenant Colonel Ritzema with his detachment departed to march around the fort.

It was pitch black in the swamp, and Ritzema's untested soldiers, remembering the ambush on the former expedition, were nervous and apprehensive. They had not proceeded far when the troops suddenly panicked and scattered, even though no shot had been fired. Apparently two units of the detachment had collided in the dark and heavy underbrush. This general confusion had so startled the other units that the entire force stampeded back toward the boats. Montgomery heard the frightened soldiers crashing through the woods back to his location and hurried to intercept them. He managed to rally the detachment and started them off again, exhorting them "to act like men" and "do your duty." They advanced about a quarter of a mile when some grapeshot fired from a British bateaux in the river landed among their ranks. Half of them again beat a hasty retreat. Ritzema and the rest of his command continued to press forward to engage a few of the enemy occupying a nearby breastwork, inflicting two casualties. By then, it was 3 A.M. and the detachment remained straggly and disorganized. Ritzema decided to withdraw his force and rejoin the covering party. The whole expedition spent the night at the landing area.[34]

Early the next morning at the request of several officers, Montgomery called a council of war. The gathering, composed of all the field-grade officers and company commanders, resolved to proceed with another effort to accomplish the planned attack on St. Johns. However, many of the officers were unsure of the obedience of their men. They felt that the state of affairs necessitated obtaining the consent of the soldiers by ballot. This method was so unmilitary and contrary to standard troop discipline as Montgomery knew it that he was appalled at its suggestion. He acceded to it only because of the exigencies of the situation. After the rank and file added their vote to continue the operation, the detachment prepared to move out. However, just then, a lieutenant who had been scouting up the river, returned and spread word that the *Royal Savage* was bearing down on their location. While Montgomery and his officers considered this latest development, half of the New England troops became unnerved and embarked on the boats without orders, intent on retreating posthaste down the river. In disgust, Montgomery ordered the demoralized expedition to return to Isle aux Noix.[35]

After withdrawing from St. Johns, a deep sense of disappointment beset Montgomery. Such an ignominious retreat was inexcusable in his thinking, and he decided to make another attempt to salvage the mission. After his column had gone a few miles, he ordered the boats put to shore so that he could test the temper of the troops regarding their marching from that point against St. Johns. While he and his officers were conferring, one of the men called out that an enemy vessel was approaching. The troops were hardly restrained from pushing off without their officers in their haste to escape, which dashed all chances of persuading the soldiers to continue operations. Back to the relative safety of Isle aux Noix they went.[36]

The disgraceful and mutinous behavior of the soldiers mortified Montgomery. "Such a set of pusillanimous wrenches never were collected," he wrote his wife. "Could I, with decency, leave the army in its present situation, I would not serve an hour longer." He wondered whether the "general character of the people has been too justly represented." After venting his exasperation, he then conceded, "there are some whose spirit I have confidence in . . . and they flatter me with hopes of prevailing on them to retrieve their characters."[37]

Turning first to the traditional remedy, Montgomery requested Schuyler to appoint a court-martial board to deal with the most flagrant cases of insubordination and unmilitary conduct. Charges were hard to prove, however, because most soldiers were reluctant to testify against their comrades. When the court completed its work three days later, it had handed out more acquittals than convictions. The punishments imposed involved a sergeant reduced in rank for deserting his post during action, a man sentenced to thirty-nine lashes for "cocking and presenting his firelock" to an officer, and another man assigned to fatigue duty for the duration of the campaign because he "fled in fear of enemy pursuit."[38]

In addition to the application of military justice, Montgomery employed other methods to instill some measure of discipline and fighting mettle in the troops. He felt that the behavior of the soldiers could be "palliated by saying they were young troops," and believed that their rough edges would "wear off by a little practice." "I have endeavored to make them ashamed of themselves, and hope that this won't happen again." He considered their general response of self-abasement and contriteness as a promise of better conduct in the future. Montgomery told Schuyler that the men were "unable to bear the reproach of their late unbecoming behavior." Therefore, he was determined to motivate the men into redeeming themselves.[39]

An opportune enemy attack also helped to buoy the men's sagging spirits. A hostile boat approached the American base and opened fire, but the patriot gunners scored a direct hit that sank the enemy vessel. This incident served to infuse optimism throughout the ranks. Shortly, morale and enthusiasm returned to the members of the expedition. Schuyler and Montgomery wanted to capitalize on the upswing of troop attitude and prepared for a renewed attack on St. Johns. However, several days of bad weather delayed initiation of the operation.[40]

The onset of rain exacerbated prevalent unhealthy conditions surrounding the patriots' encampment. Isle aux Noix was a low island with poor drainage and disease-breeding backwater, chosen as a base for strategic rather than environmental reasons. Illness caused by inclement weather, inadequate shelter, insufficient rations, and unsanitary surroundings swept through the camp. Six hundred men were on the sick list and could not engage in normal duties. Schuyler's condition also grew worse. He had been directing operations from his bed for more than a week, but now he realized that he could not continue. Bad weather had finally ended his hopes for a recovery at Isle aux Noix, so he decided to return to the healthier confines of Ticonderoga for recuperation. On September 16, he was put into a covered boat and left Isle aux Noix.[41]

With the departure of Schuyler, command of the expedition devolved upon Montgomery. It was not an enviable position. His motley collection of troops had demonstrated little courage and prowess in previous combat situations. Also, the Americans' undisciplined style of soldiering was disconcerting to Montgomery because it contrasted sharply with what he had known in the British army. Even though he expected his men to give a better account of themselves in the future, disease now sapped their strength. Time also played a detrimental role. Winter was not that far away in this northern clime, and St. Johns still stood impregnable as ever. Nevertheless, patriot aspirations for the conquest of Canada rested on the shoulders of this man. Montgomery accepted the challenge and gazed steadily northward.

CHAPTER EIGHT

Struggle and Success against St. Johns

Six weeks before St. John's they lay,
While cannon on them constant play,
On cold and marshy ground;
When Preston forced at length to yield,
Aloud proclaimed it in the field,
Virtue a friend had found . . .
To Montreal he winged his way,
Which seemed impatient to obey
And opened wide its gates,
Convinced no force could e'er repel
Troops who had just behaved so well,
Under so hard a fate.[1]

As the formidable responsibility of invading Canada settled on his shoulders, Montgomery quickly took stock of the situation. The terrain was familiar to him. Fifteen years earlier, he had campaigned in this same area while in the British army. The circumstances, however, had changed dramatically. Then, he served as an officer in a crack regiment of tightly controlled and disciplined soldiers, trained to strict obedience. Now, he found himself on the other side of the battle line in charge of an army of rebels that were quite different from the professional soldiers to whom he was accustomed. Clearly, Montgomery would have to make numerous adjustments to accomplish his crucial mission.

The arrival of more troops provided one piece of good news. These additional levies helped to compensate for the rampant sickness that had attacked and disabled almost half of his campaigners. Reinforcements arriving on August 16 included Lt. Col. Seth Warner with 170 of his Green Mountain Boys and Col. Timothy Bedel with 100 New Hampshire Rangers. Capt. John Lamb's New York artillery company, with its much-needed cannons and gunnery expertise, would also appear soon. Montgomery's troop strength was nearing two thousand soldiers.

When Schuyler returned to Ticonderoga, he immediately began to push forward additional troops to bolster Montgomery's force. Colonel Easton with two hundred of his troops and the 1st New York Regiment were soon en route from Ticonderoga to Isle aux Noix. Schuyler's diligent mobilization of reinforcements and the procurement of provisions from the rear echelon probably contributed more to the campaign than he could have otherwise accomplished at Montgomery's side. Circumstances had swept the two officers into a command arrangement that matched the capabilities of both.[2]

A few of the reinforcements, however, offered little help to the campaign. Pleading personal reasons or some other excuse, they requested to go home on furlough. Montgomery granted leaves to two irresolute company commanders, a Captain Doolittle of Connecticut and Capt. John Quackenbush (Quackenbos) of New York. Shortly afterward, he remarked wryly to Marinus Willett, another company commander: "When we get rid of the 'do-littles' and 'quakes-in-the-bush' I hope we shall have none left but fighting men on whom I can rely."[3]

Unhesitatingly, Montgomery initiated another expedition against St. Johns on September 16, the same day that Schuyler departed to return to Ticonderoga. He organized his fourteen hundred effectives into a combined strike force. First, he sent a naval component, consisting of a schooner, a sloop, ten bateaux, two row-galleys (each with a twelve-pound cannon), and 350 troops to lie in the river and counter any maneuver by the *Royal Savage*. Then, he embarked the rest of his troops in bateaux and landed them once more near St. Johns on September 17.[4]

The British garrison, commanded by Maj. Charles Preston, awaited the latest American offensive. Ironically, Preston was the same officer who had purchased the majority commission over Montgomery four years earlier. A twist of fate had confronted these two men once again—

this time on the field of battle. Preston, a competent and tenacious commandant, would be a worthy adversary for Montgomery.[5]

Carleton's entire force of regulars amounted to 376 troops of the 7th Regiment (the Royal Fusiliers) and 263 soldiers of the 26th Regiment (the Cameronians). Less than two hundred men drawn from these two regiments, along with a few artillerymen and Indians, garrisoned St. Johns at the time of the Americans' first abortive attempt upon it. Shortly afterward, Carleton strengthened the defenses at St. Johns with 225 men he had managed to provide: an augmentation of regular troops to total 500; about 100 Canadian volunteers; and a 70-man Royal Highland Emigrants company, made up of veteran Scottish soldiers who had emigrated to Canada. This additional personnel strength increased the garrison-manning level to approximately 725 troops altogether. Carleton posted another ninety officers and men from the 7th Regiment at nearby Chambly.[6]

Montgomery and his troops spent the first night near the landing area under sporadic bombardment from the fort. The next morning, he ordered Major Bedel to occupy a position north of St. Johns, taking with him the Green Mountain Boys and part of Hinman's command in addition to his own New Hampshire Rangers. As the soldiers prepared to depart, they heard distant gunfire from the direction of their intended objective. Montgomery noticed that some of the men showed signs of the same apprehension that had foiled the two earlier attacks. Determined to avoid similar results this time, Montgomery decided to lead the advance personally. With the Green Mountain Boys at the head of the column, he maintained the troops in close formation during the approach march. As the firing grew louder, Montgomery quickly maneuvered his soldiers to close in on the source of commotion.

On September 14, Montgomery had sent Maj. John Brown with one hundred Americans and thirty to forty Canadian recruits to reconnoiter the vicinity of Chambly. Brown learned that a British supply train was on its way to St. Johns. On the night of September 17, he and his troops waylaid a convoy of eight wagons loaded with stores about two miles north of its destination. The next morning, some two hundred British regulars and volunteers with two fieldpieces commanded by Capt. John Strong of the 26th Regiment emerged from the fort at St. Johns to attack him. Amid a considerable exchange of fire, Brown's force withdrew into a nearby wood with their captured booty. This constituted the firefight that Montgomery and his force of five hundred troops happened upon.

"The grape shot and musket balls flew very thick," Capt. John Fassett serving with the Green Mountain Boys recorded in his diary; but both sides suffered few casualties. When Montgomery's troops converged on the noisy battlefield, many succumbed to fear again and hung back. Yet under their general's field leadership, they managed to rebound and rout the British party back into the fort. "The enemy, after an ill-directed fire for some minutes, retired with precipitation, and lucky for them they did," Montgomery later reported, "for had we known their situation, which the thickness of the woods prevented our finding out till it was too late, there would not a man of them returned."[7]

While Brown's contingent continued foraging, commandeering twelve more wagons of supplies, Montgomery left Bedel in charge of this task force to entrench itself about a mile north of St. Johns. Montgomery sent other forces to establish posts at Longueuil and La Prairie to guard these two approaches from Montreal. Then he positioned his other units to surround the fort. The troops busied themselves preparing entrenchments and erecting gun emplacements. The siege of St. Johns had begun.[8]

Except for brief, specific missions like countering Brown's raid on the supply train, Preston preferred to retain his troops within the protective walls of the fort and rely largely upon his gunners to keep the Americans at bay. He had a large and effective battery numbering forty-two pieces of artillery, including two twenty-four-pounders, and plenty of ammunition. Therefore, he chose to exploit this advantage that he enjoyed over the besiegers. During the first weeks of the siege, Preston's rate of fire achieved a ten-to-one preponderance over that of the Americans, and the British maintained this superiority until Schuyler could send more and heavier guns from Ticonderoga.[9]

Montgomery's forces concentrated on improving their siege works. In three or four days, they erected two batteries. The Americans located one between eight hundred and nine hundred yards south of the fort in which they mounted two nine-pounders. They established the other about six hundred yards east of the fort and emplaced two small mortars there. While the besiegers attempted to strengthen their investment, the British gunners maintained a steady cannon "salute" upon them from the fort.[10]

On September 22, Montgomery narrowly escaped death from this determined bombardment as he supervised the work of his soldiers. The energetic general "sprung upon the top of the breastwork to see if it was as it should be, and the instant he struck his feet on top, a cannon shot passed him and cut off the skirt of his coat and turned him round, and he pitched into the breastwork but struck upon his feet." The experience served to enhance Montgomery's battlefield leadership image with the troops as they observed "this did not seem to hurt or frighten him."[11]

Montgomery endeavored to hold all of his officers to the high standard of conduct that he set for himself. He had little tolerance for those who failed to measure up. When recommending that Colonel Bedel take disciplinary action against his commissary officer for not accounting for captured stores, Montgomery plainly stated his conviction: "The ignorance of the common soldier may sometimes excite mercy, but the officer cannot plead in the same manner." An incident that exemplified this credo occurred shortly after Montgomery's near fatality. "The other night, Captain Motte [Gershom Mott], of the First Regiment of Yorkers, basely deserted the mortar battery, without ever having been attacked," Montgomery reported to Schuyler, "and made me a formal report that the enemy had rushed into the work, and his men had left him." "An hour after this, his Lieutenant came in," Montgomery continued, "and honestly told me there had been no enemy there." "Were I furnished with powers for that purpose, he should not live an hour after his trial, if the court condemn him: but I must transmit the court-martial to you."[12]

Montgomery was much more concerned with other aspects of command than his personal safety. One source of vexation involved maintaining a coherent organization. Some of the officers assigned to his force tended to be free-spirited and intractable. Ethan Allen, the rejected leader of the Green Mountain Boys, was such a rugged individualist. Montgomery had never approved of Allen's irresponsible military style. When Seth Warner superseded Allen as commander, Montgomery characterized the move as "a change which will be very acceptable to our convention."[13] Later, Schuyler consented with much reservation in allowing Allen to join the expedition as an unassigned officer. Montgomery deployed the zealot on various long-range missions into Canada to keep this unpredictable officer out of the immediate area of operations.

On this occasion, Montgomery had sent Allen on to Chambly to recruit and take command of a group of Canadian volunteers. John Brown had gone to La Prairie for a similar purpose. Allen collected about 250 Canadians under arms and optimistically reported to Montgomery that he could muster many more. "I swear by the Lord I can raise three times the number of our army in Canada." "To fail of victory will be an eternal disgrace, but to obtain it will elevate us on the wings of fame," wrote the glory-seeking officer with a new command.[14]

On September 24, Allen's ramblings in Canada took him to the south shore of the St. Lawrence River opposite Montreal. There he reconnoitered the largest city in Canada with a population of nearly nine thousand that served as the field army headquarters of Governor Carleton. However, it was not strongly held, because the British chose to make their stand at St. Johns and committed most of their military resources to that location. As a result, less than sixty regulars defended the city. Allen deemed Montreal as a ripe victory just waiting to be plucked.

Unfortunately, Allen's recruits proved to be unreliable and all but eighty of them melted away. But Brown chanced upon the scene with two hundred troops that he had assembled. Both of these ambitious men heard opportunity knocking on the door. Montreal was just too alluring a prize for the daring officers to resist. Impetuously, they decided to join forces and capture Montreal. Their plan called for each group to make separate crossings of the St. Lawrence River that night and conduct a joint attack from opposite ends of the city in the morning.

After meeting with Brown, Allen encountered about thirty Americans whom he persuaded to join him, bringing his total strength to approximately 110 soldiers. Shortly after midnight, Allen began ferrying his troops across the river with the odd collection of canoes and dugouts he was able to find in the limited time. There were so few boats available that only one-third of his soldiers could cross at one time. In spite of choppy waters churned by a gusty wind, Allen's entire force was safely across the river and moving toward Montreal well before dawn. By daybreak, Allen had stealthily advanced his troops to about a mile north of the city. There, he waited for a prearranged signal from Brown of his arrival and readiness to commence the attack. The signal never came. For some reason, Brown and his force failed to make the rendezvous.[15]

Allen and his party found themselves alone and stranded. It was too late to retreat and make the three requisite crossings again. Their activity in broad daylight would be promptly discovered by the enemy and elicit a counterattack. Two-thirds of the troops left on the Montreal side of the river while the first contingent crossed would be too weak a force to defend themselves. Allen decided to deploy his soldiers in a defensive position two or three miles from the city and wait for the British onslaught that would surely come. After the surprised inhabitants learned of Allen's presence around mid-morning, rampant confusion and panic broke out. However, when the intruders failed to menace the city, Carleton was able to restore order and rally a substantial number of volunteers to augment his regulars. By two o'clock that afternoon, a force of over three hundred troops under the command of Maj. John Campbell sallied out of Montreal to offer battle to Allen's hapless, outnumbered party. A sharp firefight ensued, and the British forced Allen and his followers to surrender after two hours of fighting. "I thought to have enrolled my name in the list of illustrious American heroes, but was nipped in the bud" was the way Allen later represented his actions.[16]

Allen's reckless sortie and his summary defeat was definitely harmful to the American cause in Canada. The fiasco heartened the loyal Canadians and disheartened some of those who were leaning toward supporting Montgomery's expedition. Seth Warner apprised Montgomery of Allen's failed attempt and noted that "his defeat hath put the French people into great consternation." James Livingston also informed Montgomery of the setback and concluded: "Mr. Allen should never have attempted to attack the town without my knowledge, or acquainting me of his design, as I had it in my power to furnish him with a number of men." Major Bedel reflected his embarrassment over the situation when he wrote Montgomery: "I am sorry things were not done more prudently."[17]

Montgomery was generally aware that his long-range forces were considering Montreal as an objective, but he expected to be kept current on any plan that developed so a concerted and coordinated effort could be made. In a letter, he told Schuyler that "Allen, Warner, and Brown are at La Prairie and Longueuil with a party of our troops and some Canadians. . . . They have a project of making an attempt on Montreal." Later the same day, Montgomery received the news concerning Allen's disaster, and he reported to Schuyler in a second letter: "I have to lament Mr. Allen's imprudence and ambition, which urged him to this affair single handed."[18]

Schuyler enclosed Montgomery's report when he wrote the president of Congress: "I am very apprehensive of disagreeable consequences arising from Mr. Allen's imprudence." "I always dreaded his impatience of subordination; and it was not until after a solemn promise . . . that he would demean himself properly, that I would permit him to attend the army."[19]

George Washington added his denouncement of Allen's conduct. He wrote Schuyler: "Colonel Allen's Misfortune will, I hope, teach a Lesson of Prudence and Subordination to others, who may be too ambitious to outshine their General Officers, and regardless of Order and Duty, rush into Enterprizes, which may have unfavorable Effects to the Publick, and are destructive to themselves." [20]

Most patriot public opinion joined Montgomery, Schuyler, and Washington in condemning Allen's ill-advised activity. A representative newspaper account read: "The expedition was a thing of the colonel's own head, without orders from the general [Montgomery]; and from whom, as well as others, he receives much censure. If they had been appraised of it, they could have put him in a situation to have succeeded without much danger. But Allen is a high flying genius, pursues every scheme on its first impression, without consideration, and much less judgment." [21]

Montgomery knew that he had to overcome Ethan Allen's bungling and the psychological boost it gave the British defenders of Canada. He believed that many Canadians "are anxious for our success, but have been intimidated much by our weakness, lest by a miscarriage they should be left to the vengeance of tyranny." However, in spite of his doggedness, the siege of St. Johns was progressing excruciatingly into a stalemate. Montgomery lacked the manpower to directly assault the stronghold without a reduction of its defenses, and his artillery was too weak to breach the fort's walls or cause much damage within. "Had we twice or thrice as many men," Montgomery noted, "everything would long ago have been settled." A disgruntled officer wrote: "It is amazing to me that the Colonies should have so little sense of importance of this expedition, as not to give us a good large Army, well furnished . . . which indeed would have nearly settled the controversy." [22]

The slowness of the campaign became a cause for concern of the commander in chief, which added more pressure on Montgomery to expedite his operations. In a letter to Schuyler, Washington professed his utmost confidence in him and Montgomery. However, he suggested a plan of bypassing St. Johns in an effort to capture Montreal promptly and march on Quebec to link up with Arnold's force. Montgomery felt that a release of his siege on St. Johns in order to advance on Montreal would place his command precariously between the two British threats. This would allow Preston's troops to break out and ravage the Americans from their rear. Montgomery maintained his field commander's prerogative. He continued to rely on his previously formulated strategy that held the reduction of St. Johns as the key to the defeat of Montreal. [23]

In addition, the weather and terrain severely hampered the campaign.

It was growing progressively colder, and heavy rains set in. The chilling, wet elements quickly turned the area of operations into a quagmire. "Our men Sometimes have been Wet near Twenty Days together," a Connecticut chaplain recounted. "We have been like half-drowned rats crawling thro' the swamp," Montgomery wrote to his wife. "Whenever we attempt to erect batteries, the water follows in the ditch, when only two feet deep," a participant complained.[24]

The stormy weather matched the mood of the campaigners. With their advance bogged down, internal dissensions flared among the soldiers. Although the troops admired Montgomery for his courage under fire as a battlefield leader, they continued to resist conforming to conventional military practices such as unity of command. Sectionalism remained the root of much tension among the soldiers. Traditionally, the New Englanders disliked the Yorkers, and the Yorkers distrusted the New Englanders. Lieutenant Colonel Ritzema, commanding the 1st New York, blamed the New England troops, who displayed a "dastardly spirit," for the two earlier abortive attempts on St. Johns. Maj. John Brown of Massachusetts thought "New York have acted a droll part, and are determined to defeat us, if in their power."[25]

Most of the troops felt more loyalty to their home colony and officers than to the Continental army. Some of the New England officers fumed over the fact that Montgomery, a New Yorker in their minds, commanded an expedition made up of a large majority of New Englanders. Col. Benjamin Hinman, a Connecticut regimental commander, wrote: "New York abounds with officers, but I have not had my curiosity gratified by the sight of one private." Col. Samuel Mott, another regimental commander from Connecticut, noted: "For all the pretensions of New York, there has not been one head Colonel of a Regiment seen in the Army this year; and out of their three thousand five hundred men, we have never had more than six hundred down here until these four days." Many of these officers regularly reported directly to their respective provincial authorities, commenting freely on the general and how they thought the campaign was being conducted. Colonel Mott remarked: "I have no great opinion of Montgomery's generalship, although I believe him to be a man of courage; that is but a small (though essential) qualification of a General."[26]

Montgomery's insistence on holding his officers to exacting performance standards might have rankled some. Still, he applied the criteria in a comprehensive and evenhanded manner. When his wife suggested that

Montgomery promote her brother, Capt. Henry (Harry) Beekman Livingston, who was serving as aide-de-camp to the general, he could not while remaining true to his principles. Although Montgomery had formed a close friendship with his brother-in-law, he felt that Livingston, who had been commissioned only three months, was not yet ready for higher rank. "I most certainly might have advanced Harry to a majority," he answered his wife's inquiry, but "disinterested and generous motives will forever, I hope, prevent me from serving myself or family at the expense of the publick." "Though a fine, spirited fellow," Montgomery reasoned, "he has not experience for such an important post." "I grant there are others as bad or worse," he concluded, but "it is not my doing, nor will I ever have such a weight on my conscience."[27]

Montgomery had begun some soul-searching of his own because of the difficulties that had ensued during the campaign. "I have been dragged from obscurity much against my inclination and not without some struggle, as you know," he confided to his wife, "and depend upon it, the instant I can with decency slip my neck out of the yoke, I will return to my family and farm, and that peace of mind which I can't have in my present situation." The capricious, pluralistic character of his troops continued to vex Montgomery. "The New England troops are the worst stuff imaginable," he wrote his eldest brother-in-law. "There is such an equality among them, that the officers have no authority. . . . The privates are all generals, but not soldiers." In this letter, he was equally critical of the Yorkers, whom he described out of his exasperation as "the sweepings of the New York streets." Although anguished by his situation, Montgomery's undeniable devotion to duty imposed a sense of purpose that pushed him onward.[28]

As Montgomery wrestled with the group dynamics of his command, he did not lose sight of his objective. Even with the arrival of Captain Lamb and his artillery unit on September 21, fire support for the siege continued to be a problem for the Americans. On October 5, the expedition received a thirteen-inch mortar that Schuyler had forwarded from Ticonderoga. The next day, the artillerymen embedded the gun in a position that had been laboriously raised from the swampy ground near the east battery. The besiegers expected this weapon, which they fondly dubbed the "old sow," to begin turning the artillery duel in their favor. However, the range proved too great for the gun to achieve any devastating effect on the fort and was another disappointment for the Americans.

Major Preston, the British commandant, wrote in his journal: "Anything relating to the Sow was a better Joke on them than on us."[29]

Montgomery was acutely aware of the defects of his artillery batteries. He intended to shift the emphasis from the positions on the east side and emplace another battery closer to the fort on the northwest side. There, he calculated, his artillery could fire into the stronghold with better accuracy and effectiveness. However, this proposed tactic proved unpopular with his troops. Since the selected position was located on a rise only four hundred yards from the fort, it would place them in an area more exposed to effective enemy cannon bombardment. Also, the subject site was situated on the same side of the river as St. Johns, thereby making the Americans who might occupy it more susceptible to a British ground counterassault. Montgomery drew from his skill in siege warfare that had been honed by his experience in the British army. In his estimation, these were acceptable risks that had to be taken to curtail the impasse and force the invested stronghold.

Although they respected their commander's professionalism and personal bravery, Montgomery's troops clung to a notion of free will and asserted their disapproval of this plan. "When I mentioned my intentions," Montgomery wrote Schuyler, "I did not consider I was at the head of troops who carry the spirit of freedom into the field, and think for themselves." Montgomery was learning what military commanders throughout the war would discover about the patriot soldier. Years later, Frederick von Steuben, who obtained a major-general's commission in the Continental army, wrote to a former comrade in the Prussian army and expressed this same lesson. "You say to your soldier, 'Do this,' and he doeth it; but I am obliged to say to mine, 'This is the reason why you ought to do that;' and then he does it."[30]

Major Brown told Montgomery that many men would desert if the general ordered them to occupy the intended position. Montgomery called a council of his field-grade officers to explain and garner support for his strategy. "Upon considering the fatal consequences which might flow from the want of subordination and discipline, (should this ill-humour continue), my unstable authority over troops of different Colonies, the insufficiency of the military law, and my own want of power to enforce it, weak as it is, I thought it expedient to call the Field-Officers together."[31]

The officers sided with the troops and unanimously recommended against Montgomery's plan. The general stated that was contrary to his judgment, but to quiet and satisfy the troops he would give his consent to continue concentrating the siege on the east side of St. Johns. He realized that an accommodation had to be made to preserve his command. However, Montgomery felt deep humiliation. "I cannot help observing to how little purpose I am here," he lamented to Schuyler. "Were I not afraid the example would be too generally followed, and the publick service might suffer, I would not stay an hour at the head of troops whose operations I cannot direct."[32]

Others in this situation might have quit in disgust. This general, however, possessed too much pragmatism to submit to such a fate. He remained goal oriented and did not allow his emotions to divert him from his overall purpose. By inspiration, exhortation, chastisement, or conciliation, he was willing to do whatever it took to motivate his troops in accomplishing their mission. When faced with personal rebuffs such as this, Montgomery managed to control his temper. He maintained a stoic bearing with his soldiers, while using letters to Schuyler and close family members as a safety valve to vent his frustrations.

Montgomery ordered Col. James Clinton with part of his 3rd New York to build the new battery. They completed the position on October 14, and Lamb's cannoneers opened fire with the two twelve-pounders emplaced there. The *Royal Savage*, warped to the shore close to the fort, became the primary target of opportunity. By the morning, the ship received so many hits that it sank in place. Thus, the floating menace that had struck fear in the hearts of Montgomery's raw recruits was finally neutralized, providing much-needed encouragement for the Americans.[33]

Schuyler, back in Ticonderoga, was sympathetic about Montgomery's troop discipline problems. He was experiencing much of the same. A spirit of independence prevailed in Gen. David Wooster's behavior as commander of the Connecticut troops, much to Schuyler's chagrin. At sixty-four years old, Wooster was an anachronism in an army of much younger officers. A militia veteran with thirty years of service, he was piqued at being passed over for higher rank in the Continental army by younger men with less military experience. Schuyler's senior by birth by twenty-two years and Montgomery's by more than a quarter century, Wooster seemed to shun military subordination and protocol.

In September 1775, the Continental Congress relieved Wooster and his troops of the defense of New York City and ordered them northward to join the Canadian expedition. En route, he circumvented the chain of command, conducting a court-martial at Fort George without Schuyler's required authorization. Upon learning of the incident, Schuyler wrote to Wooster for an explanation of "a conduct I cannot account for, unless you consider yourself my superior." Wooster attempted to smooth over matters with Schuyler by replying that his action "was never designed . . . to contradict or counteract your authority. . . . I have the cause of my Country too much at heart to attempt to make any difficulty or uneasiness in the Army, upon whom the success of an enterprise of almost infinite importance to the Country is now depending." Relations between the two men, however, remained strained.[34]

Wooster's soldiers followed his example and were reluctant to take orders from anyone but him. When 250 Connecticut troops reached Ticonderoga in advance of Wooster, Schuyler, anxious to reinforce Montgomery, ordered them forward to St. Johns. They answered that they did not choose to move until Wooster arrived. "Do not choose to move! Strange language in an Army," Schuyler wrote to the Continental Congress, "but the irresistible force of necessity obliges me to put up with it." Schuyler planned to retain Wooster at Ticonderoga to keep this source of disruption away from the critical field operations, where he was afraid Wooster would clash with Montgomery over rank and authority. With the refusal of the Connecticut men to advance without their leader, Schuyler had no choice but to send Wooster forward with his troops and hope for the best.[35]

Meanwhile, Montgomery endeavored to bring the siege of St. Johns to a climax. James Livingston had enlisted about three hundred Canadians and suggested to Montgomery that they might be successfully employed in an attempt against Chambly. The general recognized the strategic importance of Chambly as a source of resupply and a potential back-door entrée to St. Johns. He approved the plan and ordered John Brown with fifty Americans to join Livingston's force. During the night of October 16, the American detachment and the Canadian contingent with two nine-pounders slipped past the guns of St. Johns and converged on Chambly.

The fort's commander, Joseph Stopford, son of an Irish earl and a major in the 7th Foot, lacked the mettle of Major Preston. Chambly's defenders were protected by a castlelike stone structure, but its high walls were relatively thin. Although the fortress was not impregnable to artillery fire, the garrison had an ample stock of food, three mortars, a large supply of muskets and ammunition, and 124 barrels of gunpowder. The next morning, Brown and Livingston opened fire on the fort with their cannons. Two days of bombardment only resulted in shooting a few holes in the walls and knocking down a chimney but caused no casualties. However, Major Stopford abruptly surrendered his command on October 19 without further resistance. He also neglected to destroy the considerable military stores contained within the fort before he capitulated.[36]

The capture of Chambly gave the Americans fresh confidence and replenished their depleted supplies. Schuyler wrote Washington that the expedition might have run out of ammunition within "a very few days" if the British had prolonged their defense of Chambly. After the fort's reduction, Montgomery informed Schuyler: "We have gotten six tons of powder which, with God's blessing, will finish our business here." The colors of the 7th Royal Fusiliers were among the spoils taken at Chambly. Montgomery sent them as a battle trophy to Schuyler, who forwarded them to the Continental Congress. These were the first standards of a British regiment to be captured by the Americans during the Revolution and were a source of pride to Montgomery's troops.[37]

News of Chambly was reason for celebration when it reached General Washington's headquarters outside Boston. Washington sent congratulations to Montgomery on his success and his wish "that his next letter be dated from Montreal." A list of items captured by Montgomery was forwarded to Washington and provoked a lighthearted moment for the usually reserved commander in chief. The inventory ended: "Royal Fusiliers, 83; Accoutrements, 83." "We laugh at his idea for classing the Royal Fusiliers with the stores," Washington wrote to Schuyler. "Does he consider them as inanimates or as a treasure?"[38]

The surrender of Chambly's garrison also gave Montgomery an opportunity to satisfy his humanitarian impulse. He had received reports of the rough treatment that the British imposed on Ethan Allen after his capture. Brig. Gen. Richard Prescott was particularly vindictive toward Allen, threatening to hang him before clapping him in heavy irons aboard the warship *Gaspé* at Montreal. Although he personally disliked Allen and resented his recent military blunder, Montgomery was still concerned over his welfare as a British prisoner. The general felt an obligation to the errant officer who had been attached to his command. Intending to use the prisoners taken at Chambly as leverage to exact better conditions for Allen and other captives held by the British, he presented a letter to Major Stopford. In it, Montgomery stated that he had "information from different quarters, that Governor Carleton treats his unfortunate prisoners with the most cruel severity, loading them with irons, and that Colonel Allen himself meets with the same indignity." He then requested Stopford to write Carleton "acquainting him with your situation, and representing the fatal consequences which must attend the carrying on so barbarous a war." Montgomery dispatched a letter to Carleton similar to the one he gave Stopford. A few days later an American detachment escorted the British captives to Ticonderoga. From there, they went to Connecticut to await parole or exchange.[39]

Carleton received Montgomery's letter concerning prisoners of war and forwarded it to the American Secretary, Lord Dartmouth, with his comments. " 'Tis true the Rebels have been in irons, not from choice but necessity, we have neither Prisons to hold nor Troops to guard them, so that they have been treated with as much humanity as our own safety wou'd permit. . . . I wish to explain this matter to your Lordship, but I shall return no answer, nor enter into any correspondence with Rebels. I shall treat all their threats with silent contempt."[40]

Montgomery seized upon the success at Chambly and the audacious spirit that it imbued in his troops to make another attempt in establishing a forward battery northwest of St. Johns. With the mood of the soldiers on the upswing, there was no opposition to the plan this time. Montgomery issued orders to begin preparations for the new position. The work was in progress on October 26 when General Wooster and his 335 Connecticut men accompanied by 225 troops of the 4th New York arrived. These reinforcements raised Montgomery's force to over two thousand effectives. For the first time since the siege began, the general felt the tide of battle turning in his favor.[41]

However, Wooster's presence introduced another potentially disruptive influence on the expedition. Although Wooster assured Schuyler before he left Ticonderoga that he would recognize Montgomery's position of authority, the Connecticut general was unpredictable. Montgomery decided to employ tact and diplomacy to gain the crusty, aged veteran's cooperation. When the two generals met, Montgomery explained, "My commission is older than yours, and I must command." "I am but a young man, and you are an old man, experienced in war," he continued, therefore "I shall always take your advice as a son would that of his father." With his ego comforted, Wooster accepted Montgomery's leadership and joined the effort against St. Johns.[42]

The day after his arrival, Wooster and his men deployed around the site of the artillery position under construction. Montgomery intended to concentrate his force in the vicinity of the new battery that was nearing completion. He shifted the bulk of his strength to the northwest side of St. Johns, leaving only the 3rd New York with a few gunners on the east side to guard and offer fire from the battery there. The British defenders observed Montgomery's troops busily engaged in establishing their forward position just 250 yards from the fort. They maintained a heavy bombardment upon the Americans, but the artillery fire resulted in few casualties. With the siege tightening around his stronghold, Major Preston became increasingly concerned over the possibility of a relief force to help extricate him from his predicament.[43]

Carleton had been working for some time in Montreal to assemble a counterstrike force. Reports told him that the situation at St. Johns was becoming desperate. Something had to be done without further delay. The governor sent instructions to Col. Allan MacLean at Quebec to assemble all available men immediately and march to St. Johns. Meanwhile, Carleton quickly pressed into service a force comprised of some 800 Canadian militia, 130 Royal Highland Emigrants and Fusiliers, and 80 Indians. He intended to combine the Quebec party with the troops raised at Montreal to break the siege of St. Johns. Carleton elected to lead the operation personally, and he embarked his soldiers in boats that would take them down the St. Lawrence River to link up with MacLean's contingent.[44]

On the afternoon of October 30, Carleton and his troops reached Longueuil on the St. Lawrence River a little below Montreal. There, he encountered Seth Warner with three hundred of his Green Mountain Boys and soldiers of the 2nd New York. When Warner saw Carleton's forty-boat flotilla approaching his position, he hurried his four-pounder to the water's edge and deployed his soldiers in woods bordering the river. Warner's troops commenced firing when the enemy's boats came into range. The British force answered in kind against its hidden adversary. "The Enemy had cannon and bomb shells aboard, which they gave us a plenty of, . . . and the Musket balls came close to our heads in great plenty," recorded an American soldier. Yet, the amphibious force remained thwarted in its efforts to disembark and assault the rebel position. Carleton tried repeatedly to force a landing, only to be turned back each time by a barrage of small arms and cannon fire. After about five hours of heated fighting, Carleton ordered his fleet to put about and withdraw back to Montreal. In the confusion, two Canadians, Jean Baptiste Despins and a barber named Lacoste, found themselves left behind and were captured by Warner's soldiers. The British lost about twenty-one men killed and fifty wounded, but the Americans amazingly suffered no casualties in the repulse.[45]

MacLean and his party had pushed forward as far as Sorel when news of Carleton's defeat at Longueuil reached them. He halted his approach and placed his troops on the defensive while awaiting further instructions. The failure to advance from Montreal certainly dampened the prospects of relieving St. Johns, but Carleton was not easily discouraged. He still hoped that something could be done to alleviate Montgomery's increasing hold on the outpost that guarded Montreal. The governor continued to dispatch spies and patrols to probe for weak spots where the siege lines might be penetrated.

On November 1, everything was in readiness for the opening of the newly erected battery northwest of St. Johns. It contained four twelve-pounders, three nine-pounders, and five mortars. Utilizing the bonanza of munitions captured at Chambly, Montgomery was able to conduct a sustained bombardment of the fort. With the four-gun eastern battery joining in, firing commenced in the morning and continued uninterrupted throughout the day. The British guns returned counterbattery fire of equal intensity, but they were less effective than those of the Americans. From its improved vantage point, Montgomery's artillery could now inflict serious damage inside the fort. Colonel Ritzema elatedly noted that the protracted cannonade "knocked every Thing in the Fort to Shatters."[46]

Although the American artillery salvos resulted in considerable structural damage, they caused few casualties. However, the continuous, proximate firing began to wear on the defenders' nerves. Combined with dwindling rations and mounting despair about a relief effort, the cannonade sapped the morale of the beleaguered garrison. Still, Major Preston resisted yielding his command. His assigned mission instructed him to defend St. Johns "to the last extremity." As a dedicated, resolute, professional officer, he was determined to hold out or delay for as long as possible while waiting for reinforcements.

At sundown, the Americans ceased their shelling and Montgomery dispatched a demand for capitulation. The letter informed Preston of Carleton's defeated relief force and urged him "to spare the lives of a brave garrison." Montgomery concluded, "Should you continue . . . to persist in a defense which cannot avail you—I . . . shall deem myself innocent of the melancholy consequences." Lacoste, the barber taken prisoner at Longueuil, carried the letter so that he could attest to the hopeless situation that attended further defense of the fort.[47]

About midnight, one of Wooster's troops on picket duty challenged someone who stumbled into the American's lines in the dark. The sentry saw the man put something in his mouth upon capture but could not ascertain what it was because of the diminished visibility. He escorted his prisoner to Wooster and related the circumstances of the incident to the general. After searching and questioning the prisoner to no avail, Wooster forced the man to ingest a physic and ordered his soldier to guard him closely. A few hours after taking the purgative, the prisoner discharged a silver ball. With examination, the Americans discovered that it "went together with a screw, and on taking it apart it contained a small bit of paper on which were written these words: 'Hold out and you shall be relieved.' " Thus, the besiegers compromised Carleton's last-ditch effort to offer hope to the grim defenders of St. Johns.[48]

Uninformed of Carleton's aspirations, but well aware of his own deteriorating defense, Preston felt increasing pressure to yield. "Not a Syllable of Intelligence from General Carleton arrived altho' we sent repeated Messengers to Montreal," the hard-pressed St. Johns commandant agonized. Still, he remained proud and defiant to the end. After receiving Montgomery's letter, he replied that Lacoste was known for having "fits of insanity." Therefore, the Montreal barber was an unreliable source of information. Preston submitted a counterproposal that he would surrender the garrison if the fort was not relieved within four days. Montgomery was concerned about his delayed time schedule with respect to subsequent plans to capture Montreal and Quebec before winter halted military operations. He answered by stating "the advanced season of the year will not admit your proposal." The general offered to make available Despins, the other prisoner captured at Longueuil, to substantiate Lacoste's testimony. Having "acquitted my conscience," Montgomery warned, "if you do not surrender this day, it will be unnecessary to make any future proposals; the garrison shall be prisoners of war, without the honours of war."[49]

On November 2, Preston sent several officers, including Lt. John André, to confer with Despins, who was in custody aboard the *Enterprise*. During their meeting Despins convinced André that St. Johns was indeed in a hopeless situation. Upon his return, André reported his findings to Preston who, despairing of relief, agreed to surrender. Montgomery and Preston drew up and adjusted the terms of capitulation: the garrison would be allowed the honors of war, officers could keep their side arms, each soldier would retain his personal baggage, but all the prisoners would be interned in the colonies.[50]

The next morning, Preston paraded his command out of the battered fort to ground their muskets and formally surrender. Then, the vanquished troops boarded boats for their journey to Connecticut and detention. Preston had held out as long as reasonably could be expected without sacrificing his command to senseless bloodshed. During the siege, the defenders suffered forty-three casualties, including twenty killed. American battle losses were also relatively light. Captain Lamb recorded that his artillery company had been rather unfortunate because it lost five killed and six wounded, "which is as great a loss as has been sustained by the whole Army, except for the first skirmish with the Indians." Disease had cut down Montgomery's troops in far greater numbers. By October 12, 937 soldiers in the expedition had been discharged as unfit for duty.[51]

Although the siege of Fort St. Johns was successful, it cost the expedition valuable time. Preston's stubborn resistance delayed the American advance on Canada for two months. An American campaigner summed up the situation when he wrote his wife: "St. Johns is a very Strong Hole, and as bad to come to at as any what ever." On the other hand, it is to Montgomery's credit that he managed to hold together his ragtag command and mold his troops into a combat force capable of overcoming determined British regulars holding a fortified position.[52]

Now it was time for Montgomery to direct this wave of victory toward his next objective. Some twenty miles northwest of St. Johns lay Montreal. It was still as vulnerable as when Ethan Allen made his impromptu bid for its capture. The eventual fall of St. Johns opened the road for the American expeditionary force to march on this important prize, and Montgomery immediately began preparations for its reduction.

On to Quebec

His noble declaration to the inhabitants of Montreal,
"that the continental armies . . . being come for the
express purpose of giving liberty and security" . . . did
honour to himself, and to that delegated body under
whose authority he acted.[1]

With scarce one third of his force
Then to Quebec he bent his course.[2]

It was important for Montgomery not to allow his troops to rest on
their accomplishments and delay their advance on Montreal. Weather
would become an increasing liability to his enterprise as winter set
in. In addition, Arnold, whom he planned to join in attacking Quebec,
had been six weeks on his approach march through the Maine wilderness
by this time.

As Montgomery attempted to quickly consolidate his command after
the fall of St. Johns, he encountered more problems with his troops.
Many of the recruits, particularly the Connecticut men, had endured
their fill of a combat soldier's hardships, and they wanted to return home.
Montgomery was "obligated . . . to promise all such their dismission as
chose it, to coax them to Montreal." The American troops were also ill
equipped for the Canadian cold. When Montgomery allowed the St.
Johns garrison to retain its reserve of clothing to wear during captivity, a
mutiny nearly rose among the New York troops. The American soldiers

wanted to claim the garments as the spoils of war and use them to augment their own ragged and inadequate uniforms. However, the high-minded Montgomery faced down his troops. "I would not have sullied my own reputation, nor disgraced the Continental arms, by such a breach of capitulation," he wrote. "There was no driving it into their noodles, that the clothing was really the property of the soldier, that he had paid for it."[3]

The latest incident with his soldiers over the captured clothing led Montgomery to "wish some method could be fallen upon of engaging *gentlemen* to serve; a point of honor and more knowledge of the world, to be found in that class of men, would greatly reform discipline, and render the troops much more tractable." As this lamentation illustrates, Montgomery did not consider himself a common person. Although his remark could be construed as one of an elitist, Montgomery had been equally critical of aristocrats whom he felt were not living up to their leadership obligations. An internally driven individual with a strong personal code, he did not fit comfortably into any of the stereotypical social classes. Thus, he could not condone unacceptable behavior by his troops in order to gain their popularity. His detached brand of leadership was one of setting an example to be looked up to and emulated by his soldiers—not establishing close familiarity with the rank and file, as the crowd leaders turned military commanders tended to do. Montgomery believed that people, in general, were not inherently virtuous and needed to be held to a higher standard. He had earlier confided to his wife that "I am unfit to deal with mankind in the bulk. . . . I feel too sensibly the rascality, ignorance and selfishness so common among my fellow creatures."[4]

On the night of November 3, an early winter storm with intermittent snow and rain that left the ground "in a manner drowned with water" beset the operation. It soon turned the eighteen-mile road on which the Americans would march to La Prairie into a quagmire. Three days later, the lead elements of the expedition trudged forward in "Water sometimes midleg high." "Under our feet we had Water, Snow and Ice," a partici-pant recorded. "Over our heads were thick Clouds, and the snow and Rain came pouring down upon us." With a note of astonishment, he noted: "It was remarkable to See the Americans after almost infinite Fatigues and Hardships marching on at this advanced Season, badly clothed, and badly provided for to Montreal, pressing on to New Seiges and new Conquests." "In about four days," Colonel Bedel wrote the New

Hampshire Committee of Safety, "we shall have either a wooden leg or a golden chain at Montreal."[5]

Meanwhile, MacLean remained at Sorel trying to decide his next move after his unsuccessful attempt to merge with Carleton and relieve St. Johns. Forces under Easton, Brown, and James Livingston found him there. Montgomery had sent the detachment to block any escape of British troops from Montreal to Quebec. After a brief exchange of fire, MacLean's troops withdrew to their vessels in the St. Lawrence River. On November 8, both ships sailed away under heavy cannon fire from the pursuing Americans. The *Providence* with a contingent of regulars headed for Montreal to reinforce Carleton, and the *Snow Fell* with Mac-Lean and his Royal Highland Immigrants prudently returned to resume the defense of Quebec.[6]

For three days, Montgomery's expedition slogged toward La Prairie. From his position on the outskirts of Montreal, Montgomery sent a message to the inhabitants, advising them to persuade Governor Carleton to surrender the city or suffer "the dreadful consequences of a bombardment." Carleton appreciated the hopelessness of his situation after the capitulation of St. Johns. Lacking adequate defenses and experiencing eroding support from a populace sobered by Montgomery's imminent warning, he knew it was only a matter of time before Montreal would also fall. Carleton left the surrender negotiations to the Montrealers while he prepared to salvage or destroy whatever he could of the military stores and retrogress the garrison to Quebec.[7]

As a major fur-trade center, Montreal contained a sizable population of about eight thousand noncombatants. Under existing circumstances, loyalty of the alarmed and dispirited residents toward the British waned, replaced by a feeling of self-preservation. They were desirous of seeking the best terms possible to protect their lives and property. Civilian leaders quickly established contact with Montgomery's expedition to draw up an agreement whereby they would hand over Montreal to the Americans.

While Montgomery tightened his hold on Montreal and entered negotiations for its capture, weather conditions forced Carleton to delay his evacuation. The governor had completed loading hastily assembled military stores aboard his vessels, but contrary winds prevented the departure of his ships from Montreal for several days. On November 11, a fair breeze facilitated Carleton's flight. The governor, with his 130-man garrison, embarked in the *Gaspé* and two other armed vessels and set sail for Quebec. Eight smaller craft loaded with provisions accompanied the warships when they slipped out of the harbor. For several hours, the British flotilla made good progress. The next day, Carleton's luck changed once again when one of his ships ran aground. By the time she was afloat, the wind shifted and forced the fleet to anchor near Sorel. With his retreat stymied, Carleton waited for favorable winds to continue his voyage.[8]

Shortly after Carleton's narrow escape from Montreal, civil representatives and Montgomery agreed upon terms for its capitulation. On November 13, Montgomery's army marched through the city gates and took possession of Montreal. Unaware that Carleton had fled, they immediately launched a search for the governor, whom they believed was hiding somewhere in the city. Soon they discovered that he had eluded them. Montgomery ordered some of his troops to embark in bateaux with mounted cannons in pursuit of their quarry.[9]

Carleton had narrowly escaped Montreal, but he was not yet out of American clutches. Before the amphibious force from Montreal could close with him, his fleet encountered the provincial batteries at Sorel that had earlier thwarted MacLean's operations. On November 15, the fire from these guns forced the British ships to shift their anchorage up the river to remain out of range. While Carleton waited for a change in the wind and assessed his situation, a boat from the patriot position rowed out under a flag of truce. A messenger carried an ultimatum from the American commander, Colonel Easton, demanding that the governor unconditionally surrender with all his ships, troops, and supplies. "If you will Resign your Fleet to me Immediately without destroying the Effects on Board," the message read, "You and Your men shall be used with due civility together with women and Children on Board—to this I expect Your direct and Immediate answer. Should you Neglect You will Cherefully take the Consequences which will follow."[10]

With *Gaspé* and his other vessels hampered from continuing their passage, Carleton weighed his next move. His predicament was far from one of despair. His armed ships mounted thirty cannons that could be used to suppress the American batteries if he elected to run the blockade. However, the governor remained uncertain about the size of the threat. Although the Americans boasted of massive fire superiority over his force, he could not observe their disposition from his position. Therefore, he had no accurate way of confirming the number and strength of the guns confronting him.

Carleton called his senior officers together to consider their options.

Everyone agreed that the governor's presence at Quebec was essential, since Canada's fate depended now upon the successful defense of the capital. Jean Baptiste Bouchette, a captain of one of the sloops, suggested a plan to take Carleton aboard a small boat and sneak him past the enemy blockade. Bouchette, a seasoned French-Canadian pilot who was respectfully known as the "Wild Pigeon," had intimate knowledge of the river. Carleton decided to abandon his fleet and put his trust in the risky scheme. On the night of November 16, the governor disguised himself in the garb of a Canadian peasant and slipped over the side of the *Gaspé*. Bouchette waited alongside in a whale boat to receive him. Oars were muffled, but as the boat passed near the batteries, the crew paddled silently with their bare hands. Their stealth and the murky darkness prevented discovery by the Americans as they made good their escape. The next day, Carleton and his boatmates continued downstream until they came upon the *Snow Fell*. The British warship transported the fortunate governor and his party to Quebec, arriving November 19.[11]

With the governor's departure, command of the *Gaspé* and accompanying fleet passed to Carleton's deputy, General Prescott. Before he left, Carleton instructed him to dump all cannons, powder, and balls into the river if he could not avoid capitulation. Pressed by the Americans to surrender, the general expressed skepticism concerning the claimed invincibility of the blockade. Maj. John Brown invited Prescott to appoint one of his officers to come ashore and verify the batteries for himself. Employing his Yankee wiles during the conducted tour, Brown convinced the gullible British officer that the batteries contained many more cannons than actually existed. Prescott believed what the officer reported back to him and decided that forcing the blockade would be disastrous to his ships. On November 19, Prescott dumped the gunpowder and cannonballs into the river and ordered the fleet to strike its colors without firing a shot.[12]

Montgomery was pleased with the success of his troops in capturing the British fleet. However, from a professional military standpoint, he condemned his counterpart's fainthearted surrender. "I blush for His Majesty's troops!" he commented. "Such an instance of base poltroonery I never met with! and all because we had half-a-dozen cannon on the bank of the river to annoy him in his retreat." Still smarting from Prescott's harsh treatment of Ethan Allen, Montgomery heaped scorn upon the British general whom he regarded "a cruel rascal." "I have treated him with the sovereign contempt his inhumanity and barbarity merit," he noted.[13]

Actually, Montgomery's contempt for Prescott was expressed only in his attitude toward the captured general. The humanitarian side of Montgomery toward the prisoners of war prompted several of his own officers to censure the general, registering their concern that "the publick safety may be in danger." The incident sparked what Montgomery considered to be a challenge to his authority. "A number of officers presumed to remonstrate against the indulgence I had given some of the officers of the King's troops," Montgomery wrote to Schuyler. "Such an insult I could not bear, and immediately resigned." "Today they qualified it by such an apology as puts it in my power to resume the command."[14]

Montgomery blamed a disgruntled Captain Lamb for stirring up this unrest. The former radical patriot street leader had been a source of aggravation to Montgomery since he first joined the expedition in September. At that time, Lamb objected to the attachment of his unit to an infantry regiment, and he threatened to resign his commission if the Congress did not designate his command as an independent artillery company. Now, he was displeased with the amount of his pay and entertained his resignation once more. He felt that the captain's salary was "such a trifle" that he had to consume his personal funds to maintain himself and eventually his family "must starve at home." Montgomery regarded Lamb as "a reckless genius, and of bad temper," who was "brave, active and intelligent, but very turbulent and troublesome." However, the general realized that "He is absolutely necessary with this Army, if we are to have artillery," and tolerated his disruptive nature as best he could.[15]

Although Lamb was a habitual malcontent, his grievance concerning military pay reflected the hardship from inadequate compensation that most of the soldiers in the army bore. Congress required officers to purchase items for their own use. However, officers in the Canadian expedition were hit particularly hard by inflated prices for these commodities. The long distance in which goods had to be transported to reach the northern wilderness raised their price substantially from what officers stationed in the colonies paid for the same article. Montgomery understood his officers' plight. In a letter written the month before, he briefed Schuyler on the problem: "The very high prices which officers must pay here for everything brought from Ticonderoga, are far above what their scanty pittance of pay will allow of . . . which displaces them entirely from the footing of the troops . . . in the midst of a plentiful country." At that time, Montgomery recommended a pay augmentation or gratuity, especially to the junior-grade officers, to offset this financial burden. In the latest episode with Lamb, Montgomery appealed to Congress on his officers' behalf.[16]

Prescott's surrender yielded an unexpected windfall for Montgomery's troops. As a result of the capitulation, the Americans seized additional vessels—some with mounted cannons—to transport themselves down the St. Lawrence River to Quebec. Sundry other captured supplies found in the ships' cargo fortified the expedition's war chest, including a stand of small arms, clothing, and two hundred pairs of shoes. Montgomery also borrowed £5,000 from James Price, a successful Montreal merchant sympathetic to the Americans. He used this money to purchase warm clothing for his men, compensating for the contested British uniforms that he denied them after the fall of St. Johns.[17]

In spite of these positive developments, Montgomery had to contend with another crisis with his homesick troops. At St. Johns, some of the Connecticut men threatened to return home, and Montgomery promised them a discharge after Montreal. It was the only way, he thought, to retain them in service as long as possible. Now, they held him to his word, requesting immediate separation from further duty. This action of a few soldiers encouraged other New England troops that had not received the general's assurance to extort their own release. "Most of the New England Men embraced the Opportunity," Colonel Ritzema commented, but "the Yorkers in general resolved to see an End to the Campaign."[18]

Although their enlistments ran until the end of the year, many of the New Englanders felt that they had borne their share of hardships and were entitled to return home. Montgomery urged them to reenlist until mid-April or until reinforcements arrived. Otherwise, they would "lay him under the necessity of abandoning Canada; of undoing in one day what has been the work of months; and of restoring to an enraged and hitherto disappointed enemy the means of carrying a cruel war into the very bowels of their Country." Few heeded his continued call to arms. "The troops," Chaplain Trumbull noted, "are averse to enlisting and long to be dismissed home." They believed that they had discharged their military obligation, and patriotic appeals could not sway them.[19]

With the exception of two hundred soldiers who remained with Wooster, the Connecticut contingent quit the expedition after the capture of Montreal. Most of the other New England troops joined in the mass exodus. Seth Warner left with nearly all of his Green Mountain Boys. Bedel and a majority of his New Hampshire Rangers also departed. Easton and many of his Massachusetts troops headed home. Schuyler attributed the decision of the New England troops as an affirmation of nonvirtuous and unprofessional Continental soldiers. "They have such an intemperate desire to return home that nothing can equal it," Schuyler wrote to Congress. "It might have been expected that men influenced by a sense of liberty would not have required such a promise, and that others, to whom it was not immediately intended, would not have taken advantage of it," he anguished. "But all this," he warned, "flows from the same unhappy source with the other disorders too prevalent in our troops —a want of subordination and discipline, an evil which may prove fatal to us."[20]

The departure of these soldiers greatly disappointed Montgomery, who took it as another personal rebuke from members of his command. As with the other instances of recalcitrance from his troops, the general felt betrayed and unappreciated. Spurning self-aggrandizement, Montgomery had hoped to relinquish his field leadership of the expedition to more aspiring officers. "Will not your health permit you to reside at Montreal this winter," he wrote Schuyler. "I am weary of power, and totally want that patience and temper so requisite for such a command." "I wish [Charles] Lee could set off immediately for the command here," he wrote in another letter.[21]

This series of incidents involving his troops progressively wore down Montgomery's forbearance and pragmatism. He could attribute some of the earlier problems to novice soldiers who lacked military experience. However, he could not comprehend the seeming lack of public virtue and patriotism of the troops that returned home before their enlistments were completed. Montgomery yearned for relief from his command, but his sense of responsibility would not allow him to turn over the expedition to General Wooster, who he felt was not equal to the task. This latest vexation over troop defections drove Montgomery to tender his resignation from the service while awaiting a suitable replacement.

Troops that refused to continue with Montgomery in Canada soon began to arrive at Ticonderoga on their trek home. There, Schuyler also attempted to dissuade the disaffected horde from leaving but met no more success than Montgomery. In revulsion, Schuyler decided to follow

Montgomery's example in resigning his commission. "Gentlemen in command find it very disagreeable to coax, to wheedle, and even to lie, to carry on the service," he wrote to Washington. "Habited to order, I cannot without the most extreme pain see that disregard of discipline, confusion, and inattention, which reigns so general in this quarter, and am therefore determined to retire." "Of this resolution, I have advised Congress," he concluded. In communicating Montgomery's complaints and retirement intention to Congress, Schuyler added: "My sentiments exactly coincide with his." "I shall, with him, do everything in my power to put a finishing stroke to the campaign," he vowed, "and make the best arrangement in my power, in order to insure success to the next." "This done, I must beg leave to retire," he resolved.[22]

The proffered resignations induced conciliatory replies from the Congress. These letters praised the efforts of both men and urged them to change their minds. Members of the Congress "beg you will not insist on a Measure, which at once deprive America of the future Benefits she expects from your Zeal and Abilities, and rob you of the Honor of compleating the glorious Work you have so happily and successfully begun," John Hancock communicated to Schuyler. "The Loss of so brave and experienced an officer will be universally regretted as a Misfortune to all America. But they [members of Congress] still hope, that upon reconsidering the Matter, the same generous and patriotic Motives, which first induced you to take so capital a Part in opposing the unprovoked Hostilities of an unnatural Enemy, will prompt you to persevere in the Cause," the president of Congress wrote to Montgomery.[23]

Although the laudatory correspondence from Congress would certainly flatter any person, letters from General Washington, inspired by kindred sympathies, probably produced a greater effect on Schuyler and Montgomery. The commander in chief was experiencing the same problems with his troops at the siege of Boston. Washington reported to Congress the "egregious want of Public Spirit" in his soldiers. "Instead of pressing to be engaged in the cause of their Country," he wrote, "I find we are likely to be deserted at a most critical time." "It will be next to an impossibility to keep them under any degree of Descipline, and that it will be very difficult to prevail on them to remain a moment longer than they chuse themselves; It is a mortifying reflection to be reduced to this dilemma."[24]

Washington wrote Schuyler urging him and Montgomery to remain in command. "When is the Time for brave Men to exert themselves in the

Cause of Liberty and their Country, if this is not?" he posed. "Should any Difficulties that they may have to encounter, at this important Crisis, deter them?" "God knows, there is not a Difficulty that you both very justly complain of, that I have not in an eminent Degree experienced, that I am not every Day experiencing," he professed, "but we must bear up against them, and make the best of Mankind as they are, since we cannot have them as we wish." Washington then requested that his two generals "lay aside such Thoughts, Thoughts injurious to yourselves, excessively so to your Country, which calls aloud for Gentlemen of your Abilities."[25]

Washington's personal appeal was too poignant for Schuyler and Montgomery to turn down. They realized that their problems with the troops were not isolated, but were endemic throughout the Continental army. This relieved them of their self-reproach and restored their sense of individual honor as military leaders. In his letters, Washington also revealed an intimate insight into overcoming conditions inherent in the Continental army. Combined with an emotional solicitation to their civic responsibility, Washington's arguments engendered a positive response from his discouraged generals. Schuyler decided to retain overall command of the Northern Department, despite his incessant debilitating physical condition. Montgomery committed himself once again as field commander of the American expedition and determined to employ whatever resources were afforded him in its mission to capture Canada. Thus, Washington's persuasiveness and the receptivity of Schuyler and Montgomery to continued self-sacrifice averted a command crisis in the Canadian campaign.

Schuyler's health would not permit him to join the expedition or even remain any longer at Ticonderoga. With the forward command in the trusted hands of Montgomery, Schuyler decided to direct his rear support function from his home at Albany. He hoped that the comfortable surroundings there would be more conducive to his recovery. Before leaving Ticonderoga in charge of Col. James Holmes of the 4th New York in early December, Schuyler endeavored to put the activities at the post on as good footing as possible. He disposed of all the prisoners sent to him by forwarding them under guard to be retained in Connecticut or Pennsylvania. Then, he made arrangements for the transfer of captured cannons to Col. Henry Knox. Washington had sent Knox to transport the ordnance to Boston to reinforce the siege against British forces there.[26]

On December 7, Schuyler established his headquarters in Albany. His first order of business was to meet with an Indian delegation that was waiting for him. Managing Indian affairs in the Northern Department was one of Schuyler's finest accomplishments during the Canadian campaign. Through adroit negotiations, he was able to prevail upon the natives to maintain their general neutrality during the hostilities. Although Lord Dartmouth officially sanctioned the use of Indians, Carleton declined to loose them in any major effort against the Americans. However, some British Indian agents and loyalist leaders such as Guy Johnson and Sir John Johnson were actively engaged in trying to recruit Indians for the British cause. Their activities were thwarted by the Canadian invasion, which served to cut off British supplies to potential Indian allies. As a result, the Indians proved to be a nondeterminant factor in the Canadian campaign.[27]

Montgomery concerned himself with securing Montreal, reorganizing his scaled-down command, and preparing to close in on Quebec. "I need not tell you," he wrote his brother-in-law, Robert R. Livingston, "that, until Quebec is taken, Canada is unconquered." However, an attack of Quebec was a troublesome proposition for Montgomery. He knew by experience that his artillery and the size of his force were probably inadequate for a successful siege or investment of the city. So, even at this early planning stage, Montgomery was favoring a storming of the British defenses.[28]

Carleton's presence at Quebec also worried Montgomery. "The Governor escaped—more's the pity!," he told his wife. In contemplating future operations, Montgomery held a high opinion of Carleton as a tactician. While reviewing the historical precedent of the successful British assault against the French at Quebec during the Seven Years' War, he did not expect the same miscalculation by the present defender. "Wolfe's success was a lucky hit, or rather a series of hits," he wrote. "All sober and scientifick calculation was against him, until Montcalm, permitting his courage to get the better of his discretion, gave up the advantages of his fortress and came out to try his strength on the plain." "Carleton, who was Wolfe's Quartermaster-General, understands this well, and it is feared, will not follow the Frenchman's example," Montgomery theorized.[29]

Out of his meager force, Montgomery had to provide a garrison to occupy Montreal. He put Wooster in charge of the occupation, commanding what remained of his Connecticut troops. He augmented the Montreal garrison with several Yorker units under Colonel Ritzema.

Montgomery also sent Col. James Livingston forward to raise a Canadian partisan unit. On November 28, Montgomery and three hundred New Yorkers, newly outfitted in captured or purchased uniforms, embarked for Quebec aboard several of their prize ships. These "vessels Mr. Prescott made us a present of," as Montgomery phrased it, included the sloop *Gaspé* and the schooner *Mary*. He also took with him part of Captain Lamb's artillery company with four field pieces and six mortars. James Livingston, with his Canadian recruits, and Maj. John Brown, who led the remnants of Easton's command, joined the expedition at Sorel.[30]

In the evening of December 2, Montgomery and his men joined Arnold's force, awaiting them at Point aux Trembles about eighteen miles up the river from Quebec. Bringing with him much-needed clothing and supplies, Montgomery was hailed as a hero when he arrived. Arnold's soldiers were immediately taken with the general who assumed command of the combined field forces. After a short but "energetic and elegant" speech, as one private described it, answered with frequent huzzahs, most of the men formed a very favorable initial impression of Montgomery. "He is a gentle, polite Man, tall and Slender In his make, bald on the top of His Head, Resolute, mild, and of a fine Temper and an Excellent General," one of the troops noted. "Though his face was much pockmarked," another observed, he was "well limbed, tall and handsome," with a manner that "designated the real soldier." General Montgomery "was born to command," still another added, "his easy and affable condescension to both officers and men, while it forbids an improper familiarity, creates love and esteem; and exhibits him the gentleman and soldier. He is tall and very well made; and possesses a captivating address." Montgomery's presence raised the spirits of Arnold's troops. One soldier expressed this optimism that their new commander engendered: "Now new life was infused into the whole of the corps."[31]

Montgomery was equally impressed with Arnold's soldiers. Many of them had tasted combat at the siege of Boston before volunteering for their hazardous mission. Starting in Massachusetts, they had marched through 350 miles of rugged wilderness to reach Quebec in forty-five days. Of the original force of eleven hundred, only approximately six hundred survived the rigors of the march. Displaying remarkable endurance over incredible hardships, these troops even won the respect of the Quebec defenders. One British observer wrote: "There are about 500 Provincials arrived. . . . Surely a miracle must have been wrought in their favor. It is an undertaking above the common race of men. . . .

They have traveled through woods and bogs, and over precipices . . . attended with every inconvenience and difficulty, to be surmounted only by men of indefatigable zeal and industry." Montgomery wrote to Schuyler: "I must say that he [Arnold] has brought with him many pretty young men. . . . I find Colonel Arnold's corps an exceeding fine one, inured to fatigue, and well accustomed to cannon shot. . . . There is a style of discipline among them, much superior to what I have been used to see this campaign."[32]

The two commanders promptly established a close rapport when they joined forces. Earlier, Montgomery had suspected Arnold of being a flamboyant glory seeker in the Ethan Allen mold. Arnold's sharp dispute with Allen over who should assume leadership of the May assault of Ticonderoga could have led to Montgomery's concern. During initial planning of the dual invasion against Canada, Montgomery wrote to Schuyler, anticipating the eventual convergence of the two forces. "Should Arnold come into my neighborhood," Montgomery inquired, "has he orders to put himself under my command? You know his ambition. I need not point out the bad consequences of a separate command." Schuyler clarified the prospective command roles with Arnold. When the two officers did merge their columns, the problems with Arnold that Montgomery had contemplated never materialized. After meeting Arnold, Montgomery described him as "active, intelligent, and enterprising." As the senior ranking officer, Montgomery assumed command of the combined field force, and Arnold rendered his complete cooperation. Each officer realized and appreciated the military competency of the other, and this soon developed into an amiable working relationship on both a professional and personal level.[33]

Montgomery devoted December 3 to the distribution of supplies and organizing his little army that now numbered about a thousand men. The next day, the expedition made its way down the St. Lawrence to take up positions before Quebec. Montgomery deployed the troops to blockade the land sides of the fortress city. He stationed the soldiers that he had brought from Montreal on the right wing of the line, where the Plains (Heights) of Abraham formed a plateau to the west of the city's wall. The general assigned Arnold and his men the left wing at St. Roch, a suburb just north of the city.

Quebec stood on a promontory in a bend of the St. Lawrence River. On the southeastern or St. Lawrence side, the city was guarded by a precipitous, rocky cliff that rose more than three hundred feet above the river. Along the northeastern base of the cliff, the terrain presented a more gentle slope to the water's edge. The Lower Town or commercial section was located here. The Upper Town or main part of the city occupied the upper level of the promontory. Quebec was completely fortified by a thirty-foot-high wall, from which six bastions with mounted heavy cannons projected. Four gates—Palace Gate at the northern end, St. John's Gate at the northwestern quadrant, St. Louis Gate in the center section, and Prescott Gate between the lower and upper towns— allowed controlled access to the city.

Lieutenant Governor Cramahé and Colonel MacLean had initiated measures for the defense of Quebec with the resources at their disposal. They evacuated the inhabitants of the Lower Town to within the more secure confines of the walled city. They also leveled nearby buildings outside the wall to deprive attackers of cover and afford British gunners with clear fields of fire. Finally, they pressed into service every man who was willing to take up arms in the defense of the city. After his return to Quebec, Governor Carleton immediately reviewed these preparations and began to finalize his defensive plan. There were about five thousand people inside the walls of Quebec. Stored provisions were available in sufficient quantity, if carefully rationed, to sustain this number of individuals until the middle of May. Therefore, Quebec could withstand a six-month siege without undue hardship. Carleton expected reinforcements from England before then.

The total occupants of Quebec included a 1,248-man armed defensive force consisting of disparate components of British regulars, artillerists, marines, seamen, and militiamen; Canadian militiamen and volunteers; and the Royal Highland Emigrants. However, the loyalty of many civilians was suspect. Like the Montrealers, many of Quebec's inhabitants feared that an attack on their city would result in wholesale destruction of their homes and personal property, if not their own lives. They viewed capitulation as a means of saving those things they held dear. For this reason, some of them were aiding and abetting the American seizure of Quebec. Lt. Col. Henry Caldwell, British militia commander, stated: "We could guard against open and avowed enemies, but not against those lurking about town."[34]

To rid the city of these security risks and solidify public support against the American threat, Carleton issued a proclamation. "In order to rid the Town of all useless, disloyal and treacherous persons," the edict read, those eligible men who would not join in the defense of Quebec by serving in the militia were to "quit the Town in four days" and the limits of the District of Quebec by December 1 "under pain of being treated as Rebels or Spies, if . . . found within the said limits." Although it prompted some citizens to flee the area and drove a few into Montgomery's camp, Carleton's purge of unreliable elements had a salutary effect. According to Caldwell, "that order strengthened the garrison considerably" and everyone now "seemed zealous for the public service." Under the threat of banishment, Carleton induced some two hundred British and three hundred French inhabitants to volunteer for militia duty.[35]

Carleton planned no offensive action. His strategy was to force Montgomery to bring the battle to him. He had enough resources so that he could winter behind the walls of Quebec and await reinforcements that would come with the spring breakup of ice in the frozen St. Lawrence river. Until then, he would stand behind his formidable fortifications and defy the Americans to take Quebec.

Montgomery was well aware of the difficulties facing him. The frozen ground would not allow him to dig trenches and engineer proper siege lines. The lightness of his artillery would not permit him to breach the defensive wall. The expiration of enlistments for all of Arnold's New England troops at year's end and the threat of British reinforcements by April precluded a protracted operation. Montgomery thus had no intention of relying on classic siege tactics. Instead, he planned to capitalize on a few expedients that he hoped to turn to his advantage. When writing to his brother-in-law from Montreal, he revealed some of his thinking for combating Carleton in Quebec: "The extensiveness of his works, which in case of investment, would favour him, will, in the other case [storming], favour us. . . . We may select a particular time and place for attack, and to repel this, the garrison must be prepared at all times and places; a circumstance which will impose upon it incessant watching and labour, by day and by night, which in its undisciplined state, must breed discontents that may compel Carleton to capitulate."[36]

As soon as the envelopment of Quebec was complete, Montgomery initiated a war of nerves with Carleton. On December 7, he sent an ultimatum to the governor designed to plant the seeds of doubt concerning a continued defense of Quebec. "The feelings of humanity induce me," he began on a consolatory note, "to save you from the Destruction which hangs over you." "I am well acquainted with your situation," he claimed, describing it as "a great extent of works in their nature incapable of defence, manned with a motley Crew of Sailors the greatest part of our friends, of Citizens who wish to see us within their Walls, and a few of the worst Troops who ever stiled themselves Soldiers." "I am at the head of troops," he postured, "accustomed to success, confident of the Righteousness of the Cause they are engaged in; inured to danger and fatigue, and of the ungenerous means employed to prejudice them in the minds of the Canadians; that it is with difficulty I restrain them till my Batteries are ready, from insulting your works which would afford them the fair opportunity of an ample vengeance and just retaliation." "Should you persist in an unwarrantable defence," Montgomery warned, "the consequences be on your own Head."[37]

Montgomery employed an innocuous noncombatant, an old woman, to deliver the message to Carleton. She approached the Palace Gate and told the guard that she carried an important dispatch for the governor. Except to raise his ire, the bluff made no impression on Carleton, who determined to continue his previous decision not to communicate with the rebels. With a dramatic air to demonstrate his indignation after scanning the communiqué, Carleton summoned a drummer. He ordered him to take Montgomery's message with fire tongs, so as to avoid contamination from the vile prose, and ceremoniously consign it to the flames in his fireplace. The governor then had the messenger ousted from the city so that she could report to Montgomery how the communication was received.[38]

A few days later, Montgomery tried another ploy. This time, he wrote a direct appeal to the Quebec merchants, assuring them that his army had come "with the professed Intention of eradicating Tyranny, and giving Liberty and Security to this oppressed Province, Private Property having ever by us been deemed sacred." Montgomery chose another woman to smuggle this solicitation into the city. However, Carleton soon discovered the plot and clapped her in the city jail to repent her indiscretion. As a last resort, Montgomery directed that copies of his previous message to Carleton be enclosed with the proclamation to the merchants and that they be shot over the wall into Quebec by bow and arrow. This tactic met with no more success than the earlier attempts to intimidate and discredit Carleton. By this time, the governor had tightened his control over the inhabitants remaining in the city. The merchants were too wary now to risk accommodation with the Americans.[39]

Montgomery never put much hope for success on his psychological warfare against Quebec, but he felt that it was an option that had to be tried before resorting to more daring action. At this juncture, however, required expedience would not afford him the luxury of continuing this type of operation. The present situation called for direct military efforts against the city to dislodge Carleton's obstinate defense.

Attack on Quebec

The situation of his army pressed dispatch;
snows and frost only quickened his motions.
He hoped by one successful stroke, before
the arrival of succours to the garrison,
to complete his plan.[1]

But yet, what-reck, he at Quebec,
Montgomery-like did fa', man,
Wi' sword in hand, before his band,
Amang his en'mies a', man.[2]

Thus fell our worthy and brave General.
Weep America! for thou hast lost one of
thy most virtuous and dearest sons.[3]

After receiving no satisfaction in his attempts to arrange a peaceful capitulation of Quebec, Montgomery turned to an artillery cannonade of the city. Erecting batteries with the guns he had brought from Montreal, he emplaced five small mortars behind protective buildings in St. Roch, a few hundred yards from the walls of Quebec. Shelling of the city commenced on December 9 to provide a postscript to the unanswered messages of conciliation that Montgomery had sent to the inhabitants.

Several days of sustained firing, however, failed to make a serious impact on the garrison or civilian population. Capt. Thomas Ainslie of the British militia crowed, "Their shot had no more effect upon our walls, than pease wou'd have against a plank." "Before they gave us a sample of their savoir faire in the bombarding way," Ainslie remarked, "the towns people had conceived that every shell wou'd inevitably kill a dozen or two of people, & knock down some two or three houses . . . but after they saw that their bombettes as they called them, did no harm, women and children walked the streets laughing at their former fears."[4]

The ineffectiveness of Montgomery's six-, nine-, and twelve-pounders was due largely to their light weight and limited range. It soon became apparent to the Americans that their batteries were not in a position to compete with the thirty-two-pounders in the fortress. This British fire superiority manifested itself in the casualties and damage suffered by the Americans from counterartillery fire. A hostile cannon barrage drove Arnold from his headquarters in St. Roch when his house was riddled with shot. Carleton's cannoneers nearly killed Montgomery when a shell decapitated his horse and demolished his sleigh a few minutes after he had alighted to confer with his aides.[5]

Despite the disadvantages from which the American artillery endured, Montgomery ordered the emplacement of another battery that hopefully could give a better account of itself. The Plains of Abraham offered the most advantageous firing location, but it offered little natural cover from outranging counterbattery shelling. In addition, the hard frozen ground would not permit digging or the construction of earthworks to protect the guns or gunners. Nevertheless, the Americans accepted the challenge and risk. Captain Lamb chose a site on the Plains about seven hundred yards from St. John's Gate. Working by night in the biting cold, his men prepared the new position. It took the name of the "ice battery," because its breastworks were constructed with snow that had been wetted down with water and allowed to form into walls of ice. On December 15, Lamb's men mounted five six-pound and twelve-pound cannons and a howitzer in the battery, and trained the weapons on Quebec.

With this show of force, Montgomery decided to issue still another appeal to the British defenders. A party consisting of Colonel Arnold, Capt. John Macpherson (one of Montgomery's aides-de-camp), and a drummer advanced under a flag of truce. They carried a letter from Montgomery promising Carleton and Cramahé safe conduct to England if they would capitulate. Holding true to his stance of nonnegotiation with the rebels, Carleton turned away the American representatives without meeting with them or receiving their communication.[6]

Thwarted once again in his attempt to parley a peaceful solution to the siege, Montgomery resumed bombardment of Quebec. The "ice battery" joined in pouring a vigorous volume of fire upon the walled city. The overall effectiveness of the cannonading, however, was little improved.

At first, Carleton's gunners were frustrated in their attempts to answer the latest challenge to their artillery primacy. Intervening houses in the adjacent suburb of St. John's blocked their line of fire to the new American battery. Carleton ordered the obtrusive structures destroyed, and the British cannoneers soon brought their heavy thirty-two-pound guns to bear on the "ice battery." The big guns systematically laid waste to the installation.

Counterbattery fire quickly silenced two of Lamb's guns, killing three of his men and wounding several others. Still, the Americans persisted in continuing their artillery operations in the face of adversity. Montgomery arrived at the battery in the midst of the ruinous shelling. After experiencing the dismounting of a cannon and disabling of its crew by incoming fire, the general turned to Captain Lamb. "This is warm work, sir," he remarked to Lamb. "It is indeed," was the reply, "and certainly no place for you, sir." "Why so, Captain?" the general asked. "Because there are enough of us here to be killed without the loss of you, which would be irreparable," Lamb answered. Montgomery and Lamb apparently had reconciled their differences.[7]

Lamb and his men displayed courageous military conduct in carrying out their duties while their battery disintegrated around them. In spite of these heroics, Montgomery knew that his gunners could not compete with the British cannons. He did not wish to sacrifice any more of his men and weapons to a futile effort, so he instructed Lamb to evacuate the position.

Montgomery indicated his grand strategy for assaulting Quebec in a letter to Wooster. "I never expected any other advantage from our artillery than to amuse the enemy and blind them as to my real intention," he wrote. Montgomery then revealed his underlying aim: "I propose the first strong northwester to make two attacks at night: one, with about a third of the troops, on the lower town; . . . the other upon Cape Diamond bastion."[8]

Although Montgomery claimed to be "fully convinced of the practicability" of his plan, his decision was undoubtedly influenced by several situational factors. A traditional siege could not be effectively conducted. The American guns were clearly inadequate to the task of breaching the walls of the city or of undermining the morale of its inhabitants. Montgomery also felt pressure for the speedy capture of Quebec from his superiors, who presumed that he would continue his string of military conquests in Canada with its culmination at the capital city. Schuyler informed Washington, "I make no doubt but that it [Quebec] will be in our possession before any troops can come to its relief." Washington answered, "I flatter myself that your next Favour will give me an account of General Montgomery's joining Colonel Arnold and that Quebec is or soon will be reduced to our possession." Henry Knox added to the general anticipation by impetuously reporting to Washington during this time that "I have very little doubt that General Montgomery has Quebec in his possession."[9]

Congress had also become impatient. In November, it sent a committee north to assess the progress of the Canadian campaign. Advancing no farther than Ticonderoga, the committeemen did not catch up with Montgomery. However, in their report they expressed confidence in him and recommended that Congress provide reinforcements for his enterprise. Montgomery's conquests of St. Johns and Montreal were the only victories won by the Continental army during the first six months since its organization. Bolstered by Montgomery's previous triumphs, members of Congress relied on the continuation of his momentum to secure Quebec and were slow to act on requests for augmentation. Benjamin Franklin reflected an anxious Congress when he wrote: "[We] have now reason to expect that whole Province [Quebec] may soon be in our possession."[10]

The prospect of a Canadian alliance also prodded Montgomery in his decision. He wrote Schuyler: "I fear the Canadians will not relish a union with the Colonies till they see the whole country in our hands, and defended by such a force as may relieve them the apprehensions of again falling under the Ministerial lash."[11]

Considerations of support from his soldiers added another factor to Montgomery's concept of operations. "I am not certain whether or no the troops relish this mode of proceeding," he admitted. "Should it not appear in the same advantageous light to the men, I shall not press it upon them, well knowing the impossibility of making troops act with the necessary vigour on such an occasion, if their minds are possessed with imaginary terrors." Montgomery induced his troops with an order that directed that "the Effects of the Governor, Garrison, and of such as have been acting in misleading the Inhabitants and distressing the Friends of

Liberty" would be auctioned and the proceeds divided among the invading soldiers. Some of the troops took a much wider view when they interpreted this directive concerning the spoils of war. "All that get safe into the city will live well," one man wrote, "for they are allowed to plunder and take what they please." [12]

The New England troops under Arnold presented a potential problem to the operation. Because their enlistments expired at the end of the year, many were contemplating getting an early start for home. A Pennsylvania soldier condemned them by observing: "The patriotism of the summer of seventy-five seemed almost extinguished in the winter of seventy-six." Although Montgomery had expedited his plan of attack on Quebec to accommodate the impending termination of enlistments, he was now concerned over the possibility of losing half of his troop strength even before year's end. [13]

On Christmas Day, Montgomery spoke to Arnold's troops, assuring them "nothing was wanting to insure victory but the exercise of that valor" that they had "so triumphantly displayed" thus far. He concluded that their success "would rescue a province from the British yoke" and obtain "immortal honor" for themselves. "The address was sensible and concise," one private noted, "the engaging oratory of the General highly enraptured us." "We answered him with a cheer, declaring that whatever his Excellency was pleased to command we were ready to obey." Although another private considered the plan to storm Quebec "rash and imprudent," he did not think it proper to make any objections, "lest I should be considered wanting in courage." "The fire of patriotism kindled in our breasts," he recalled, "and we resolved to follow wherever he should lead." Montgomery reported to Schuyler that "I then had reason to believe the troops well inclined for a coup-de-main." [14]

The recent communication from Montgomery also alleviated Schuyler's "distressing anxiety" over his greatest fear. A false, malicious report circulated at his headquarters "that General Montgomery was killed, Colonel Arnold taken prisoner, and our Army totally defeated." After hearing from Montgomery, a relieved Schuyler wrote to Congress to belie the rumor. Yet, the ominous hearsay would prove to be strangely prophetic. [15]

Meanwhile, dissension between Arnold and some of his officers brought another crisis with which Montgomery had to deal. Some animosity arose between Arnold and one of his company commanders, with whom two others soon sided. John Brown also fomented the dispute by encouraging the malcontent captains. Brown had detested Arnold since their feud over command of the combined force that captured Ticonderoga in May. So, Brown used this incident to provoke his old antagonist. As a condition to their continued service, the three company commanders insisted upon being released from Arnold's command and reorganized into a separate contingent under Major Brown. This cabal placed Montgomery in a very delicate position. "This dangerous party threatens the ruin of our affairs," Montgomery wrote Schuyler. "The three discontented companies are within a few days of being free from their engagements," he explained. "I must try every means to prevent their departure, and in this matter I am much embarrassed." "Their officers have offered to stay provided they may join some other corps," he continued. "This is resentment against Arnold, and will hurt him so much that I do not think I can consent to it." Although he risked divesting his force of three companies, Montgomery stood behind Arnold in the controversy. He had no intention of contravening the authority of his assistant commander whose abilities he respected. The general met with the involved officers and managed to defuse the situation. He persuaded them to put aside their differences, forego their unreasonable demands, and support the operation against Quebec.[16]

With these difficulties settled, Montgomery began final preparations for the assault. He numbered "not much above 800 men fit for duty exclusive of a few ragamuffin Canadians," but he hoped to penetrate Carleton's thinly stretched defenses by employing the advantage of surprise. He had written earlier to Schuyler: "Fortune often baffles the sanguine expectations of poor mortals. I am not intoxicated with the favors I have received at her hands, but I do think there is a fair prospect of success." His plan called for the New Yorkers and four of Arnold's companies to storm the Cape Diamond bastion by escalade while the remainder of his force made a secondary attack on the Lower Town.[17]

On December 27, a snowstorm descended upon the city—the kind of weather conditions that Montgomery wanted in order to conceal his operations from the enemy. He issued orders for his troops to check their weapons, ready scaling ladders, and stand by for action. Because some of his men wore confiscated British uniforms, he instructed them to attach twigs of hemlock to their hats to distinguish them from their adversaries during battle. Soon after midnight, however, the snow stopped falling and the weather suddenly turned clear. Montgomery called off the attack, telling his soldiers "it was with the greatest reluctance he found himself

Call'd upon by his duty to repress their ardor, but should hold himself answerable for the loss of those brave men whose lives might be Saved by waiting for a favourable opportunity."[18]

Montgomery soon learned that the change in weather and his decision to postpone the operation saved his troops from almost certain disaster by a forewarned enemy. Joshua Wolf, Colonel Caldwell's clerk taken prisoner by the Americans, had escaped back to Quebec and informed Carleton of Montgomery's plan of attack. His intelligence was corroborated by a Sergeant Singleton, an American deserter who defected to the British at the same time. In the morning, an observed shift of the garrison defenses to counter an attack at the designated location confirmed that the plan had been compromised. In order not to play into Carleton's hands, Montgomery changed his strategy to concentrate his main effort on the Lower Town.[19]

Carleton maintained his garrison on twenty-four-hour alert. The defenders were confident in their ability to defeat any assault upon their ramparts. "Above a thousand men were ready to oppose the Rebels in case of an attack," Ainslie recorded in his journal. "The rest of the Garrison lay in their cloaths with their arms and accoutrements lying beside them." "Can these men [Americans] pretend that there is a possibility of approaching our walls loaden with ladders," he wrote with an assured air. "Shall we be looking on cross arm'd?" "It will be a fatal attempt for them," he predicted. "They will never scale the walls."[20]

In spite of the delay, most of the American troops remained in high spirits. Even an outbreak of smallpox failed to dampen their enthusiasm. Medical personnel encouraged inoculations and evacuated confirmed cases to a facility three miles away in an attempt to limit the contagion. Some of the men in Capt. Simeon Thayer's company confronted four fellow soldiers who had feigned sickness to avoid mustering for the attack. They paraded the impugned shirkers with "halters round their necks," exposing them to the ridicule of the rest of the company "as a punishment Due to their effeminate courage, who after suffering in their fatigues to a degree of spirit as yet known to be equal'd, timorously withdrew from the Laurels they were ready to gather."[21]

As Montgomery waited for advantageous conditions to launch his operation, he revised his plan of attack. Leading his three hundred New Yorkers from the Plains of Abraham, he would descend to the St. Lawrence and follow the narrow path beside the river, passing below Cape Diamond to get into the Lower Town from the southwest. Arnold would approach from St. Roch with some five hundred of his own men, fifty artillerymen under Captain Lamb, and about forty Canadians and Indians, entering the Lower Town from the opposite direction. After effecting a linkup, Montgomery and Arnold would force their way up the steep, connecting roadway through Prescott Gate into the Upper Town, thereby rupturing the city's walled defenses. Once the Americans were inside the inner city, resistance would crumble. To throw Carleton off balance and guessing as to where the main attack would materialize, Montgomery planned two feints. Colonel Livingston's contingent of Canadians would threaten St. John's Gate, setting it on fire; and a detachment of Massachusetts men under Capt. Jacob Brown (John Brown's brother) would engage the guard at the Cape Diamond bastion. In order to coordinate the movement of the two primary assault forces, Brown's party would also fire rockets to signal Arnold that Montgomery had initiated his approach. In an attempt to confuse the defenders further, Montgomery slated Capt. Isaiah Wool's battery of five mortars at St. Roch to throw shells into the town while the diversionary feints were conducted.[22]

Montgomery selected the Lower Town for the real assault because it was the least fortified part of Quebec, lying outside the towering city walls. Carleton knew this vulnerability and had taken precautions by building a network of barricades and obstacles there. Montgomery calculated that his troops could overcome these obstructions. He also did not rule out the possibility that if his force could gain possession of the Lower Town or commercial district, the English merchants would prevail upon Carleton to surrender to prevent destruction of their property.

This was an ambitious plan born out of desperate circumstances. Intrinsic and external exigencies—lack of heavy artillery, short-term enlistments, threat of enemy reinforcements, and high expectations of superiors—combined in compelling Montgomery to take precipitous measures against Quebec. With his experience in siege warfare, he could weigh the odds as well as anyone. The British garrison outnumbered his force by more than two to one and had established fire supremacy over his artillery. The chances for success were less than convincing. He would have liked clear superiority in troop strength and firepower to go against a stubborn enemy defending a fortified position, but he realized that he must play the hand that fate had dealt him. From his military experience, he also knew that the imponderables of warfare—surprise, tactical mistakes, heroism of the soldiers, and sheer luck—often determined the tide of battle, and he hoped these advantages would fall his way. As he had written his brother-in-law, Robert R. Livingston, a few weeks before, "*Audaces fortuna juvat*—Fortune favors the bold."[23]

Although he appeared effusive and unabashed to his troops to help maintain their spirit, Montgomery seemed pensive and preoccupied in his headquarters at Holland House. As with all military leaders just before committing their soldiers to the uncertainties of a deadly contest against the enemy, Montgomery felt the awesome weight of command—responsibility for the lives of others—on his shoulders. During these private moments of reflection, he engaged in some quiet soul searching, running the operation through his mind while trying to make it as perfect as humanly possible.

Others prepared for battle in their own personal way. Capt. John Macpherson, Montgomery's aide-de-camp, composed a letter to his father in Philadelphia. An ardent, twenty-year-old patriot, Macpherson appended instructions for his letter to be mailed only in case he did not survive. "If you receive this, it will be the last this hand will ever write you," the poignant text read. "Orders are given for a general storm of Quebec this night; and Heaven only knows what may be my fate; but whatever it be, I cannot resist the inclination I feel to assure you that I experience no reluctance in this cause, to venture a life which I consider is only lent to be used when my country demands it." Capt. Jacob Cheeseman, a company commander in the 1st New York Regiment, also penned a letter to his father: "I can't tell when I shall return home, for I can't do like many of my fellow-citizens—after putting my hand to the plow, look back; especially now, when my country calls loudly for assistance." Cheeseman expressed these patriotic sentiments despite a premonition of his impending death on the battlefield. After dressing, he placed five gold coins into his pocket so that they could be used to pay for a proper burial when his body was recovered.[24]

With the onset of another snowstorm on the night of December 30, which promised to be fiercer than the previous one, Montgomery issued the order for attack that his troops anticipated. At two o'clock on the morning of the 31st, the Americans gathered at their designated assembly areas—the New Yorkers on the Plains of Abraham, Arnold's force at St. Roch, Livingston's Canadians in vicinity of St. John's Gate, and Brown's men opposite the Cape Diamond bastion. Around four o'clock, Montgomery led his column down toward Wolf's Cove located beside the river. As he began the steep one-mile descent, Brown's detachment launched its rockets and began firing upon the Cape Diamond bastion. Livingston's contingent of Canadians approached St. John's Gate. Observing the rockets in the snow-choked sky over Cape Diamond, Arnold started his advance. The long-awaited onslaught against Quebec had commenced.[25]

The rockets served as a signal to the Americans, but they also alerted the British that the city was under attack. Capt. Malcolm Fraser of the Royal Highland Emigrants, who commanded the main guard that night, was conducting a tour of the guard posts on the western wall when the rockets burst in the sky. Sensing that this meant an imminent attack, he immediately spread the warning. Drums beat to arms, town bells rang the alarm, and officers ran through the streets rushing troops to their posts. British artillery roared in reply to the American mortars that began to fall. In short order, the entire garrison stood ready to oppose the attack, but they had not determined where the main thrust would be made. The defenders extended lanterns affixed to poles over the walls and heaved ignited fire balls from the battlements to illuminate the ground outside. The two feints were not convincing enough to be taken very seriously. Livingston's demonstration amounted to a timorous action by the Canadians. They were not able to mount any intimidating encounter and failed to set the gate afire. Although Brown's men maintained a spirited fusillade on their objective, they did not attempt to close upon the position.[26]

In the midst of the clamor, Carleton waited patiently for the situation to clarify. The unruffled veteran British general decided not to commit his main reserve until the fog of battle lifted sufficiently so that he could fix the location of the primary attack. Suspecting that what they had experienced so far was merely a diversion for the real attack, Carleton sent Colonel Caldwell and a detachment of militia to investigate the gunfire near the Cape Diamond bastion.

About this time, Montgomery reached Wolfe's Cove, where the famed British general had landed sixteen years before during his conquest of the French in Quebec. The American general had no time to consider the irony of the occasion, for the heavy blizzard and rough terrain were putting him behind his time schedule. Bitter cold and deep snowdrifts called for Herculean efforts to move forward. Turning downstream, he continued to lead his men in their advance along the edge of the St. Lawrence. Here, he encountered even more distressing conditions. Upheaval of the frozen river had piled onshore huge masses of ice that repeatedly blocked their path, forcing them to claw their way up the cliff to get around the obstructions. This was particularly difficult for the men carrying scaling ladders. Almost two miles of this stretched ahead before they reached the first defenses of the Lower Town. The troops slogged onward but lost precious minutes of darkness during the ordeal. Toward the rear of the column was Col. Donald Campbell, Montgomery's quartermaster general. Campbell would later describe the route as "the worst Path I ever traveled, being obliged in several places to scramble up the slant of the Rocks & then descending by pulling the Skirt of our Coats under us & sliding down 15 or 20 foot, & this repeated several times before we got to the first Barrier."[27]

Campbell and Montgomery were a study of contrasting personalities. It is difficult to understand why they got along so well. Perhaps there was a kindred feeling because Campbell was a Yorker who had previously served as an officer with the British army. However, Campbell's case demonstrates the diverse backgrounds and purposes of the members of the expedition. The colonel was a vociferous braggart who ostentatiously carried a large claymore—a two-edged Scottish broadsword—into battle. Unlike Montgomery, Campbell's object for serving in the patriot cause was motivated by selfish reasons. He owned ten thousand acres of land in New York awarded to him by the British Crown as compensation for his father's disputed land holdings and services in quelling the Scottish rebellion of 1745. After receiving this grant, Campbell incurred many debts by living in English high society beyond his means while trying to uphold an affluent image. To save himself from debtors' prison, he used his inheritance and social connections to persuade a number of influential English friends, including a member of Parliament, to insure his debts. He then summarily departed for America, leaving his backers to make restitution for what he owed. His ex-friends sued in British courts for his title to the New York lands to recoup their losses. With this threat of personal ruin hanging over his head, Campbell embraced American independence as a means to rid himself of private legal and financial difficulties.[28]

On the other side of Quebec, Arnold's column braved the raging storm as it marched into battle. Like Montgomery, Arnold led the way—both had learned that it was vital to take such chances when commanding raw American soldiers in combat. Seeing their leaders in the fore steadied the nerve of the troops, but the practice also increased the exposure of these officers to enemy fire. Like all good field commanders, Montgomery and Arnold were willing to risk their lives in the execution of their duties.

Behind Arnold and his advance party, Captain Lamb and his cannoneers dragged a six-pound cannon lashed to a sled. The main body of rifle companies followed. A contingent of Canadians and Indians brought up the rear.

Their route took them past the Palace Gate north of the city. Arnold's vanguard circumvented the gate undetected, but his main body of troops drew heavy fire from the alerted British guards atop the wall. For a third of a mile they ran a gauntlet of musket balls rained upon them from above. "Here we lost some brave men," Priv. John Joseph Henry remembered, because he and his fellow soldiers "were powerless to return the salutes we received, as the enemy was covered by his impregnable defenses." "They were even sightless to us," he groaned. "We could see nothing but the blaze from the muzzles of their muskets."[29]

In the ensuing rush toward the Lower Town, Lamb's unwieldy sled became mired in a deep snowdrift and the cannon had to be abandoned. The artillerists continued the march armed only with their muskets. Finally, Arnold and his troops reached the first barricade in the Lower Town, which was defended by a detachment of militia and two light cannons. One of the British artillery pieces hastily fired. A badly aimed load of grapeshot whistled over the Americans' heads with little effect. Snow had wet the powder of the other gun causing it to misfire. Then, a hail of musket fire exploded from the emplacement. Arnold originally planned to take this barrier under fire with his own cannon while separating his force into left and right envelopments to defeat it from the rear. Deprived of his field piece, he had to resort to more direct and daring tactics. Arnold ordered a frontal assault against the position before another volley of cannon shells could be leveled against his troops. While leading the charge, he felt a stab of pain and fell to the ground. Amid the withering fire, a bullet had ricocheted into his path, lodging in his left leg below the knee. Trying to continue, he slumped against a wall, barely able to stand. Several soldiers ran to his assistance. With a man under each arm, Arnold shouted encouragement to his troops as he limped reluctantly from the field of battle.

Seeing their leader wounded and unable to carry on, many of Arnold's men became dispirited. "We are sold" echoed down the troop line. The command was in danger of crumbling. Another officer had to assert himself quickly to maintain the momentum of the assault. Capt. Daniel Morgan and his Virginia riflemen accepted the call to duty. Morgan was a natural leader and was respected for his military prowess by the troops.

His superior officers—a lieutenant colonel and two majors—had not reached the scene, so he took the initiative. Making his way to the fore, he exhorted the soldiers to follow his lead. While the enemy attempted to reload, Morgan flung himself at the barrier. Men with scaling ladders ran beside him while dodging musket fire. Closing upon the fifteen-foot-high barricade, Morgan was the first one to mount a ladder, calling for the rest to heed his example. As he reached the top, a blast of fire erupted in his face. The stunned captain toppled backward off the ladder into the snow below. Upon a quick personal inspection, he discovered several bullet holes through his clothing and his face blackened by burned gunpowder. Miraculously, he was unhurt and sprang back up the ladder without hesitation. This time he vaulted over the wall, and his comrades flocked after him. The startled British militiamen surrendered without much further resistance. Morgan had overcome the strongpoint and taken over a hundred captives, while losing one killed and six wounded. His opponents suffered comparable casualties.[30]

As the troops rounded up their prisoners, Morgan advanced to the second barricade situated three hundred yards ahead. Surprisingly, he found it undefended, and the way looked open to the Upper Town beyond. Morgan rejoined his force and urged them to push on through the next barrier without delay. To his disappointment, he found them unwilling to advance. They expressed concern over the size of their assembled force. The prisoners outnumbered their captors at this point, and some expressed fear that the captives might try to overpower their guards. In addition, some companies had become separated from the assault party and were still trying to find their way through the narrow, winding streets on the other side of the first barricade. The officers told Morgan that they wanted to wait there until more of their straggling column caught up and Montgomery's force joined them. Morgan decided not to press the matter further, for he "was overruled by hard reasoning." However, he feared that a great opportunity for quick victory had slipped between their fingers. "To these arguments I sacrificed my own opinion and lost the town," Morgan later lamented.[31]

The Americans used this interval to take stock of their state of affairs. Many of them discovered that their weapons had become wet and useless. While shielding them from the elements with their coat lappets, the warmth of their bodies melted the accumulated snow on their clothes, soaking the firelocks. They gratefully exchanged them for arms seized from the British captives. "These were not only elegant," Henry described them, "but were such as befitted the hand of a real soldier." It was about daybreak when the major part of the column arrived and the Americans re-formed for an attack on the second barrier.[32]

Meanwhile, Colonel Caldwell and his detachment had reached Cape Diamond bastion and "saw that there was nothing serious intended" there by the Americans. On his own volition, he then led his men to St. John's Gate. During his tour, he concluded that no real threat was developing from the Plain and the guards manning the wall were capable of handling the demonstrations of Brown and Livingston. While at St. John's Gate, he learned of Arnold's attack on the other side of the town. Augmenting his militia with some Royal American Emigrants under Capt. John Nairne, Caldwell headed toward the Lower Town.

MacLean was also active in sorting out what the Americans' intentions were and preparing to counter them. He informed Carleton of the serious action developing in the Lower Town. Carleton had, therefore, ordered some two hundred Canadian militiamen to occupy and hold that sector.

When Caldwell reached the second barricade, he was joined by Captain Anderson leading about fifty sailors. Caldwell came upon a scene of confusion at the defensive position. "I found things, though not in a good way, yet not desperate," he described the situation. He said that the Canadians were "shy of advancing toward the barrier," and he "was obligated to exert myself a good deal." Caldwell quickly restored order and readied his men to receive the Americans. As he was accomplishing this, Captain Anderson led his detachment through the barricade gate. Seeing Morgan on the other side, Anderson called for him to surrender. Morgan aimed his rifle and shot him through the head. Anderson's party retreated behind the barricade dragging the dead body of their officer with them.[33]

Seizing the moment, the Americans initiated their assault against the barrier. Men positioned ladders against the wall and Morgan clambered to the top. He was driven back by hostile fire. In spite of repeated attempts, no one was successful in climbing over the heavily defended barricade. Efforts to outflank the barricade by breaking into adjacent buildings also met with failure. Some were shot off the ladders while trying to scale the wall. Others were killed or wounded in the narrow, confined streets from the murderous fire laid down by Caldwell's troops. Captain Lamb suffered a major wound when a part of his face was torn away by grapeshot.[34]

The tide of war had turned against the Americans. The officers considered the alternatives left them. Some felt that Montgomery surely would join them at any moment, and they wanted to hold their position until reinforced. The majority had given up hopes of relief from the New York troops and viewed their situation as untenable. They decided to abandon the attempt and withdraw.

However, Carleton took action to prevent that. By this time, the British commander was confident that the only threat to his defense rested with the forces presently opposing him at the second barricade in the Lower Town. Seizing the initiative at the critical moment, he decided to commit his reserves by ordering Capt. George Laws with five hundred men to sally forth out of the Palace Gate and strike the Americans from their rear. Spilling out the gateway, Laws followed the path left by Arnold's troops as they earlier skirted the gate and proceeded toward the Lower Town. Shortly, he collided with Captain Dearborn's "lost company." Because of a delay in starting their approach march, Dearborn and his men had become separated from Arnold's main force and were still trying to find their way to join the rest of the column. One of the British pickets saw Dearborn in the murky distance and challenged him to identify himself. "A friend," the captain replied to the shadowy figure. When asked who he was a friend to, Dearborn answered, "to liberty." The soldier then exclaimed, "God damn you" and lunged to fire at Dearborn. The American hurried to give his adversary "his due." "But to my great mortification," Dearborn recounted, "my Gun did not go off . . . nor one in Ten of my men could get off our Guns they being so exceedingly wet." Surrounded and outnumbered by six to one, Dearborn surrendered after a brief stand. British troops marched him and his men under guard into the Upper Town.[35]

Anxious to cut off the American retreat, Captain Laws continued to charge toward the Lower Town. Upon nearing the chaotic engagement there, he called for the first Americans he saw to capitulate. They jeered at the suggestion of surrendering to a lone officer. Laws looked around and discovered that his men were nowhere in sight—in his excitement he had outrun them. Although the captain insisted that his command would arrive "in a twinkling," the disbelieving Americans disarmed the overzealous officer and made him their prisoner. A short time later, Laws's men did appear in such numbers as to force his release and cause much consternation to the stalled American assault force.[36]

The fresh British troops quickly recaptured the first barricade, preventing any chance of withdrawal by the rebels. Heartened by the appearance of Laws's force, the British prisoners also turned on their former American captors. Trapped between the two barricades, what was left of Arnold's column held out until nearly ten o'clock. One in five of the Americans had been killed or wounded. Their spirit flagged as their numbers were reduced. They finally despaired of being relieved by Montgomery's force and began surrendering. Morgan, however, was defiant to the end. Backed against a wall, he refused to relinquish his sword to the British soldiers who encircled him and demanded it. Even when they threatened to shoot him on the spot if he did not submit, he scornfully stood his ground. The deadly impasse was broken when Morgan sighted a priest in the crowd of British troops. He handed the surprised clergyman his sword, angrily announcing, "Not a scoundrel of those cowards shall take it out of my hands." Thus ended the three-hour fight in the Lower Town. The Americans had come almost within reach of their objective, but it had eluded their grasp.[37]

Montgomery and his column of Yorkers were very much on the minds of Arnold's troops during their desperate struggle. The plan called for a combined effort against the British defenses in the Lower Town. They could not understand why the general had failed to keep his rendezvous and forsaken them in their hour of need. Not yet known to them, another catastrophe had befallen Montgomery and his men.

At about six o'clock earlier that morning, Montgomery and his men reached a timber palisade blocking their way into the Pres de Ville section of the Lower Town. There was no sign of any defenders at the obstacle, so Montgomery called on his pioneers to use their saws and axes in cutting an opening through the fifteen-foot-high picket fence. Leaving half of the pioneers there to finish the job for the main body, the general and his vanguard slipped through the breach and continued about a hundred yards to a second palisade. Still unchallenged by any sentries, Montgomery again ordered the pioneers to remove some pickets in the barrier to allow passage. He was concerned with advancing his troops past these obstacles as quickly as possible because he knew that every moment's delay increased their chances of discovery. He also worried about the slowness of his advance and wanted to link up with Arnold's force as soon as possible. In his impatience, Montgomery pushed several of the half-sawed posts out of the way with his own hands and edged through the opening. His aide, Captain Macpherson; the first company commander, Captain Cheeseman; and several others in his advance party accompanied him. Behind them, the main force had reached and began negotiating the first palisade. Peering through the snowy gloom Montgomery discerned the outlines of a two-story blockhouse guarding the entry to Pres de Ville.

The two palisades were so intimidating and the house in such an advantageous location to cover the open area before it, that the defenders apparently felt no need to place guards forward of these sites. Therefore, the house was the first occupied position Montgomery encountered. It was a simple frame structure near a potash works. The British converted it into a stronghold by cutting loopholes in the walls for muskets and mounting four small cannons in the upstairs windows. A motley garrison manned the fortified house. Some thirty Canadian militiamen and a handful of British seamen-gunners comprised the guard force. One of the militiamen observed Montgomery and his men passing through the barrier and alerted his comrades. The guardsmen made their cannons ready to fire and took up positions at the firing ports with readied muskets. They decided to hold their fire until the Americans advanced close enough to present a target that would be difficult to miss.

Back at the barricade, Montgomery heeded the sudden clamor and flurry of activity in the blockhouse. It was now obvious to him that the enemy knew of his presence and was preparing to repel his advance. He decided to attack the strongpoint before his adversaries had any more time to gird themselves for an engagement. Montgomery drew his sword and turned to the men behind him. "Come on, my good soldiers, your General Calls upon you to Come on." Leading the charge, Montgomery was less than fifty yards from the blockhouse when the hostile cannons began to roar. Grapeshot, followed by a fusillade of musket fire, downed most of the Americans who were in the front. The advance party was cut to pieces. Montgomery was killed during the first volley with grapeshot through the head and both thighs. Captains Macpherson and Cheeseman lay dead a few feet behind. Other bodies were sprawled nearby in the snow. A few dazed survivors fled back to the barricade.[38]

With the death of Montgomery, command fell on the shoulders of Colonel Campbell. At the sound of gunfire, he had hurried forward from his position with the main body. Upon reaching the second barricade, he surveyed the grisly scene before him—a battlefield littered with bodies from the advance party and under the guns of the blockhouse. The troops milling about him were demoralized over the loss of their general and their predicament. However, the outcome of the engagement was yet to be decided. The full weight of the American resources had not been brought to bear on the blockhouse. The main force of the column had not reached the second barrier and was still uncommitted to combat. This situation called for someone to rally the soldiers and press forward with the attack. Campbell proved incapable of the task thrust upon him.

Soldiers of the American army derived much of their courage from that of their leaders, and with Montgomery killed and Campbell unable to muster the mettle to replace him, the New Yorkers became an irresolute armed assemblage rather than an effective fighting force. Several unnerved officers joined Campbell and advised him against continuing. He readily agreed and ordered an immediate retreat. Turning his back on the Lower Town, he abandoned Arnold's force, leaving it to fend for itself. Reversing the column in its tracks, Campbell directed it back the way it had come, while taking charge of the rear guard.[39]

Leaving the unrecovered remains of Montgomery and his party on the battlefield only added to the disgrace of Campbell's action. The lifeless forms of Montgomery and the men who fell with him began accumulating a shroud of falling snow where they lay on the now silent field of battle. Macpherson did not live to receive the promotion for which he had been recommended. Montgomery never learned of his advancement to major general that Congress conferred on December 9 in recognition of his victorious leadership of the northern army.[40]

CHAPTER ELEVEN

Aftermath of Quebec

Every Tongue is loud in celebrating his Praises, and
lamenting his Fate; and on every Breast his distinguished
merit is written in Characters indelible. Among the first
Patriots and Heroes, the faithful Page of History will
perpetuate the name of Montgomerie.[1]

If a Martyr's sufferings merit a Martyr's Reward his
claim is indisputable. . . . He now rests from his Labour
and his Works can't but follow him.[2]

The bodies of Montgomery and his men lay undisturbed where
they fell for the rest of the day. The blockhouse guards did not
realize the significance of the action in which they had been
involved—that one prong of the American army had been turned back
and its commanding general slain. They could observe some of the attackers fall under their guns and the survivors withdraw, but they had no
way of discerning the extent of damage they had inflicted on their assail-
ant or whether the opposition would launch another attempt at their
position. Later that morning, when word came that an enemy force had
penetrated the Lower Town, several of the nervous guardsmen would
have abandoned their outpost if cooler heads had not prevailed. Although
Montgomery's death was not yet known to the British, it became apparent to all by that afternoon that they had repulsed a major attack by the
Americans on the city.[3]

Flush with his success in defending Quebec, Carleton sent a task force into the suburb of St. Roch to seize Wool's mortar battery, acquiring Lamb's derelict cannon on the way. They managed to rout the Americans from the battery but encountered unexpected resistance when they attempted to pursue them through the narrow streets. The artillerymen were joined by some reserve troops and improvised a holding action in the hamlet. Meanwhile, some soldiers ran to Arnold's headquarters in the general hospital to warn the colonel of an impending British attack. Bedridden after having the bullet removed from his leg, Arnold received the news with typical audacity. He ordered a gun issued to every wounded man in the hospital to resist the British, and he readied his brace of pistols and sword so that he could wield them from his bed. "He was determined to kill as many as possible if they came into the room," the doctor observed with awe. However, the British officers in St. Roch decided not to press the issue further. The task force returned to Quebec with the captured field pieces after setting fire to several houses.[4]

Once Wool reported the departure of the British from St. Roch, relative calm returned to Arnold's headquarters. The colonel dispatched a letter to General Wooster in Montreal, informing him of Montgomery's death and his failed attempt on Quebec. He also appraised his current situation as critical and requested immediate assistance from Wooster, who was now the ranking American officer in Canada. On his return from Pres de Ville, Campbell had sent Edward Antill to also notify Wooster of the American defeat at Quebec. In a series of subsequent letters to Wooster, Arnold continued his plea for reinforcements. "For God's sake, order as many men down as you can possibly spare, consistent with the safety of Montreal, and all the mortars, howitzers, and shells, that you can possibly bring." Despite his vulnerable plight, Arnold vowed to fight on. "I have no thoughts of leaving this proud town," he wrote his sister, "until I first enter it in triumph."[5]

In Quebec, the British celebrated their victory. "The Flower of the rebel army fell into our hands," Captain Ainslie elatedly depicted the battle. Another officer took a religious tone when accounting for their military success: "The Lord of Hosts severely smote our enemy; they were overwhelmed as with a whirlwind, and left us triumphant to gather them up and lead them into captivity." Colonel Caldwell predicted that the Americans' loss would discourage similar enterprises in the future: "The Quebec expedition will make them heartily sick of engaging in war out of their Provinces."[6]

On the morning of January 1, the British ventured outside the walls of Quebec to survey the battle sites and retrieve the dead. James Thompson, overseer of works in the engineer department of the garrison, accompanied a party from Pres de Ville. He was there to inspect the damage done to the barricades and order their repair. He also supervised the removal of the dead Americans. As the men found the frozen corpses and pulled them from the knee-deep snow, they came across an upward-thrust arm protruding from a white mound. After uncovering the body and upon closer examination, Thompson determined by the quality of his uniform that the man was a high-ranking officer. A bloody fur cap marked with the initials R. M. led Thompson to believe that these were the mortal remains of Montgomery. One grapeshot ball had entered the head through the chin, another had lodged in the groin, and a third had shattered the thigh bone. Beside the crumpled body lay a sword where it dropped when the violent, fatal impact of cannon fire wrenched it from Montgomery's outstretched arm. The ornate sword, fashioned with an ivory handle and a silver dogs-head pommel that befitted a general, heightened Thompson's suspicion that the recovered remains belonged to the rebel leader. He had the corpse carried inside Quebec, where it was recognized by the Widow Prentice, who operated an inn that Montgomery had patronized while serving with the British army. Carleton brought in some American prisoners to confirm her identification of their slain general.[7]

Although on opposite military sides at this time, Carleton respected the man that he had soldiered with in the war against France. The entire garrison admired Montgomery as an individual, even if they could not approve of his political transgressions. Few used harsh words when relating the death of their enemy. "Those who knew him formerly in this place, sincerely lament his late infatuation," Captain Ainslie wrote in his journal. "They say he was a genteel man, and an agreeable companion."[8]

Carleton ordered Montgomery buried with dignity but without elaborate ceremony in Quebec. While the governor wanted to treat Montgomery's remains with respect, he did not wish to further the cause of the rebellion by contributing to the mystique that he feared would be built around Montgomery's mourned demise. Thompson employed a craftsman to build a suitable coffin for the occasion. Many of the American prisoners grieved as they saw the general carried to his grave. "My heart was ready to burst with grief at viewing the funeral of our beloved general," wrote Private Henry. "Montgomery was beloved, because of his manliness of soul, heroic bravery, and suavity of manners." "He had the voluntary love, esteem, and confidence of the whole army," Major Meigs noted. "His death, though honourable, is lamented, not only as the death of an amiable, worthy friend, but as an experienced, brave general, whose country suffers greatly by such a loss at this time." At sunset on January 4, the British committed Montgomery's remains to a grave inside the St. Louis Gate. Macpherson and Cheeseman were also interred without coffins in the same plot. The Reverend de Montmollin, the garrison chaplain, performed the graveside service, with Carleton and a few British officers and Quebec citizens in attendance.[9]

It was difficult to ascertain the total casualties suffered during the assault. Although the British scavenged the battlefield, some bodies remained hidden by the snow until the spring thaw. Private Henry noted that "of commissioned officers we had six killed, five wounded," but he overestimated the figures for the rank and file as "at least one hundred and fifty killed and fifty or sixty wounded." Captain Dearborn probably rendered a more accurate accounting: "The Sergeants, Corporals, and privates, kill'd & wounded according to the best accounts I could obtain, Amounted to about one Hundred men, the number kill'd on the Spot, about 40." The British casualties were comparatively light. Carleton reported only one officer (Captain Anderson) and six enlisted men killed, with eleven rank and file wounded.[10]

In addition to the casualties, the Americans lost some four hundred men, fit and wounded, including thirty officers, who were captured by the British. Carleton proved to be a magnanimous captor. He imprisoned the Americans in the Upper Town, segregating the officers from the enlisted ranks. All the prisoners experienced good treatment. Carleton allowed the recovery of their baggage, arranged humane accommodations, and provided medical care for the wounded. Most of the captured Americans were apprehensive over the possibility of being sent to England and tried for treason. So, they were appreciative of Carleton's forebearing and benevolent attitude toward them. Henry referred to the governor as "an ornament such as would grace any nation." He even placed the British general in the company of his revered American personages. "If such men as Washington, Carleton, and Montgomery, had the entire direction of the adverse war, the contention, in the event, might have happily terminated to the advantage of both sections of the nation."[11]

With Henry and his fellow prisoners languishing in captivity, Arnold confined to his bed, and Campbell demoralized, the Americans understandably reflected on the events that led to the failure of their attack. The loss of both field commanders during the early stages of the assault suddenly and unexpectedly placed the American operation in jeopardy. When a debilitating wound forced Arnold out of action, Morgan admirably picked up the reins of leadership. He aggressively continued the assault in the Lower Town to overrun the first barricade. There, the Americans halted their advance to await reinforcements. If Morgan and his men had immediately pushed forward beyond the undefended second barricade, they might have been able to break into the Upper Town with little opposition. The breach could have caused enough panic and confusion for the British to induce their submission. Unfortunately, in a moment of indecision, they let the opportunity expire. During the crucial time in which the assault party regrouped, the British managed to assemble an impregnable defense of the barrier. If Arnold had been spared his injury and retained the command, it is difficult to believe that this pugnacious warrior would have allowed the assault to pause after reduction of the first barricade.

Colonel Caldwell, who was chiefly responsible for galvanizing the British effort in that sector, admitted: "Had they acted with more spirit, they might have pushed in at first and possessed themselves of the whole of Lower Town, and let their friends in at the other side, before our people had time to have recovered from a certain degree of panic, which seized them on the news of the post being surprised." Captain Ainslie, however, disagreed and offered a more optimistic scenario: "Allow for a moment that they had carried the Lower Town, they would have been but little advanc'd towards getting possession of the upper town, from whence we can burn the houses below us at any time. Shells wou'd soon have reduced it to a heap of rubbish." Still, most of the Americans believed that the Lower Town was the key to the walled city above. Possession of the second barricade undoubtedly would have encouraged them to seriously threaten the Upper Town. Their success would have been decided by the unpredictable situation created at that time.[12]

The conditions for an American victory certainly would have improved with the arrival of Montgomery's column in the Lower Town. The culmination of this force with that of Morgan, even after the initial opportune moment had slipped away, would have offered a significantly stronger challenge to the invincibility of the second barricade. The weight of this combined thrust might have provided enough impetus to tip the scales of battle in the Americans' favor. With Montgomery's untimely death, this challenge against the British defenses never materialized with its planned intensity. If Montgomery had survived or another instinctive leader such as Morgan had sprung forward to take his place, the New York contingent stood an excellent chance of defeating the blockhouse at Pres de Ville and linking up with their comrades in the Lower Town. All that was needed at this critical juncture was for someone to provide a steadying influence on the soldiers to continue the attack. The guard-house, manned by an ill-assorted group on the verge of panic and greatly outnumbered by the Americans, stood as the only remaining obstruction between the column and Quebec. A forceful assault by the Yorkers probably would have sent the defenders fleeing and opened the way to their objective. Instead, it was the Americans who fled when Campbell showed his lack of courage under fire. The troops saw through his previous facade of bluster and posturing and refused to follow him. With no redeemer forthcoming after Montgomery's death, the American effort died at Pres de Ville, a failure that ultimately doomed the entire opera-tion. Arnold expressed this contention when writing of Montgomery: "Had he been properly supported by his troops, I make no doubt of our success." [13]

As Arnold lamented what could have been and scribbled letters while propped up in his bed, he also began to plan for future operations. Fearing a counterstrike from Carleton, some of his officers urged him to withdraw into the countryside. Arnold would not entertain such tactics. He ordered a blockade of the city with what meager forces he had left while waiting for reinforcements. Some six hundred men were available to Arnold after the failed attack on Quebec. Of these, more than one hundred whose enlistments had expired left for home. They were joined by a number of deserters who had experienced their fill of war. "I hope you will stop every rascal who has deserted from us and bring him back again," Arnold wrote Wooster. Arnold also wanted someone more active to assume command of the expedition while he recuperated from his wound. At first, he selected Colonel Campbell to relieve him. However, Arnold soon heard the details of Campbell's conduct at Pres de Ville and took back the command. For two months, the wounded combatant ran the emaciated army and the blockade of Quebec from his bedside. [14]

The men who participated in the assault on Quebec composed a microcosm of the Continental army in 1775. There was Montgomery in the lead charging into the mouth of the enemy's cannon. He represented the purists or idealists who sought no personal reward from the war but fought because they believed in the principles of the cause. Beside him was Arnold, the confident and adept officer who characterized those who embraced the military as a means to satisfy their pent-up ambitions. Behind came Campbell and men of his ilk, with hidden, personal agendas for their involvement in the enterprise and questionable staunchness of character. Also along was Morgan, portraying the troops who joined the army to vent their physical aggressiveness. Lamb, who personified the radical revolutionary, was prominent as well. Then, there was the seventeen-year-old Henry, symbolizing the restless young men who enlisted in a quest for adventure and maturity. Still, there were nameless others who were composites of these sundry traits. Collectively, they pointed out the multisided character of the first Continental soldiers and shattered the myth of the monolithic duty-filled patriot freedom fighter.

Carleton was content to remain within the confines of Quebec after repulsing the American attack. Although his available forces now had a four-to-one advantage over that of the Americans, the governor rejected any offensive action against the tenuous blockade that Arnold defiantly maintained. Carleton was generally hailed as the savior of Quebec, yet even some of his officers criticized him for not delivering a coup de grace to the American expedition after their abortive attack. "The general did not choose to risk anything further," wrote Colonel Caldwell. "His ideas seemed entirely to centre in the preservation of the town, certain of succours arriving in the spring; nor did he seem to carry his views towards the operations of the summer campaign, which might have been much forwarded by the entire rout of the enemy." Cautious by nature, Carleton interpreted his primary mission as a defensive one of safeguarding Quebec proper. Uncertain of how many troops Arnold still fielded, he was not willing to venture a major engagement with the Americans on their terms. To send his soldiers outside the safety of the walled city in pursuit of Arnold's force would be a foolhardy dereliction of duty, he reasoned. He surely also considered that this was the blunder by which the French had lost Quebec in 1759. Successful so far in his defensive strategy, it made good sense to Carleton to continue holding the Americans at bay until British reinforcements arrived in April.[15]

If Carleton was not disposed toward destruction or dispersal of the Americans surrounding Quebec, Arnold certainly had no means to force the situation to a climax. Therefore, the Quebec campaign settled into an impasse that would last for the winter.

In spite of Arnold's pressing requests for reinforcements, Wooster was unwilling to immediately leave Montreal. He had a garrison of only five hundred to six hundred troops to hold that city, as well as Chambly and St. Johns, and he feared a Canadian uprising. He was also concerned with securing Montreal to provide a route of withdrawal from Quebec if retreat became necessary. So, he dispatched an urgent appeal to Seth Warner to send his Green Mountain Boys to Canada "as fast as they are collected." Then, Wooster sent Antill and Moses Hazen with a letter to Albany to inform Schuyler of the failed attack on Quebec. "I shall not be able to spare any Men to reinforce Colo: Arnold. . . . I have therefore sent Colo: Clinton and Mr. Price who I think may be of great service to him." [16]

Schuyler was overwhelmed by the news of Montgomery's death. He had valued him as his personal friend as well as his able field commander. Schuyler was concerned that the loss of Montgomery cast future Canadian operations in great peril. He sent a letter to Congress, explaining the tragedy, and he also wrote a "melancholy account" to Washington. "My amiable friend, the gallant Montgomery, is no more; the brave Arnold is wounded; and we have met with a severe check, in an unsuccessful attempt on Quebec. May Heaven be graciously pleased that the misfortune may terminate here." Schuyler's inability to send support to Quebec compounded his grief. His hopes for prompt relief of the Canadian expedition rested with Washington. In Schuyler's letter to his commander, he stated: "I tremble for our people in Canada . . . nothing . . . seems left to prevent the most fatal consequences, but an immediate reinforcement, that is nowhere to be had, but from you." [17]

Washington received Schuyler's letter on the evening of January 17. He also deplored the demise of one of his most competent generals. "In the Death of this Gentleman," Washington wrote to Schuyler, "America has sustained a heavy Loss, as he had approved himself a steady Friend to her Rights and of Ability to render her the most essential Services." The next day he called a council of war to consider the crisis in Canada. The council resolved "that in the present feeble state of the Regiments here, It was improper to detach any force from these Lines to Quebec or Canada." The siege of Boston, like that of Quebec, had turned into a seemingly endless stalemate that sapped the morale of the American soldiers. Rampant desertions combined with low recruitment rates to undermine the combat efficiency of the Continental army. In addition, Washington was engaged in a major reorganization of his army while trying to maintain pressure on the British in Boston. This rebuilding program was necessary to compensate for the short-term militia units that were leaving en masse now that they had completed their original commitment. "It would give me the greatest Happiness, if I could be the happy Means of relieving our Fellow Citizens now in Canada," Washington replied to Schuyler. "But it is not in my power." "In short I have not a Man to spare," he groaned. A reallocation of some of the units to be raised for the Boston army, and a plea to Congress and the various colonies for increased military manpower, was the best that the commander in chief could do for the Canadian operation at this time.[18]

After notifying Schuyler, Antill and Hazen continued to Philadelphia to apprise Congress of the situation in Canada. On January 18, Antill, who had been with Montgomery during the assault, testified for two hours before the congressional delegates. Congress had already authorized nine battalions for the Canadian campaign on January 8, even before news of the attack on Quebec reached them. However, incentive to push the measure to fruition had been lacking. The repulse of the American forces in Canada aroused more congressional attention in considering the needs of the northern army. Congress adopted an extensive series of resolves concerning affairs in Canada during the next several days.[19]

The initial inclination of Congress in respect to Montgomery's death was to keep the loss as quiet as possible. The delegates feared that news of the disaster might plunge the patriot movement into despair or even dissolution. One member "moved in a florid Speech that the Delegates may wear Mourning (a Crape round the left Arm) for One Month for Montgomery," and another desired to arrange a sermon honoring the general's mortality. A third proposed a public monument be erected to his memory. Congress turned down these actions "on the Ground that no Mourning is ever worn by any Courts on such Accounts & that the General is already embalmed in the Heart of every good American and that such Proceeding may cause too much alarm at such a critical Juncture."[20]

The circumstances of Montgomery's tragic death provoked a widespread catharsis, calling into question the manner in which the Congress and colonial authorities had prosecuted the war. Criticism leveled at government officials ranged from a seeming lack of will in decisively conducting the patriot military effort to short-term enlistment policies and scarcity of resources allocated to support the armed conflict.

Lieutenant Colonel Ritzema, stationed with Wooster at Montreal, was one of the first to lash out in frustration against what he perceived as the government's neglect of the northern army. Stunned after hearing of the events in Quebec, he fired off a letter to Pierre Van Cortlandt, chairman of the New York Committee of Safety. "Our misfortune is in great measure owing to the anxiety some of the troops were under of returning home," he wrote. "This I trust will be a warning to America not to enlist men for any limited time." "I will venture to say," he continued, "that unless a change takes place in this respect, America must fall a sacrifice to her enemies." "We are now in a wretched plight," Ritzema observed in the letter, "our excellent general dead and defeated—a great probability that the flower of his army is cut to pieces—the soldiers mutinous, and with little discipline, not a sous to pay them with, which makes them so." "For God's sake, sir, exert yourself," he exclaimed. "I have exaggerated nothing; let us have men and money, otherwise, by Heavens, Canada is lost."[21]

Gen. John Sullivan, who was with Washington outside Boston, wrote to the New Hampshire Assembly to give his assessment of the Quebec disaster. "Upon my soul, it gives me pain to find that our Continental chest is so often empty," the general asserted, "and that parsimony and indolence, which has destroyed so many powerful States, is but too likely to destroy ours." "To this, alone, was owing that fatal defeat at Quebec, as the deceased Montgomery's letters will fully show," he concluded. "For he seemed to prophesy his defeat from the want of money to pay off the troops."[22]

Such complaints prompted the political leadership to significantly widen their concept of opposition to British rule. Congress came to regard the Canadian campaign less as an adjunct operation. Now, most delegates fixed on the possession of Canada as a vital issue in the Americans' struggle against Britain. This called for a deeper commitment to produce the assets needed to pour into an expanded war effort.

"Your Letter to Congress respecting the unfortunate Death of General Montgomery and the Disaster of his Troops pierced every Heart," a congressional delegate wrote to Schuyler. "I sincerely Sympathize with you the Loss of that brave officer." "I know your affliction must be great for in him you have lost a most Valuable Friend and an officer in whom you deservedly put the greatest Confidence," he consoled, "but Such is Heaven's Will, and let us Acquiesce in the Divine Providence." "What Aid Congress Mean to give the Northern Army you have," he assured the general. "I hope a steady Attention will be given to that important Affair." "Measures are now taken by Congress, which I trust will reduce

Carleton & his few troops before the End of February," another member wrote his provincial congress. "Had one third of the Succours been sent Montgomery, in all human probability, the Life of that brave and gallant Officer had been saved & Quebec long e'er this in our Possession." [23]

Samuel Chase, a Maryland delegate, demonstrated an early enthusiasm for backing the conquest of Canada. He wrote to John Adams: "I think the Success of the War will, in great Measure, depend on Securing Canada to our Confederation." John Adams agreed with his colleague, and most of his fellow members would shortly come to accept this precept. In a letter to his close friend in the Massachusetts Congress, James Warren, Adams expressed the overwhelming feeling in the Continental Congress: "The Unanimous Voice of the Continent is Canada must be ours, Quebec must be taken." [24]

Strangely, Montgomery's brother-in-law, Robert R. Livingston, was among the few delegates who disapproved of the Canadian campaign. "When the expedition agt. Canada was first projected I opposed it," he said. "It is indisputable that the possession of Canada will drain us of our specie, disapate without ading to our strength," he prophetically stated. The acquiescence that built in Congress toward projection of patriot military operations in Canada swept away the objections of Livingston and the small number of like-minded members. [25]

Washington had a keen understanding of the sentiments that developed in Congress during this time. He welcomed its realization of the critical outcome of the Canadian campaign and the long-needed emphasis by that body on proper military support. At the end of January, he wrote to Wooster: "I need not mention to you the Importance of Canada in the scale of our Affairs—to whomsoever It belongs, in their favour probably, will the Ballance Turn—If it is ours, success will crown our virtuous Struggles—If our Enemies, the Contest at best, will be doubtful, hazardous & bloody—Government being fully convinced of these facts, will most assuredly send a Strong & considerable Reinforcement to Quebec early in the Spring." In a subsequent letter to his confidant, Lt. Col. Joseph Reed, Washington reiterated how the recent tragedy at Quebec had been turned into a long-term military advantage for the American army: "But for the loss of the Gallant Chief [Montgomery] & his brave Followers I should think the re-buff rather favourable than otherwise; for had the Country [Canada] been subdued by such a handful of Men 'tis more than probable that it would have been left to the defense of a few, & rescued [retaken] from us in the Spring—Our eyes will now, not only be open to the Importance of holding it, but the numbers which are requisite to that end." [26]

During the first few months of 1776, momentum intensified in the government for a revived sustainment of Canadian operations. However, the issue of short-term enlistments was a different matter. Like most in the colonies, members of Congress and provincial officials possessed an ingrained fear of establishing a standing army, lest it encourage a military dictatorship and loose the troops against the civilian sector of American society. The idea prevailed that the army should be composed of part-time citizen-soldiers following the historical example of Cincinnatus, a farmer who twice joined the legion to save Rome, and both times returned to his plow as soon as the crisis had passed. Enrolling soldiers in the Continental army for extended periods of duty smacked of a menacing military establishment that the civil officials were trying to guard against. On the other hand, the Quebec experience graphically pointed out the inefficiency of the enlistment program in use. Military leaders were convinced that the high turnover rate of soldiers, leading to an undependable troop strength and organization for combat, represented the underlying bane of the army's ability to protect the country against the British. In their view, establishment of a professional army for the Americans was essential to the successful outcome of the struggle against England, because it provided the only hope to stand up to the seasoned British redcoats. [27]

Washington laid out these concerns to the president of Congress during the first part of February 1776. "The disadvantages attending the limited Inlistment of Troops, is too apparent to those who are eye witness of them to render any animadversions necessary," he wrote to John Hancock. "That this cause precipitated the fate of the brave, and much to be lamented Genl Montgomerie, & brought on the defeat which followed thereupon, I have not the most distant doubt of," he stated, "for had he not been apprehensive of the Troops leaving him at so important a crisis, but continued the Blockade of Quebec, a Capitulation, from the best Accts I have been able to collect, must inevitably have followed." Professing that "I have nothing more in view than what to me appears necessary to advance the publick Weal," Washington went on to recommend to Congress that it extend the length of service requirement for the military by obligating recruits to serve until the end of hostilities. [28]

Civilian authorities began to seriously reevaluate the enlistment issue after Quebec. Still, they harbored much recalcitrance toward the tradition-breaking action of lengthening the time for military service. On January 19, 1776, Congress defeated an initial motion that troops be enlisted for three years or as long as the war continued. An emotional discussion ensued over the issue. One delegate, Roger Sherman of Connecticut, expressed his opposition that "long enlistment is a state of slavery. There ought to be a rotation which is in favor of liberty." John Adams, a Massachusetts delegate, endorsed the proposal for long-term enlistments only if administered on a voluntary basis, "as men must be adverse to it—war may last 10 years." As arguments such as that of Washington mounted, however, Congress reluctantly moved toward extension of enlistment periods. The delegates appointed a three-person committee, comprised of Benjamin Franklin, Samuel Chase, and Charles Carroll, to go to Canada to study the situation and make recommendations. On May 17, 1776, the commission reported: "The inlisting Men for a year, or for a less time occasioned the Death of the brave Montgomery . . . & is the principal Source of all the disorders in your Army." [29]

Even with this corroboration, it was not until September 16, 1776, that Congress decided to procure enlistments in the Continental army for the duration of the war. On September 24, 1776, John Hancock, president of Congress, notified the states of these resolves to "engage the Troops to serve during the Continuance of the War." He then explained the thinking of Congress on the subject at that time. "The many ill Consequences arising from a short and limited Inlistment of Troops, are too obvious to be mentioned," he stated before citing Montgomery's reverse at Quebec as the determining case in point. "Without a well disciplined Army we can never expect Success against veteran Troops," he admonished, "unless our Troops are engaged to serve during the War." Thus, Congress opened the way for the professionalization of the American army. It might not have happened but for Montgomery's tragic death at Quebec. [30]

While debate over military enlistment policies percolated in Congress, the delegates also reconsidered the method by which Montgomery's death would be officially sanctioned. Soon after the original decision to downplay the loss, it became obvious from the amount of public mourning for the fallen general that this governmental position was untenable. Letters, popular ballads and poems, public speeches, newspaper articles, and broadsides carried the name of Montgomery throughout the colonies. The *Pennsylvania Gazette*, for example, epitomized Montgomery as the most appealing kind of soldier during that time. "The loss of General

Montgomery," wrote the editor, "who well understood the duties of a soldier and the citizen and generously endured the fatigues of one for the sake of securing the rights of the other, is greatly regretted by every lover of mankind." The traditional practice of not speaking ill of one recently deceased could account for some of the courtesy paid to Montgomery, but the magnitude of the homage far surpassed what would be expected from this social convention. To capitalize on this outpouring of popular adoration, Congress began extolling Montgomery as a martyr for the patriot cause.[31]

During this early period of the Revolution, conflicting loyalties divided the country. Many colonists maintained equivocal attitudes toward the conflict with Britain and hoped for eventual reconciliation with the mother country. Even moderate patriots such as Robert R. Livingston, who approved of some sort of independence from Britain, questioned whether the movement toward that ultimate goal was proceeding too fast and recklessly. The patriot faction needed a rallying point to pull its activism together and stimulate public opinion against Britain. Montgomery's death filled this requirement perfectly.

If someone had set out to design an ideal martyr for the cause of liberty, they could not have done better than Montgomery. He embodied all the necessary credentials for martyrdom. His personal life was beyond reproach, and his professional life commanded respect from friend and foe alike. Also, he could not be dismissed as a knee-jerk radical. Characterized by reason and temperance, his reputation appealed to a large swath of the population, both liberal and conservative. He had been on the other side while serving in the British army, but obviously he had appreciated the signs of British tyranny and joined the American patriots. His ultimate sacrifice at Quebec earned him a hero's status.

Congress hoped that Montgomery's unselfish, truly virtuous participation in the Revolution would encourage others to follow his precedent. On January 25, the delegates resolved to order a monument that would be established to Montgomery's fame. "It being not only a tribute of gratitude justly due to the memory of those who have peculiarly distinguished themselves in the glorious cause of liberty, to perpetuate their names by the most durable Monuments erected to their honour," Congress explained, "but, also, greatly conducive to inspire posterity with an emulation of their illustrious actions." The monument would serve to "express the veneration of the United Colonies for their late General, Richard Montgomery," the resolution read, "and for transmitting to future ages, as examples truly worthy of imitation, his patriotism, conduct, boldness of enterprise, insuperable perseverance, and contempt of danger and death."[32]

Congress also scheduled a state memorial service for Montgomery and selected the Reverend William Smith to deliver a eulogy. The appointment of Dr. Smith, who was the provost of the College and Academy of Philadelphia, precipitated a highly controversial event. Ironically, the loyalist faction tried to use Montgomery's fame on this occasion for their own purposes. Unbeknown to most of the members of Congress who knew him only by his professional reputation, Smith was a latent loyalist.

The ceremony on February 19, 1776, was conducted at the new Reformed Calvinist Church in Philadelphia with pomp and ceremony. A New Hampshire delegate, Josiah Bartlett, described the service in a letter to his wife: "The Congress, the General Assembly of this province, the Committees of Safety and inspection, and about 30 Clergymen of the Different Denominations in this City, with other Gentlemen, walked from the Court house, in a Body, to the Church, on Each Side walked three Regiments of the City associators. The musick was very solemn & mournful, and composed with the organs, Bass viol, 8 or 10 violins, German flutes, French horns &c, the whole was Conducted with great order & Decency." A clergyman, Henry Muhlenberg, also commented on the ritual in his journal:

> The procession was arranged as follows: (a) The students of the English Academy. (b) The preachers of all denominations in the city and the teachers of all facilities in the Academy. (c) The Congress of the united provinces. (d) The provincial Assembly. (e) The corporation of the city, i.e. the mayor, etc. (f) The committees of the city and its suburbs. (g) The battalions of the associated city militia, which marched along either side in order that the countless throngs of people might not crush the procession. All the bells in and around the city were tolled in token of mourning. But the church was much too small. In the church vocal and instrumental music was rendered, which broke into the oration several times and was intended to give an impression of various scenes in the siege, and the drums outside, in the front of the church, joined in at given signals.[33]

Smith's oration was extremely laudatory of Montgomery, but during the course of his address the minister's sentiments toward reconciliation with Britain were subtly revealed. Smith resorted to a misrepresentation of fact when he claimed that Montgomery and Schuyler shared in this loyalist view: "His [Montgomery's] principles of loyalty to his Sovereign (whom he had long served, and whose true glory consists in healing those streaming wounds) remained firm and unshaken. . . . He most ardently joined his worthy friend, General Schuyler, in praying that 'Heaven may speedily re-unite us in every bond of affection and interest; and that the British empire may again become the envy and admiration of the universe, and flourish' till the consummation of earthly things." In his address, Smith also chastised some of his fellow clergymen and academicians for their patriot leanings: "God forbid that any of the profession to which I belong, should ever . . . prostitute their voice to inflame men's minds to the purposes of wild ambition, or mutual destruction."[34]

The flagrant attempt of Smith to propagandize his oration in behalf of the loyalist faction infuriated the patriot-minded delegates. When a member moved to thank Smith for his oration on Montgomery, it "was objected to for several reasons; the chief was that the Dr. declared the Sentiments of the Congress to continue in a Dependency on G Britain which doctrine this Congress cannot now approve." John Adams voiced the outrage of the patriot faction that influenced Congress on this issue: "The oration was an insolent Performance. . . . A Motion was made to Thank the orator and ask a Copy—But opposed with great Spirit, and Vivacity from every Part of the Room, and at last withdrawn, lest it should be rejected as it certainly would have been with Indignation." "The orator then printed it himself," he noted, "after leaving out or altering some offensive Passages." Adams then conceded, "The appointment of him to make the oration, was a great oversight, and mistake." This embarrassing incident served as a reminder to the more radical patriot leadership that constant vigilance must be maintained against opposing forces lurking within their midst.[35]

Proponents of the conflict with Britain continued to take advantage of Montgomery's acclaim to build support for their cause. A theme that surfaced in the campaign of words was one of reprisal and vengeance for Montgomery's death and the humiliating failure at Quebec. "Poor Brave Montgomery! but it is not a time to cry but to revenge," Gen. Charles Lee wrote after learning that the British had killed his fellow general. This broad refrain of reprisal had been used successfully earlier by the Sons of Liberty to direct public hatred against the British after various so-called military atrocities such as the Boston Massacre. Publicists seized on Montgomery as a consummate subject to wage their rhetorical battle throughout the Revolution.[36]

Thomas Paine was the foremost of these patriot authors to incorporate Montgomery in his literature. Paine had already written his *Common Sense* before he learned of Montgomery's death. This pamphlet, which originally appeared in Philadelphia on January 10, 1776, made bold, direct attacks on the British monarchy for the first time. Previous grievances generated in the colonies had sidestepped this institution held sacred by most Englishmen and narrowly focused on the British Parliament and the ministerial army. With his next work, *A Dialogue between the Ghost of General Montgomery Just Arrived from the Elysian Fields; And an American Delegate in a Wood Near Philadelphia*, the best-known American pamphleteer amplified the idea of independence he had advanced in *Common Sense*. In this imaginary dialogue with a delegate to the Continental Congress, the ghost of Montgomery moralized: "I am here upon an important errand, to warn you against listening to terms of accommodation from the court of Britain. . . . It was no small mortification to me when I fell upon the Plains of Abraham, to reflect that I did not expire like the brave General Wolfe, in the arms of victory. But I now no longer envy him his glory. I would rather die in attempting to obtain permanent freedom for a handful of people, than survive a conquest which would serve only to extend the empire of despotism." Paine published this pamphlet in June 1776, the time when Congress appointed a committee to draft the Declaration of Independence. Paine's composition was very instrumental in blunting loyalist and conservative Whig arguments against this congressional instrument and leading public thinking toward an acceptance of independence.[37]

The next year, Hugh Henry Brackenridge published the pamphlet play, *The Death of General Montgomery*. This was a sequel to his earlier propaganda drama, *The Battle of Bunker's-Hill*, released the year before. In this latest offering, Brackenridge continued writing in the heroic tragedy style to arouse the colonists against the British. In it, he recounted the legendary deeds of Montgomery at Quebec and condemned the British for his death. The play reflects how vilification in protest rhetoric by this time had extended to Englishmen in general.

> When men far off, in civilized states . . .
> In every language, they shall execrate,
> The earth-disgracing name of Englishmen.
> And at the Last Day, when the pit receives
> Her gloomy brood . . .
> Pointing to him, the foul and ugly Ghosts

Of Hell, shall say,
That was an Englishman."[38]

In addition to mourning the loss of a fellow officer, Continental army leaders used Montgomery's self-sacrificing military prowess as an object lesson to stimulate lagging enlistments and promote military discipline and morale among their troops. Nathanael Greene, one of Washington's best generals, reflected this thinking in a letter to John Adams. "The monuments you are erecting to the great heroes Warren, Montgomery, and Mercer will be a pleasing circumstance to the army in general," he wrote, "and at the same time, a piece of justice due to the bravery of the unfortunate generals." "Patriotism is a glorious principle," he added, "but never refuse her the necessary aids." Greene also proposed that a number of medals be struck of these heroic figures "to animate the living to great and worthy actions."[39]

To honor Montgomery, the Continental military named after him one of the forts established on the Hudson River to guard against a British incursion. In addition, Congress commissioned a warship *Montgomery;* and various colonies, including New York, Maryland, Pennsylvania, and Rhode Island, christened privateers under the registry Montgomery.[40]

By 1778, as hostilities dragged on with no end in sight and revolutionary spirit very much on the wane, attempts emerged to revive the public's resolve. An instance that typified this period of appealing to the hearts and minds of the populace occurred in Boston. City officials, led by Samuel Adams, organized a civic ceremony on March 5 to commemorate the eighth anniversary of the Boston Massacre. A committee asked Jonathan Williams Austin to deliver the oration. Like so many orators before him, Austin selected Montgomery as his principal subject. In his impassioned speech intended to rekindle the ebbing emotions of the citizenry, he asked his audience: "Shall the frequent Calls of our Exalted General [Montgomery], who seems to be raised up by Heaven, to show to what height Humanity may soar; who generously sacrificing affluence and domestic life, wishes to share with you in every danger and distress, shall his frequent calls be in vain?" Then he exhorted them: "Let not the ashes of Warren, Montgomery, and the illustrious Roll of Heroes, who died for Freedom, reproach our inactivity and want of spirit, in not completing this grand Superstructure [Revolution]; the Pillars of which have been cemented with the richest blood of America."[41]

Even though Montgomery proved to be one of the most able military commanders during his brief duty in the Continental army, it would seem that he provided just as valuable service to the Revolution after his death. Patriot propagandists evoked his name throughout the conflict when calling upon their pens to augment the sword of the Continental soldier. Their effusion of patriotic spirit, call to arms, and declamation against the British earned them and Montgomery a place in the American psyche of the period.

Montgomery also had a significant impact on British perceptions of the Revolution. The Whig or opposition political faction used his virtuous example to its advantage when denouncing the government for its colonial policies. British opposition statesmen pointed to Montgomery's character to refute the ministerial argument that American rebels were nothing more than uncouth, renegade provincials. This resulted in a legitimation of the Revolution in the eyes of many Englishmen and a softening of their attitude toward the conflict. On March 11, 1776, a few days after the British government received an account of Quebec, Whig leaders Edmund Burke and Charles James Fox eulogized Montgomery in the House of Commons. Prime Minister Lord Frederick North, who was in attendance, acknowledged Montgomery's attributes but spoke against what he called "this unqualified liberality of the praises bestowed on General Montgomery by the gentlemen in Opposition, because they were bestowed on a Rebel." Fox countered by reminding the ministers that they "owed the Constitution which enabled them to sit in that House to a rebellion."[42]

The London opposition press reflected the tribute given Montgomery in Parliament by the Whigs. The *Evening Post* bordered the March 12 edition in mourning black and commented that North would never be able to convince Englishmen that Montgomery was nothing but a common rebel. *Scot's Magazine* compared Montgomery to a national hero, General Wolfe:

> In Abram's plains they lie interr'd
> the virt'ous and the brave:
> Among the rest no more preferr'd
> than bold Montgomery's grave.

The articles lionizing Montgomery became so plentiful that a loyal Londoner grew tired of reading the commendations of the American general and submitted a retort to the editor of the *General Evening Post*.

"Encomiums on the death of Montgomery having been admitted into some of the public papers, you are desired to give a place to the following Contrast in your next."

> Montgomery dies;—from his ill-boding fall,
> Ah! wisdom learn, ye mad Provincials all.
> Alike, alas! Montgomery to thee,
> The fatal bullet, or the fatal tree.
> Who fights and falls in foul Rebellion's cause,
> From Virtue's friends can ne'er deserve applause:
> Ambition's dupe, a lawless Faction's tool,
> Must live a madman, and must die a fool.
> Here read thy character, thy peril, Lee;
> A traitors name, a traitors destiny.

The *Morning Post* published another poem, "The Siege of Quebec," that ridiculed the fallen American general who had received so much public attention from the British:

> Montgomery fell among the dead.
> Arnold and Campbell—wiser—fled!
> Gen'rals surpass their troops in cunning,
> And there fore should excel in running.

Although loyal English newspapers retaliated against the widespread proliferation of respect and sympathy for Montgomery, the damage had been done. The British political opposition occupied the high ground and the conservatives could only snipe at them. The power of the press initiative remained with the Whig faction on this issue.[43]

A few years later, the Reverend James Murray published a book, *An Impartial History of the Present War in America.* In it, he summed up the sentiments of many of his fellow Englishmen toward Montgomery after Quebec. "Thus fell Richard Montgomery in the cause of liberty, fighting as he believed, and as unbiased reason will in after ages determine, for the rights of human nature and of his country, against the illegal encroachments of a British ministry. . . . His many and excellent qualities, and agreeable disposition, had procured him an uncommon state of both public and private esteem, and there was perhaps no person engaged on the same side, and few on either, whose loss would have been more regretted both in Britain and America."[44]

Scholars have long questioned why the British were ostensibly dilatory in prosecuting the Revolution. Time after time, the British army fretted away their military advantage and failed to force the Continental army into a climactic battle that would hasten an end to the rebellion. This tactical ambivalence was attended by a long succession of British military commanders. Political leadership in Parliament was similarly unstable during the conflict, evidenced by the strong opposition faction. Many have attributed these conditions to a lack of British national will to conduct the war more forcefully. General ambivalence on the English home front toward the colonial problem resulted in a fragile base to reunite the empire. Regard for Montgomery unfolded as an important factor in shaping British public opinion during this decisive period. In this respect, Montgomery's spirit transcended politics and boundaries, and was able to influence both sides of the Revolution.

Epilogue

A very distinguished Officer, who sacrificed his life in support of the liberties of America . . . the edict of the intelligent & brave Montgomery, whose name will be immortal . . . [1]

Montgomery (whose name is recorded in the annals of Fame, there to stand in conspicuous characters until time shall be no more) . . . [2]

After Montgomery's repulse at Quebec, the American government experienced an awakened intensity regarding the Canadian campaign and began funneling resources to the northern army. Slowly, troops and matériel built up. On the first of April 1776, when Wooster finally came to Quebec to assume command, the American force numbered two thousand troops. However, Arnold could not get along with Wooster because of personality conflicts. When Arnold reinjured his leg in an accident with his horse shortly after Wooster's arrival, he used this excuse to retire to Montreal, leaving his superior in charge of the siege. Wooster bombarded the city with artillery and tried to assume the military initiative, but his attempts amounted to no more than inconsequential harassment to the enemy.

On May 1, Gen. John Thomas, a more capable and active officer, superseded Wooster. Six days later, before Thomas could organize any serious action against Quebec, a British relief fleet arrived. The fifteen ships contained Gen. John Burgoyne, eight army regiments, and two thousand German mercenaries. The British had won in the race with the Americans to deliver a substantial reinforcement to Quebec. This spelled the end of the American siege of Quebec. With his increased troop strength, Carleton now felt confident in taking the fight to the Americans, who numbered about twenty-five hundred men at this time. The British commander wasted no time in launching a vigorous attack on the besiegers. Overpowered, Thomas's troops beat a hasty retreat, leaving much of their equipment behind when they fled. Exacerbating the problem, Thomas became ill with the smallpox that had helped in decimating his army. On June 2, while his force was retreating to Chambly, he died.

Field command of the Canadian campaign now devolved upon Brig. Gen. John Sullivan, who had recently arrived at St. Johns with a brigade of fresh troops. Sullivan combined his men with the remnants of Thomas's force and set out on a second march on Quebec. He was met by the British at Trois-Rivières, about halfway between Montreal and Quebec. The Americans suffered one calamity after another as the British pushed them back in a series of engagements. With their casualties mounting and in danger of being surrounded by the British, survival of Sullivan's force became critical. More and more, the American fate in Canada appeared doomed to failure. Even the relentless Arnold now advised that there was "more honor in making a safe retreat than in hazarding a battle against such superiority." "The junction of the Canadians with the Colonies, an object which brought us into this country, is now at an end," he wrote Sullivan. "Let us quit them and secure our own country before it is too late."[3]

Congress received the discouraging reports from Canada in a gloomy mood and pondered the causes of the misfortunes. In the minds of many delegates, the loss of Montgomery's military leadership dealt a fatal blow to the campaign. "Since the Death of Montgomery," John Adams reflected, "We have had no General in Command there [Canada] who Seems to have had a full and comprehensive View of the State of that Province, to have watched the Motions in every Part, or concerted his measures with any System." Sullivan might have received more criticism than he deserved for his brief, inglorious part in the Canadian campaign. As his subsequent service with the Continental army demonstrated, he was an adequately capable and courageous general. During his command in Canada, he experienced the same problems that confronted Montgomery earlier. While Montgomery found ways of working through these difficulties, Sullivan was overwhelmed by them and unable to hold his army together as an effective fighting force. His censure stemmed from instinctive comparisons drawn with Montgomery, and almost any general would pale under such a correlation. Some never fully appreciated Montgomery's ability and achievements under the circumstances he faced until the actions of his successors were beheld.[4]

On June 17, 1775, Congress ordered Gen. Horatio Gates to take command of the Continental troops in Canada. During the last of June, Sullivan's exhausted and demoralized men straggled into Crown Point. By July, the Americans had fallen all the way back to Fort Ticonderoga where the Canadian operation had begun, and Canada was once again in the hands of the British. On July 6, 1776, a grateful British government nominated Carleton for knighthood. Thus, within ten months, the army that had set out in September 1775 to conquer Canada was reduced by what Dr. Isaac Senter, a participant throughout the entire campaign, described as "a heterogeneal concatenation of the most peculair and unparalleled rebuffs and sufferings that are perhaps to be found in the annals of any nation."[5]

The Canadian campaign may be dismissed in a strict sense as a waste of resources and a dismal failure for the Americans. Yet, in a wider view, the operation can be recognized as serving a valuable end. Although Quebec was not captured or Canada conquered, Montgomery's offensive forced the British forces in Canada into a prolonged life-or-death struggle well within the interior of their northern province. By keeping Carleton's forces thus occupied, the expedition relieved the American colonies from any threat of a British aggression from the north during that period of time. Montgomery's efforts delayed the British from attempting to execute the Hudson Highlands strategy of invading New York and isolating the Continental forces in New England. This certainly eased a major concern of Washington with his army surrounding Boston. The siege of Boston resulted in the greatest American military accomplishment during the first year of the Revolution, but it was not won in Massachusetts alone. By pinning down Carleton and his army in Canada for almost a year, Montgomery precluded his coming to the aid of the beleaguered British forces in Boston. When the British government sent reinforcements from England during 1776, some were diverted to relieve Quebec. The dissipated troop deployment prevented any major reinforcement of the besieged British soldiers in Boston. This lack of troop concentration in Boston to effect a breakout helped in the British decision to evacuate the city in the spring of 1776. Thus, the American incursion into Canada played a major role in securing New England during the initial stage of the Revolution. Therefore, when considering the Canadian campaign in full perspective, even though Montgomery failed in his immediate objective, he succeeded in furthering the Revolution in an indirect way.

After the War for American Independence at last came to an end, Montgomery's spirit figured prominently in the public ceremonies that sprang up across the country in which the celebrants basked in their victory over Britain. Simeon Baldwin, who would become a member of Congress and a Supreme Court justice, cited Montgomery during his address in Albany upon the occasion. "During an unhappy Period of near 8 years we have experienced all the horrors of a War," he stated. "Nothing less than the Liberties, Happiness, & future Glory of the American World, were the lively incentives, which emboldened the Patrons of our Cause, to oppose the aspiring progress of lawless Power." "These Sons of Liberty, they are worthy of the name, even dared to assault the strongest Bulwarks of the northern realm," he continued. "Come ye who enjoy the blessings for which they fought, lend a tear to the immortal memory of your brave Montgomery."[6]

With the end of hostilities, the government finally made good on its commitment to erect a national monument to Montgomery's memory. Some years before, Benjamin Franklin had arranged for the memorial to be crafted in Paris by Jean Jacques Caffieri, sculptor to Louis XVI. Officials originally intended to locate the elegant Pyrenees marble shrine at the State House in Philadelphia; however, wartime disruptions delayed its installation. After it was finished in 1777, the monument lay in nine packing cases at Le Havre, France, awaiting shipment for nearly two years. When transported from Le Havre to North Carolina, it remained there for several more years. In 1784, Congress directed the superintendent of finance to issue instructions for its erection in New York, Montgomery's adopted state. Eventually, New York City became the site of the nation's tribute to Montgomery. In 1787, with appropriate formality, the monument was dedicated at St. Paul's Episcopal Church.[7]

Janet Montgomery outlived her husband, Richard Montgomery, by fifty-three years. During this time, she assumed the role as protectress of the Montgomery spirit. She always reverently and lovingly referred to him as "my general" or "my soldier," and scrupulously guarded his memory and reputation. In replying to a letter from Aaron Burr, who had served with Montgomery in Canada, Janet indicated the high pedestal on which she placed her spouse. "You have awakened all my sensibility by the praise you bestowed on my unfortunate Genl.," she wrote. "He was indeed an angel sent us for a moment." "Alas! for me, that this world was not more worthy of him."[8]

Like many eighteenth-century women, Janet was content to be a secondary partner while living with her husband. However, the absence of her spouse necessitated her breaking out of this mold and becoming more self-reliant and assertive. After Montgomery left for the war, Janet supervised the completion of their white-framed house near Rhinebeck that they named "Grasmere." She lived there for the next twenty-seven years.

After their traumatic separation while her husband served in the Continental army, Janet agonized over the dangers that he faced. A forlorn wife's lamentations were poignantly expressed in Janet's early letters to the man who had been torn away from her after only two years of marriage. Before long, these letters became too emotional for Montgomery to contend with while devoting himself to his military duties. "I must entreat a favor of you," he wrote from St. Johns, "to write no more of those whining letters." "I declare if I receive another in that style," the affectionate but exasperated husband stated, "I will lock up the rest without reading them." "I don't want anything to lower my spirits," he explained. "I have abundant use for them all." The death of her dearly loved husband shortly afterward was an almost insufferable personal tragedy to Janet. After Montgomery's demise, Janet entered into a period of bereavement that would last for the remainder of her life; but on another level, Mrs. Montgomery came into her own as a self-sufficient woman.[9]

As the Revolution progressed, Janet maintained an active interest in politics and the course of the war. She proudly upheld the patriot cause for which her husband gave his life and sharply criticized loyalism in any form. "Whilst life and memory are left me," she wrote to her cousin, Mrs. John Jay (Sally Livingston Jay), "his loved Idea must ever retain my whole heart and fill it with regret that my every hope of happiness is no more."[10]

Mercy Otis Warren, a well-known author who would write a patriotic history of the Revolution, sent Janet a letter of sympathy as soon as she heard of Montgomery's death. This act of kindness initiated a long friendship between these like-minded women of the Revolution.[11]

Janet also could be a harsh critic of some patriot leaders if she thought they neglected their responsibilities. She soon became a detractor of General Schuyler. Perhaps she blamed him for remaining in the rear echelon of the Canadian campaign. She might have felt that his inactivity placed an undue burden on her husband, contributing to his death. Janet's sentiments were reflected in the journal of William Smith, who was an extended guest of the Livingstons at Clermont Manor during the war and came into contact with Janet on a regular basis. "Mrs. Montgomery . . . censures Genl. Schuyler for ordering a Brigade from Below as discovering Weakness," he wrote in July 1777. "She alledges that there are 6000 Men at Ticonderoga which is thought to be Force enough for the Northern Defence—and she also faults his being at Albany."[12]

Janet also found herself heavily involved with the younger generation of Americans. Many republican mothers named their sons after Montgomery, and some of these families corresponded with Janet, requesting her to offer advice and encouragement to Montgomery's namesakes. With no children of her own, she probably relished this relationship with young devotees across the country. "There is no pleasure equal to hearing my dear little friend of the improvement you and all those who are call'd after General Montgomery make in their learning," she wrote to one, "and I will please myself that they will all strive to be good and great men." The boy died eight months later, and Janet tried to comfort the grief-stricken mother in the loss of her only son. "God is just," she wrote. "I am one that speaks from a knowledge of his goodness—tried in the Furnace of affliction by the loss of a Father and a Husband—which were the two strongest tyes of my life," she continued, "yet he did not permit me to sink under the weight of my woes—but bid me look forward to the high reputation they had left behind." "I close this with commending you to his care," she concluded, "and with assuring you that I shall ever remember with pleasure the attention you have shown for my husband's memory."[13]

Although Janet never remarried, remaining faithful to "her soldier," she had a notable courtship with another general during the summer of 1784. After the war, the charming widow in her early forties met and began corresponding with Horatio Gates, who had lost his wife the previous year. Gates was immediately captivated by Janet and entered upon an eager pursuit that he hoped would lead to their marriage. Janet valued Gates as a friend, but she was convinced that no one could ever take the place of Montgomery in her heart. Before long, she realized that Gates's intentions transcended friendship. Not wishing to give her suitor false hopes, Janet "dropped a tear" over his matrimonial proposal and gently informed Gates that a second marriage was not a possibility for her. "Sensible to your merits, I shall ever be flattered by being assured of your friendship and I would hope that in ceasing to love me—my unaffected candor may also entitle me to your esteem," she wrote, "And that you may soon, good Sir, meet with some more amiable woman, whose undivided affections will contribute to your lasting felicity." Two years later, Gates found and married the "amiable woman" whom Janet had hoped he would. Mrs. Montgomery and General Gates continued their friendship and correspondence until the general died in 1806.[14]

In 1789, Janet prepared to visit Montgomery's relatives in Ireland. She traveled to New York City and spent several months waiting for her ship to sail. During this time, her brother, Robert R. Livingston, acting in his capacity of chancellor, swore in the first president of the United States. Janet attended Washington's Inaugural Ball on May 7 and visited the Washingtons several times afterward. Washington wrote letters of introduction for Janet to some of the Irish aristocracy who had sympathized with the colonies during the Revolution. After arriving in Ireland, she stayed awhile with the brother-in-law of Bishop Samuel Provoost, the clergyman who performed her marriage to Montgomery. Then, she moved in with the Ranelaghs, the family of Montgomery's sister, for an extended visit. The Ranelaghs graciously received Janet into their home and hosted a number of guests who came to call upon her. However, the outspoken Janet frequently entered into lively discussions with the Ranelaghs over British-American politics. Eventually, these differences in opinion resulted in a falling-out between the sisters-in-law. Lady Ranelagh later wrote a sharp letter to Janet accusing her of troublemaking. "You talked much of being the bond of Peace before you came—but I must say that . . . you have not much put that Maxim in force." In 1790, Janet returned to America, thoroughly disgusted with Lady Ranelagh.[15]

As an heiress to the Livingston fortune, Janet Montgomery increased her holdings from time to time as these assets became available and were distributed after deaths in the family. As a result, she became involved with land speculation. In the 1780s, she bought a portion of the De Lancey estate in New York City as an investment. Officials confiscated the property and offered it at public sale after the De Lanceys turned loyalist and fled. Fetching it at a bargain price, the irony of this transaction—involving the De Lanceys, who were bitter political rivals of the Livingstons before the war—probably did not escape Janet's notice.[16]

After her mother's demise in 1800, Janet decided to build a more comfortable residence for herself closer to the family estate at Clermont. She purchased two hundred acres on the east bank of the Hudson River about twenty miles north of Poughkeepsie and began planning a palatial home for her later years. In 1804, construction was complete, and she moved into the magnificent French-styled stone mansion. She named her house Château de Montgomery, but it later also became known as Montgomery Place. Here at the age of sixty-one, she became the grande dame of the Livingston and Montgomery clans, entertaining friends and family members. She also continued to manage her vast estate and business affairs. Her income mostly came from land ventures and rentals of her various properties, but she also engaged in a number of agricultural activities. Some of these undertakings were quite innovative, such as raising six thousand silkworms in a silk-producing project.[17]

In the wake of another war between America and Great Britain that erupted in 1812, nationalism ran high and public spirit once again resurrected Montgomery's memory. Americans celebrated what they regarded as their second triumph over Great Britain, and grateful thoughts turned back to the hero of the preceding conflict. Many were concerned that Montgomery's remains still resided where he fell in a foreign land. It seemed fitting that Montgomery's final resting place be located in the new nation for which he had fought and died. Sensing the time was right to accomplish this long-overdue tribute to her husband, Janet started the bureaucratic wheels turning. In 1818, she wrote New York Lt. Gov. Stephen Van Rensselaer. "Having obtained permission from Gov. Sir James Westbrooke to remove the ashes of General Montgomery from Quebec, my friends supposed it would be more honorable, if the Countrey would undertake it," she said, "if my friends will have the goodness to propose it and redeem his ashes from a public gate-way—in a strange land, they will do great justice to my feelings and honor to themselves."[18]

On February 27, 1818, the New York Legislature passed an Act of Honor authorizing the relocation of Montgomery's body. Gov. De Witt Clinton of New York arranged with Sir John Sherbrooke, governor-general of Canada, for the return of Montgomery's remains to New York. State authorities commissioned Lewis Livingston, Janet's nephew, to go to Quebec and receive the remains. James Thompson, who assisted in Montgomery's interment at Quebec in 1776 and was now eighty-nine years old, participated in the exhumation and identification of the body on June 16, 1818. Lewis Livingston escorted Montgomery's remains, encased in a new mahogany casket, to the capitol at Albany on July 4, 1818, where they lay in state for two days. Then, the remains were placed on board the steamboat *Richmond* and conveyed down the Hudson River toward New York. Governor Clinton had notified Janet of the time when the *Richmond* would pass Château de Montgomery, and she went out on the veranda to view the ship carrying her general home. Forty-three years had elapsed since she and Montgomery parted at Saratoga. When pangs of nostalgia rushed over her, she requested to be left unattended on the porch. "At length, they came by," she described the scene, "with all that remained of a beloved husband, who left me in the bloom of manhood, a perfect being." The *Richmond* stopped, while a military band on board played the dead march and the honor guard fired a salute, and then solemnly continued its passage to New York City. Emotions overcame the seventy-four-year-old widow. When her companions came to find her some time later, they found Janet unconscious on the floor where she had fainted.[19]

When General Montgomery's body reached the city of New York, nearly five thousand people participated in the ceremonies that followed. Newspapers and magazines were full of articles covering the event. The *Daily Advertiser*, for instance, carried complete coverage of the function, and the *Port Folio* printed a long, doleful poem in French eulogizing Montgomery. The funeral procession consisted of military and civilian organizations such as the Society of the Cincinnati and other revolutionary veteran groups, foreign diplomats, and state and federal dignitaries headed by Vice President John C. Calhoun. Montgomery's remains were interred on July 8, 1818, next to his monument at St. Paul's Church. Only once before, upon the death of George Washington, had such a huge outpouring of public sentiment for a national hero occurred. "I am satisfied," Janet wrote. "What more could I wish than the high honor that has been conferred on the ashes of my poor soldier."[20]

Ten years later, Andrew Jackson corresponded with Edward Livingston. "Present me in the most respectful terms to your aged sister [Janet]," he wrote. "Say to her, if I ever should be within one hundred miles of her dwelling I will visit and have the honor of shaking by the hand the revered relict of the patriotic Genl. Montgomery, who will ever live in the hearts of his countrymen." "I rejoice to hear that at the age of 85 she retains all her intellectual faculties," he added. Three months afterward on November 6, 1824, Janet Montgomery died, looking forward to a reunion with her husband. She had written Mercy Otis Warren some years before: "What but the expectation beyond the grave can ever make me smile in the midst of grief; what make me suffer life after my Soldier's fall, but the blessed flattering hope of meeting him again."[21]

Although faded from the modern memory, Gen. Richard Montgomery remains an American icon. Although he and Janet left no direct descendants to carry on the Montgomery name, his deeds during the Revolution should stand in the collective consciousness to remind each generation of Americans of the sacrifices that some have made to secure independence for the new American nation. His legacy challenges the inheritors of this precious freedom to respect the liberties for which Montgomery fought.

Appendixes

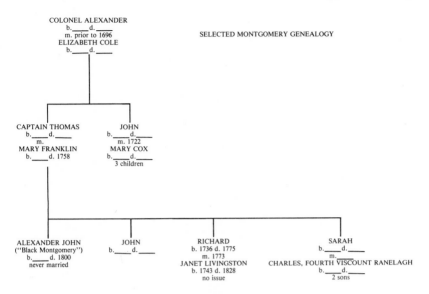

SELECTED MONTGOMERY GENEALOGY

COLONEL ALEXANDER
b.____ d.____
m. prior to 1696
ELIZABETH COLE
b.____ d.____

CAPTAIN THOMAS
b.____ d.____
m.
MARY FRANKLIN
b.____ d. 1758

JOHN
b.____ d.____
m. 1722
MARY COX
b.____ d.____
3 children

ALEXANDER JOHN
("Black Montgomery")
b.____ d. 1800
never married

JOHN
b.____ d.____

RICHARD
b. 1736 d. 1775
m. 1773
JANET LIVINGSTON
b. 1743 d. 1828
no issue

SARAH
b.____ d.____
m.
CHARLES, FOURTH VISCOUNT RANELAGH
b.____ d.____
2 sons

Appendix A: Selected Montgomery Genealogy

186 · *Appendixes*

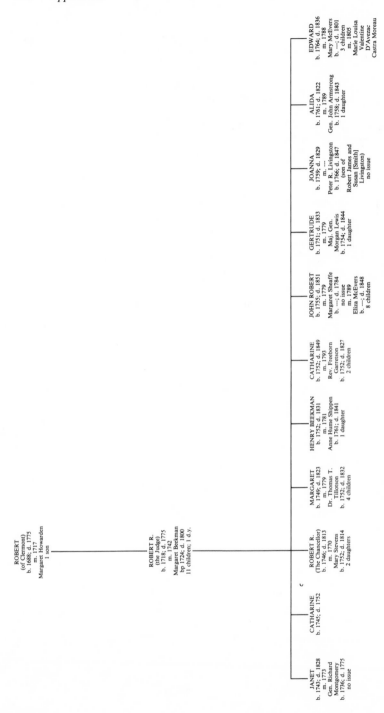

Appendix B: Selected Livingston (Clermont) Genealogy

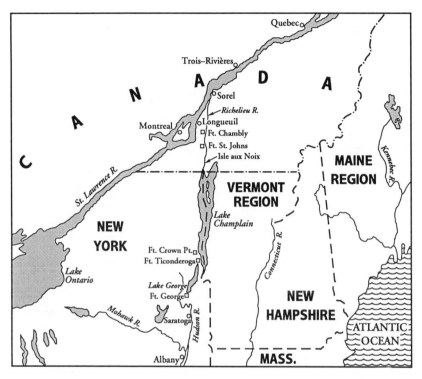

Appendix C: Canada and the Northern Campaign

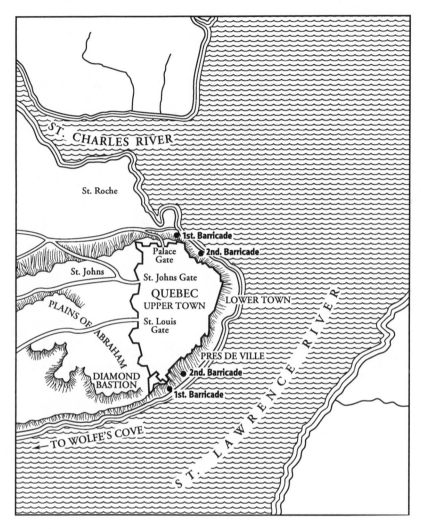

Appendix D: The Attack on Quebec

Notes

ONE   *Introduction*

1. George W. Cullum, "Major-General Richard Montgomery," *Magazine of American History* 11 (April 1884): 295.
2. From the Journal of Jeremiah Greenman, in Robert C. Bray and Paul E. Bushnell, eds., *Diary of a Common Soldier in the American Revolution, 1775–1783* (DeKalb, Ill., 1978), 23; Vincent F. O'Reilly, "Major-General Richard Montgomery," *American-Irish Historical Society Journal* 25 (1926): 186.
3. Justin H. Smith, *Our Struggle for the Fourteenth Colony*, 2 vols. (New York, 1907), 2:130.
4. Peter Force, ed., *American Archives*, 4th and 5th ser., 9 vols. (Washington, D.C., 1837–53), 4th ser., 3:765.
5. From the Journal of James Thompson, Superintendent of Military Works at Quebec, 1761–1776, quoted in William J. Anderson, "Canadian History: The Siege and Blockade of Quebec by Generals Montgomery and Arnold in 1775–76," *Literary and Historical Society of Quebec Transactions*, new ser., pt. 9 (1871/72): 62.
6. Force, *American Archives*, 4th ser., 4:589.
7. Sir Guy Carleton to Gen. Sir William Howe, January 12, 1776, in Anderson, "Canadian History," 66.
8. Thompson, quoted in Anderson, "Canadian History," 65.
9. James Grant Wilson and John Fiske, eds., *Appleton's Cyclopaedia of American Biography*, 7 vols. (New York, 1886–1900), 4:370–71.
10. Thompson, quoted in Anderson, "Canadian History," 67.
11. Quoted in Wilson and Fiske, *Appleton's Cyclopaedia* 4:371.
12. Benedict Arnold to Hannah Arnold, January 6, 1776, in Force, *American Archives*, 4th ser., 4:589.
13. Philip Schuyler to John Hancock, January 13, 1776, in Force, *American Archives*, 4th ser., 4:666.

14. [Thomas Paine], *A Dialogue between the Ghost of General Montgomery and an American Delegate in a Wood Near Philadelphia* (New York, 1865 [1776]).

15. Hugh Henry Brackenridge, *The Death of General Montgomery* (Norwich, 1777), in Norman Philbrick, ed., *Trumpets Sounding: Propaganda Plays of the American Revolution* (New York, 1972), 213–54.

16. Ibid., 50.

17. Quoted in Wilson and Fiske, *Appleton's Cyclopaedia* 4:371.

18. Force, *American Archives*, 4th ser., 4:1650.

19. Ibid., 1654.

20. Report from Benjamin Franklin, Silas Deane, and Arthur Lee to the Committee of Foreign Affairs, November 30, 1777, Francis Wharton, ed., *The Revolutionary Diplomatic Correspondence of the United States*, 6 vols. (Washington, D.C., 1889), 2:436.

21. O'Reilly, "Major-General Richard Montgomery," 189–90.

22. John Hancock to the States, September 24, 1776, in Paul H. Smith, ed., *Letters of Delegates to Congress, 1774–1789*, 17 vols. (Washington, D.C., 1976–), 5:228–30.

23. There is no definitive biography of Richard Montgomery. The only one, written by A. L. Todd, *Richard Montgomery: Rebel of 1775* (New York, 1966), was not well received by scholars. Stuart R. J. Sutherland, for example, criticized the book: "Its superficial research and naive style of writing make it of little value." Francess G. Halpenny, ed., *Dictionary of Canadian Biography*, 11 vols. (Toronto, 1966–82), 4:550.

24. Joseph Nathan Kane, *The American Counties* (Metuchen, N.J., 1972), 16. The list of persons (except for presidents and governors) for whom six or more counties have been named include: Benjamin Franklin, 23; Francis Marion, Nathanael Greene, and the Marquis de Lafayette, 17 each; Richard Montgomery, 16; Henry Clay and Anthony Wayne, 15 each; Joseph Warren, 14; Charles Carroll and Stephen Arnold Douglas, 12 each; John Caldwell Calhoun, 11; John Hancock, James Lawrence, Oliver Hazard Perry, and Zebulon Pike, 10 each; Henry Knox, Daniel Morgan, and Israel Putnam, 9 each; Thomas Hart Benton, Alexander Hamilton, William Jasper, Robert Edwin Lee, John Marshall, and Daniel Webster, 8 each; Daniel Boone, Robert Fulton, and Casimir Pulaski, 7 each; and George Rogers Clark, George Armstrong Custer, Johann De Kalb, Benjamin Lincoln, Meriwether Lewis, Nathanael Macon, and Hugh Mercer, 6 each.

25. Kane, *The American Counties*, 260–61. The full list includes: Arkansas, 1842; Georgia, 1793; Illinois, 1821; Indiana, 1822; Iowa, 1851; Kansas, 1867; Kentucky, 1796; Maryland, 1776; Mississippi, 1871; Missouri, 1818; New York, formerly Tryon County, name changed to Montgomery County, 1784; North Carolina, 1778; Ohio, 1803; Pennsylvania, 1784; Texas, 1837; and Virginia, 1776.

T W O *Ancestry and Early Life*

1. William Smith, *An Oration in Memory of General Montgomery* (Philadelphia, 1776), 16–17.

2. There is some confusion over the date of Richard Montgomery's birth. Some sources cite the date as 1736; others as 1738. The data that Montgomery was sixteen years old when he matriculated at Dublin College on June 15, 1754, in George Dames Burtchaell, and Thomas Ulick Sadleir, eds., *Alumni Dublinenses* (Dublin, Ireland, 1935), 588, substantiate 1738. Dumas Malone, ed., *Dictionary of American Biography*, 26 vols. (New York, 1928–58), 13:98–99; Leslie Stephen and Sidney Lee, eds., *The Dictionary of National Biography*, 24 vols. (London, 1968 [1949–50]), 13:767–68; Mark M. Boatner III, *Encyclopedia of the American Revolution* (New York, 1976), 726–27; *National Cyclopedia of American Biography*, 63 vols. (New York, 1898–1984), 1:100–101; Wilson and Fiske, *Appleton's Cyclopaedia* 4:370–71; Halpenny, *Dictionary of Canadian Biography* 4:545–50.

3. Cullum, "Major-General Richard Montgomery," 273.

4. Thomas H. Montgomery, "Ancestry of General Richard Montgomery," *New-York Genealogical and Biographical Society Record* 2 (July 1871): 128.

5. Ibid., 129.

6. Ibid., 128; Janet Montgomery in Louise L. Hunt, *Biographical Notes Concerning General Richard Montgomery* (Poughkeepsie, N.Y., 1876), 4.

7. Thomas H. Montgomery, "Ancestry of General Richard Montgomery," 128.

8. Janet Montgomery, in Hunt, *Biographical Notes Concerning General Richard Montgomery*, 4.

9. Paul Van Dyke, *Catherine de Medicis*, 2 vols. (New York, 1922), 1:103.

10. Hugh Ross Williamson, *Catherine de' Medici* (New York, 1973), 81.

11. Williamson, *Catherine de' Medici*, 82.

12. François Pierre Guillaume Guizot, *A Popular History of France, from the Earliest Times*, 8 vols. (New York, 1969 [1869]), 4:268; Henry M. Baird, *History of the Rise of the Huguenots of France*, 2 vols. (New York, 1970 [1879]), 1:339–40.

13. Williamson, *Catherine de' Medici*, 90.

14. Julien Coudy, ed., *The Huguenot Wars* (New York, 1969), 79.

15. James Westfall Thompson, *The Wars of Religion in France, 1559–1576* (New York, 1957), 342.

16. O. I. A. Roche, *The Days of the Upright: The Story of the Huguenots* (New York, 1965), 134–36; Duc de Castries, *The Lives of the Kings and Queens of France* (New York, 1979), 163.

17. Baird, *History of the Rise of the Huguenots of France* 2:589.

18. Thompson, *The Wars of Religion in France, 1559–1576*, 472.

19. Baird, *History of the Rise of the Huguenots in France* 2:632, 636.

20. Ibid.; Henry M. Baird, *The Huguenots and Henry of Navarre*, 2 vols. (New York, 1970 [1903]), 1:16–17.

21. Baird, *History of the Rise of the Huguenots of France* 2:634.

22. Ibid. *"Roturier"* is a French term for "commoner," "not of noble rank."

23. Baird, *The Huguenots and Henry of Navarre* 1:261–62.

24. Janet Montgomery to Edward Livingston, July 4, 1820, Janet Montgomery, "Reminiscences," ed. John Ross Delafield, *Dutchess County [N.Y.] Historical Society Year Book* 15 (1930): 73 (an unpublished manuscript copy of this document that confirms its content is in the New-York Historical Society holdings); Janet

192 · *Three: Duty in the Seven Years' War*

Montgomery, in Hunt, *Biographical Notes Concerning General Richard Montgomery*, 4; Thomas H. Montgomery, "Ancestry of General Richard Montgomery," 123, 125.

25. Baird, *History of the Rise of the Huguenots of France* 2:78; Thomas H. Montgomery, "Ancestry of General Richard Montgomery," 127.

26. Janet Montgomery, in Hunt, *Biographical Notes Concerning General Richard Montgomery*, 4.

27. John William Fortescue, *A History of the British Army*, 13 vols. (London, 1910–30), 1:307–9, 335, 390, 401, 449, 460, 489–90.

THREE   *Duty in the Seven Years' War*

1. Brackenridge, *The Death of General Montgomery*, 237–38.
2. William Smith, *An Oration in Memory of General Montgomery*, 17.
3. Among the standard works that treat the Seven Years' War in North America (French and Indian War) are: Francis Parkman, *The Battle for North America* (Garden City, N.Y., 1948 [1851–92]); and Howard H. Peckham, *The Colonial Wars, 1689–1762* (Chicago, 1964).
4. Great Britain War Office, *Annual Army Lists* (London, 1756), 270–71. The 17th Regiment numbered thirty-five officers (one commander, one lieutenant colonel, one major, seven captains, one captain lieutenant, one adjutant, one chaplain, one surgeon, twelve lieutenants, nine ensigns), and seven hundred rank and file.
5. The Irish regiments included the 1st, 17th, 27th, 28th, 43rd, 46th, and 55th. Richard Cannon, *Historical Record of the Seventeenth, or the Leicestershire Regiment of Foot* (London, 1848), 17; E. A. H. Webb, *A History of the Services of the 17th (the Leicestershire) Regiment* (London, 1911), 41; John Knox, *An Historical Journal of the Campaigns in North America*, ed. Arthur G. Doughty, 3 vols. (Freeport, N.Y., 1970), 1:16–17.
6. For studies concerning musketry and infantry tactics, consult Torsten Lenk, *The Flintlock: Its Origin and Development*, ed. John. E. Hayward (London, 1965); Howard L. Blackmore, *British Military Firearms, 1650–1850* (London, 1961); Harold L. Peterson, *Arms and Armor in Colonial America, 1526–1783* (Harrisburg, Pa., 1956).
7. For discussions of cannons and artillery techniques, see James A. Browne, *England's Artillerymen, A Historical Narrative of the Services of the Royal Artillery, from the Formation of the Regiment to 1862* (London, 1865); Albert Manucy, *Artillery through the Ages: A Short Illustrated History of Cannon, Emphasizing Types Used in America* (Washington, D.C., 1949).
8. Knox, *An Historical Journal of the Campaigns in North America* 1:16–17.
9. Cannon, *Historical Record of the Seventeenth*, 17; Webb, *A History of the Services of the 17th*, 41; J. Mackay Hitsman and C. C. J. Bond, "The Assault Landing at Louisbourg, 1758," *Canadian Historical Review* 35 (December 1954): 315–16.
10. John Forbes, *Writings of General John Forbes*, ed. Alfred P. James (Menasha, Wisc., 1938), 16.

11. Fortescue, *A History of the British Army* 2:321.

12. Hitsman and Bond, "The Assault Landing at Louisbourg, 1758," 318.

13. Fortescue, *A History of the British Army* 2:322–23.

14. Hitsman and Bond, "The Assault Landing at Louisbourg, 1757," 321.

15. Ibid., 330.

16. *London Gazette*, August 15, 1758.

17. J. S. McLennan, *Louisbourg from Its Foundation to Its Fall, 1713–1758* (London, 1918), 253; Cannon, *Historical Record of the Seventeenth*, 18; Webb, *A History of the Services of the 17th*, 44.

18. Knox, *An Historical Journal of the Campaigns in North America* 1:189–95.

19. Richard Montgomery to Col. Jacob Glen, August 24, 1758, Misc. MSS, Montgomery, New-York Historical Society.

20. As prime minister, Pitt directed the overall war effort. However, King George II was interested enough in military matters to intervene occasionally. Pitt generally appointed principal military commanders based on merit and ability, sometimes promoting promising officers such as Amherst over the heads of seniors. The king usually favored a patronage system for selection of military authorities. Abercromby represented one of the king's disappointing appointees.

21. J. Mackay Hitsman, *Safeguarding Canada, 1763–1871* (Toronto, 1968), 14; Rex Whitworth, *Field Marshall Lord Ligonier: A History of the British Army, 1702–1770* (New York, 1958), 278.

22. Webb, *A History of the Services of the 17th*, 46.

23. Ibid., 47.

24. Cannon, *Historical Record of the Seventeenth*, 19; Knox, *An Historical Journal of the Campaigns in North America* 1:403. At Lake Champlain and the St. Lawrence River watershed, geographical directions follow the flow of water. Thus, down refers to a northward heading and up indicates a southward orientation.

25. J. M. LeMoine, "General R. Montgomery and His Detractors," *New York Genealogical and Biographical Record* 22, no. 2 (April 1891): 65–66; Malcolm Fraser, *Extract from a Manuscript Journal Relating to the Siege of Quebec* (Quebec, 1927 [1868]), 13–14.

26. James Wolfe, *General Orders in Wolfe's Army during the Expedition up the St. Lawrence* (Quebec, 1875), 29. Apparently, this episode did no lasting harm to Alexander Montgomery's reputation. After quitting the army after the war, he served for a number of years as an Irish M.P. For a comprehensive study of scalping, consult James Axtell, *The European and the Indian: Essays in the Ethnohistory of Colonial North America* (New York, 1981), chaps. 2, 8. An Ensign Douville was reportedly the French officer whose scalp Washington sent to Dinwiddie.

27. Hitsman, *Safeguarding Canada*, 18.

28. Webb, *A History of the Services of the 17th*, 51–52; Cannon, *Historical Record of the Seventeenth*, 20.

29. *London Gazette*, March 23, 1762; *London Gazette*, March 24, 1762; Webb, *A History of the Services of the 17th*, 53–54; Cannon, *Historical Record of the Seventeenth*, 20–21; Fortescue, *A History of the British Army* 2:548–50.

30. Robert Burton, "Siege and Capture of Havana in 1762," *Maryland Historical Magazine* 4 (1909): 321–35; Fortescue, *A History of the British Army* 2:550–52;

Webb, *A History of the Services of the 17th*, 54–55; Cannon, *Historical Record of the Seventeenth*, 21–22.

31. Burton, "Siege and Capture of Havana," 334; Fortescue, *A History of The British Army* 2:552; Webb, *A History of the Services of the 17th*, 56.

32. Major T. Mante Journal, 425–26, 461, quoted in Webb, *A History of the Services of the 17th*, 56; Burton, "Siege and Capture of Havana," 328.

33. Rev. John Graham, September 28, 1762, quoted in Burton, "Siege and Capture of Havana," 334.

34. John Adair to General Amherst, September 18, 1762, quoted in Webb, *A History of the Services of the 17th*, 57.

35. Janet Montgomery, "Reminiscences," 74.

36. Earl of Halifax to Gen. Thomas Gage, January 14, 1764, in Clarence Edwin Carter, ed., *The Correspondence of General Thomas Gage with the Secretaries of State, 1763–1775*, 2 vols. (New York, 1969 [1931–33]), 1:11.

37. Gen. Thomas Gage to the Earl of Halifax, April 7, 1764, in Carter, *The Correspondence of General Thomas Gage* 1:21.

38. Webb, *A History of the Services of the 17th*, 57–60.

39. Charles J. Fox, who had been raised as a wealthy aristrocrat, had his own reasons for adopting Whig views. They concerned the king's personal dislike of him as a libertine and a product of the idle rich.

40. Janet Montgomery, "Reminiscences," 67.

F O U R   *Decision for the Patriot Cause*

1. William Smith, *An Oration in Memory of General Montgomery*, 19–20.

2. Richard Montgomery to John Montgomery, n.d., in Thomas H. Montgomery, "Ancestry of General Richard Montgomery," 129. Richard's eldest brother, Alexander Montgomery, received a substantial inheritance from an issue-less uncle. Therefore, the father, Thomas Montgomery, left his estate to Richard, an older brother, John, and a younger sister, Sarah, while bequeathing a nominal legacy to Alexander. Thomas H. Montgomery, "Ancestry of General Richard Montgomery," 128. The proceeds from Montgomery's commission are assumed to be £1,500—the prevailing value at that time. Eric Robson, "Purchase and Promotion in the British Army in the Eighteenth Century," *History*, new ser., 36 (February–June 1951): 60.

3. Janet Montgomery, "Reminiscences," 74. New Yorkers during that time considered the out ward to be the environs situated north of New York City, beyond the built-up area, including the scattered farms.

4. Janet Montgomery, "Reminiscences," 67, 73–74.

5. Janet Montgomery, "Reminiscences," 64–65. Of Janet's four sisters who survived childhood and for whom there is a recorded date of marriage, all but one married after the age of twenty-eight, and the average age of marriage was thirty years: Janet, thirty; Catharine, died at age seven; Margaret, thirty; Catharine, forty-one; Gertrude (the exception), twenty-two; Joanna, no record of marriage

date; Alida, twenty-eight. On the other hand, the average age of marriage for Janet's four brothers was twenty-six years.

6. Janet Montgomery, "Reminiscences," 64.

7. Richard Montgomery to Judge Robert R. Livingston, in Janet Montgomery, "Reminiscences," 47–48; Hunt, *Biographical Notes Concerning General Richard Montgomery*, 2–3; [Louise L. Hunt], "General Richard Montgomery," *Harper's New Monthly Magazine* 70, no. 417 (February 1885): 351. There is disagreement among the sources over the date of the letter. John Ross Delafield in "Reminiscences," by Janet Montgomery, transcribes the date as May 28, 1773, but Louise L. Hunt, in *Biographical Notes Concerning General Richard Montgomery* and "General Richard Montgomery," places the date at May 20, 1773.

8. Robert Livingston's will, February 10, 1723, Livingston-Redmond MSS, microfilm edition, Franklin Delano Roosevelt Library, Hyde Park, New York, roll 4.

9. John Wilson Poucher, "Dutchess County Men of the Revolutionary Period: Judge Robert R. Livingston, His Sons, and Sons-in-Law," *Dutchess County [N.Y.] Historical Society Year Book* 30 (1945): 55.

10. Judge Robert R. Livingston to Richard Montgomery, June 21, 1773, in Hunt, *Biographical Notes Concerning General Richard Montgomery*, 3–4; [Hunt], "General Richard Montgomery," 351.

11. Quoted in Julia Delafield, *Biographies of Francis Lewis and Morgan Lewis*, 2 vols. (New York, 1877), 1:184; Rivington's *Gazetteer* (New York), July 29, 1773.

12. William Alexander (1726–1783) was a notable exception to colonial patriot distaste of royal symbology. A prominent New Jersey businessman who later received a general's commission in the Continental army, Alexander endeavored to claim the earldom of Stirling in 1756. Although he was unable to secure official recognition of the British government to the peerage that he coveted, he usurped the title and referred to himself as "Lord Stirling" before and during the Revolution. For the most recent biography, see Paul David Nelson, *The Life of William Alexander, Lord Stirling* (Tuscaloosa, Ala., 1987). Nelson theorized that many colonial patriots indulged Alexander's title as an expression of spite and mockery against British arrogance (62). However, another biographer indicated that George Washington's opponents accused him of aristocratic leanings after the Revolution because of his practice of calling Alexander "Lord Stirling." Douglas Southall Freeman, *George Washington: A Biography*, 7 vols. (New York, 1948–57), 6:212–13.

13. Janet Montgomery, "Reminiscences," 67–68. Quotation from the recollections of Catharine Livingston Garretson's daughter, by Susan Warner, "Life of the Rev. Freeborn Garretson," unfinished MS, 19, in Katherine M. Babbitt, *Janet Montgomery: Hudson River Squire* (Monroe, N.Y., 1975), 10–11.

14. Janet Montgomery, "Reminiscences," 68.

15. Quoted in Delafield, *Biographies of Francis Lewis and Morgan Lewis* 1:215.

16. Richard Montgomery to Lt. Perkins Magra, [after April] 1774, Montgomery MSS Collection, Clements Library, University of Michigan. Also published in Clements Library Associates, *Major General Richard Montgomery: A Contribution toward A Biography* (Ann Arbor, Mich., 1970), 12–15. The "hobby horse" refers

to his country life; the "skittish nag" is the British army in which Montgomery served for fifteen years.

17. George Clymer to Josiah Quincy, Jr., July 29, 1773, Josiah Quincy, *Memoir of the Life of Josiah Quincy, Jun.* (New York, 1971 [1825]), 114. Clymer, later a delegate to the Continental Congress, was just slightly less caustic in his criticism toward his native province: he referred to Pennsylvania as only a moderate in its revolutionary spirit. Quincy was a fellow lawyer and Massachusetts friend of Clymer.

18. Paul A. Gilje, *The Road to Mobocracy: Popular Disorder in New York City, 1763–1834* (Chapel Hill, N.C., 1987), 52–58; Edward Countryman, *A People in Revolution: The American Revolution and Political Society in New York, 1760–1790* (Baltimore, 1981), 63–66.

19. Henry B. Dawson, *The Sons of Liberty in New York: A Paper Read Before the New-York Historical Society, May 3, 1850* (New York, 1850), 112–18; Martha J. Lamb, *History of the City of New York*, 3 vols. (New York, 1877), 1:746–47; Ellis H. Roberts, *New York: The Planting and the Growth of the Empire State*, 2 vols. (New York, 1887), 2:376–79. The Sons of Liberty replaced the destroyed liberty pole with a new one erected nearby on property obtained for that purpose. This sixth and last liberty pole stood until the British capture and occupation of the city in the summer of 1776. For a definitive treatment of the Golden Hill and Nassau Street riots, consult Lee R. Boyer, "Lobster Backs, Liberty Boys, and Laborers in the Streets," *New-York Historical Society Quarterly* 57, no. 4 (October 1973): 281–308.

20. The *Nancy*, commanded by Captain Lockyer, was the first tea ship to arrive at New York. Capt. James Chambers was the master of the *London*, which became involved in the New York "Tea Party." New York decided that subsequent shipments would be impounded until the tea could be sold at auction. Force, *American Archives*, 4th ser., 1:249–50; New York State, *The American Revolution in New York: Its Political, Social, and Economic Significance* (Albany, N.Y., 1926), 32–33, 312–13; Leopold S. Launitz-Schurer, Jr., *Loyal Whigs and Revolutionaries: The Making of the Revolution in New York, 1763–1776* (New York, 1980), 106–8; Bernard Mason, *The Road to Independence: The Revolutionary Movement in New York, 1773–1777* (Lexington, Ky., 1967), 19–22; Malcolm Peter Decker, *Brink of Revolution: New York in Crisis, 1765–1776* (New York, 1964), 141–44; Carl L. Becker, *The History of Political Parties in the Province of New York, 1760–1776* (Madison, Wisc., 1968), 95–111.

21. L. H. Butterfield, ed., *The Adams Papers: Diary and Autobiography of John Adams*, 4 vols. (New York, 1964), 2:103. For a comprehensive study of the Livingston family, consult Cynthia A. Kierner, *Traders and Gentlefolk: The Livingstons of New York, 1675–1790* (Ithaca, N.Y., 1992).

22. Poucher, "Dutchess County Men of the Revolutionary Period," 55.

23. Patricia U. Bonomi, *A Factious People: Politics and Society in Colonial New York* (New York, 1971), 180. For a comprehensive study of the 1766 land riots in New York, refer to Sung Bok Kim, *Landlord and Tenant in Colonial New York: Manorial Society, 1664–1775* (Chapel Hill, N.C., 1978), 346–415. The manorial tenancy system in provincial New York had its roots in the semifeudal patroon-

ship institution of New Netherland. In 1664, the English conquered this Dutch holding and established the colony of New York in its stead. However, land ownership practices in the newly formed province borrowed heavily from the earlier model. The resultant tenancy method became the basis of long-standing landlord-tenant tensions. This adversary potential broke out into violent confrontations on numerous occasions throughout the colonial period and well beyond the Revolution. Finally, in 1846, a revised state constitution opened the way for tenants to obtain titles to their farms.

24. The British officer was Capt. John Montresor. John Montresor, *The Montresor Journals*, ed. G. D. Skull, Collections of the New-York Historical Society, no. 14 (New York, 1882), 363.

25. Judge Robert R. Livingston to Robert Livingston, Jr., May 14, 1776, Livingston-Redmond MSS, microfilm edition, Franklin Delano Roosevelt Library, roll 8. Two members of the Livingston family were named Robert Livingston, Jr. One was the first proprietor of Clermont (Janet's grandfather). The one involved in this correspondence was the son of Philip Livingston (from the Livingston Manor branch).

26. Richard Henry Lee to a "Gentleman of Influence in England," March 27, 1768, in James Curtis Ballagh, ed., *The Letters of Richard Henry Lee*, 2 vols. (New York, 1911–14), 1:27.

27. Launitz-Schurer, *Loyal Whigs and Revolutionaries*, 50–51. For an in-depth treatment of this episode, see Nicholas Varga, "The New York Restraining Act: Its Passage and Some Effects, 1766–1768," *New York History* 37, no. 3 (July 1956): 233–58; Lee E. Olm, "The Mutiny Act for America: New York's Noncompliance," *New-York Historical Society Quarterly* 58 (1974): 188–214.

28. Bonomi, *A Factious People*, 261–62. William Livingston became a New Jersey delegate to the First Continental Congress, serving until June 5, 1776. He then took command of the state's militia as a brigadier general but resigned his commission on August 31, 1776, upon election as governor. He held this office for fourteen years.

29. Janet Montgomery, "Reminiscences," 68–69.

30. Thomas Jones, *History of New York during the Revolutionary War*, 2 vols. (New York, 1968 [1879]), 171–72. John R. Livingston volunteered as an army officer during the Revolution but was never commissioned. He was in charge of the powder mills built by his father in 1775 to supply the American army, and his critical services in this capacity were probably of far greater value to the Revolution than they would have been as a soldier.

F I V E   *Service in the Provincial Congress*

1. William Smith, *An Oration in Memory of General Montgomery*, 19.

2. New York State, *The American Revolution in New York*, 27–46.

3. Cadwallader Colden to the Earl of Dartmouth (William Legge), July 6, 1774, Edmund B. O'Callaghan and Berthold Fernow, eds., *Documents Relative to the Colonial History of the State of New York*, 15 vols. (Albany, N.Y., 1856–57),

8:469–70. Cadwallader Colden (1688–1777) was born in Scotland and combined the practice of medicine and merchandising in Philadelphia before moving to New York. There, he attained the position of senior councilor before his appointment as lieutenant governor in 1760. Although widely respected as a distinguished scientist and scholar, Colden's efforts to enforce the Stamp Act in 1765, during one of the several times he assumed the role of acting governor, aroused the resentment of many New Yorkers. This resulted in his being hanged and burned in effigy. William Tryon (1729–1788) served as the royal governor of North Carolina for six years (1765–1771) before his transfer to New York in July 1771. While in North Carolina, he was instrumental in supressing the "Regulators," a movement brought on by East-West sectionalism and challenge to established governmental jurisdiction. In his military capacity (commissioned in 1751, he maintained his officer status in the British army), Tryon led the militia to eventually defeat the Regulators in the Battle of Alamance on May 16, 1771. After his transfer to New York, he became popular with many of the residents on a personal level. In 1772, the provincial government organized Tryon County and named it in his honor. However, increased resistance by the patriot movement against his official status and royal authority soon forced Tryon on the defensive. In April 1774, he departed to discuss his problems with the English government, leaving Colden in charge. For the most recent biography of Tryon, see Paul David Nelson, *William Tryon and the Course of Empire: A Life in British Imperial Service* (Chapel Hill, N.C., 1990).

4. New York State, *The American Revolution in New York*, 27–46.

5. Ibid., 47–48. This source states that the counties of Tryon, Gloucester, Cumberland, and some districts of Queens did not send representatives to the New York Provincial Convention. However, Becker, *The History of Political Parties in the Province of New York*, 186–92, indicates the noncompliant counties as Tryon, Gloucester, Cumberland, Richmond, and Charlotte. The Provincial Convention carefully inspected the credentials of the proposed members before seating them. Eventually, forty-one members signed the official minutes of the convention.

6. *New York Journal*, April 13, 1775; William M. Willett, ed., *A Narrative of the Military Actions of Colonel Marinus Willett* (New York, 1969 [1831]), 30–31, 54–55; Isaac Q. Leake, ed., *Memoir of the Life and Times of General John Lamb* (Albany, N.Y., 1970 [1857]), 101–2; Force, *American Archives*, 4th ser., 2:347–49, 364.

7. Cadwallader Colden to Lord Dartmouth, May 3, 1775, O'Callaghan and Fernow, *Documents Relative to the Colonial History of the State of New York* 8:571–72; Force, *American Archives*, 4th ser., 2:448, 459–61; William H. W. Sabine, ed., *Historical Memoirs from 16 March 1763 to 25 July 1778 of William Smith*, 2 vols. (New York, 1958), 1:221.

8. *Pennsylvania Journal*, April 26, 1775.

9. *New York Mercury*, May 1, 1775; *New York Journal*, May 4, 1775; Cadwallader Colden to Lord Dartmouth, June 7, 1775, in Cadwallader Colden, *The Colden Letter Books, 1760–1775*, 2 vols., New-York Historical Society Collections, no. 10 (New York, 1877–78), 2:400; Force, *American Archives*, 4th ser., 2:400, 427, 448–49, 468, 471, 605. Various associations were created by the patriots during the prerevolutionary period as a means of consolidating political strength.

The General Association should not be confused with the Continental Association, both of which are commonly referred to as merely the "Association." The First Continental Congress signed the Continental Association on October 20, 1774, as a nonimportation, nonconsumption, and nonexportation agreement against British goods. This association also established enforcement committees to seize goods that violated the terms of the instrument and to publicize the names of those who failed to comply with the association's stipulations. By April 1775, all colonies had adopted the association. It was enforced in New York by the Committee of Sixty, the Committee of One Hundred, and the Provincial Congress. The Continental Association generated great pressure on English merchants to encourage the British government toward reconciliation with the colonies. Other associations of a different sort appeared in early 1775. Unlike those created as an economic weapon, these endeavored to gain support of the colonists to the patriot cause. The General Association in New York emerged as one of these types of conventions.

10. Cadwallader Colden to Capt. George Vandeput, May 27, 1775, in Colden, *The Colden Letter Books* 2:413–14.

11. Force, *American Archives*, 4th ser., 2:470–71, 481, 529–30, 617–18, 636–37, 670–71.

12. Provincial Congress MSS, New York State Archives; New York Secretary of State, *Calendar of Historical Manuscripts Relating to the War of the Revolution,* 2 vols. (Albany, N.Y., 1863–68), 1:67.

13. Ibid. Roger J. Champagne, *Alexander McDougall and the American Revolution in New York* (New York, 1975), 86.

14. Provincial Congress MSS, New York State Archives; New York Secretary of State, *Calendar of Historical Manuscripts Relating to the War of the Revolution* 1:85–86.

15. Richard Montgomery to Robert R. Livingston, June 3, 1775, Robert R. Livingston Papers, New York Public Library. Janet Montgomery, "Reminiscences," 69. For a comprehensive discussion of patriot ideological divisions, refer to Mason, *The Road to Independence*, 71–72.

16. For a definitive study of the composition and group dynamics of the New York Provincial Congress, consult Becker, *The History of Political Parties in the Province of New York*, 201–10.

17. On May 8, 1775, the British forces commander, Gen. Thomas Gage, sent a message to the commander of Fort Ticonderoga, Capt. William Delaplace, warning him of the possibility of a raid on his position. Lt. Jocelyn Feltham arrived twelve days before the attack with the advance element of a twenty-man reinforcement that Gen. Guy Carleton was sending from Canada. The only casualty was Colonel Easton, who received a slight wound by a sentry's bayonet during the initial encounter. Prisoners consisted of two officers and forty-eight enlisted men. Ethan Allen to the Massachusetts Congress, May 11, 1775, and Benedict Arnold to the Massachusetts Committee of Safety, May 11, 1775, in Force, *American Archives*, 4th ser., 2:556, 557; Allen French, *The Taking of Ticonderoga in 1775: The British Story; A Study of Captors and Captives* (Cambridge, Mass., 1928), 42–45; Benson J. Lossing, *The Pictorial Field Book of the Revolution*, 2 vols.

(New York, 1851–52), 1:124; Christopher Ward, *The War of the Revolution*, ed. John R. Alden, 2 vols. (New York, 1952), 1:72. Benedict Arnold (1741–1801) was born in Norwich, Connecticut. He was apprenticed to a druggist at the age of fourteen. After the death of his parents, the twenty-one-year-old Arnold sold the family property and moved to New Haven. There he opened a shop to sell drugs and books. Marrying his first wife in 1767, he became a successful merchant and trader. When Lexington and Concord broke out, he raised a company of Connecticut militia and marched for Boston. On May 3, 1775, Massachusetts appointed Arnold a militia colonel and approved his plan to attack Fort Ticonderoga.

18. Because of indecision on the part of Congress, directives concerning relocation of armament at Fort Ticonderoga were delayed. By the time an initiative was taken, severe winter weather and scarcity of adequate transportation combined to further impede their removal. A detail under Col. Henry Knox, the newly appointed Continental army chief of artillery, utilizing oxen drawn sleds, finally delivered the cannons (52–59 weapons weighing a total of about 119,900 pounds) from Ticonderoga to the vicinity of Boston on January 24, 1776. For accounts of Knox's cannon transportation operation, see Henry Knox, "Knox's Diary during His Ticonderoga Expedition," *New England Historical and Genealogical Register* 30 (1976): 321–22; North Callahan, "Henry Knox, General Washington's General," *New-York Historical Society Quarterly* 44 (1960): 150–65; Alexander C. Flick, "General Knox's Ticonderoga Expedition," *New York State Historical Association Quarterly Journal* 9 (1928): 119–35.

19. After the Revolution, the territorial dispute resumed. Finally, an accord was reached whereby Vermont paid New York $30,000 for the contested lands and the state of Vermont entered the Union in 1791. For a thorough treatment of the New Hampshire Grants controversy, consult Irving Mark, *Agrarian Conflicts in Colonial New York, 1711–1775* (Port Washington, N.Y., 1965), 164–94.

20. For a comprehensive discussion of the Fort Ticonderoga affair, refer to Justin H. Smith, *Our Struggle for the Fourteenth Colony* 1:119, 166–71, 178–92.

21. The Hudson River was also known as the North River during this time. In June–October 1777, the British army employed this Hudson Highlands strategy when Gen. John Burgoyne launched an invasion from Canada down the Lake Champlain–Lake George–Hudson River route in an attempt to geographically separate the colonies and deal with them in a piecemeal fashion. This offensive failed when Burgoyne lost the Battle of Saratoga and surrendered his forces.

22. Richard Montgomery to Robert R. Livingston, June 3, 1775, Robert R. Livingston Papers, New York Public Library. Guy Carleton (1724–1808) was a career British army officer, rising to the rank of major general before he received his most recent appointment as governor of Quebec Province on January 10, 1775. He had served in the same capacity during the 1766–1770 period. For a comprehensive biographical study of Carleton during the American campaign in Canada, see Perry Eugene Leroy, "Sir Guy Carleton as a Military Leader during the American Invasion and Repulse in Canada, 1775–1776," 2 vols. (Ph.D. diss., Ohio State University, 1960).

23. Worthington Chauncey Ford, ed., Library of Congress, *Journals of the*

Continental Congress, 1774–1789, 34 vols. (Washington, D.C., 1904–37), 2:57, 59–61, 73–75.

24. William Douglas to Hannah Douglas, July 19, 1775, in William Douglas, "Letters Written during the Revolutionary War by Colonel William Douglas to His Wife Covering the Period July 19, 1775, to December 5, 1776," *New-York Historical Society Quarterly Bulletin* 12 (1929): 150.

25. Force, *American Archives*, 4th ser., 2:516–17; Major Isaac Hamilton to Cadwallader Colden, May 26, 1775, June 5, 1775, in Cadwallader Colden, *The Letters and Papers of Cadwallader Colden*, 9 vols., New-York Historical Society Collections, no. 56 (New York, 1918–37), 7:297, 299–300.

26. Willett, *Narrative*, 58–65.

27. Richard Montgomery to Robert R. Livingston, June 7, 1775, Robert R. Livingston Papers, New York Public Library.

28. Colden, *The Colden Letter Books* 2:426–28; Force, *American Archives*, 4th ser., 2:1285, 1290, 1626–27; O'Callaghan and Fernow, *Documents Relative to the Colonial History of the State of New York* 8:646. For an excellent commentary on the relationship between the Provincial Congress and popular disorder, see Gilje, *The Road to Mobocracy*, 61–64.

29. *Journals of the Provincial Congress of the State of New York*, 2 vols. (Albany, N.Y., 1775), 1:31, 33, entries of June 7, 1775; New York Secretary of State, *Calendar of Historical Manuscripts Relating to the War of the Revolution*, 1:101; Force, *American Archives*, 4th ser., 2:1248, 1265, 1267, 1272, 1273, 1278–80, 1284, 1286, 1287, 1299, 1301.

30. Richard Montgomery to Robert R. Livingston, June 7, 1775, Robert R. Livingston Papers, New York Public Library.

31. Abigail Adams, for example, found herself in similar circumstances when her husband, John Adams, left to serve in the Continental Congress, compelling her to manage their Braintree, Mass., farm.

32. Janet Montgomery to Lt. Perkins Magra, May 25, 1775, Montgomery MSS Collection, Clements Library. Also published in Clements Library Associates, *Major General Richard Montgomery*, 18–23. The two sisters referred to in the poem were the maiden sisters who resided with Janet Montgomery during this time. Richard Montgomery's only sister, Lady Sarah Ranelagh, lived with her husband, Charles, fourth Viscount of Ranelagh, in Ireland.

33. The colonial patriots philosophically aligned themselves with the British opposition faction in England (Whigs), calling themselves "whigs" after that political party. The patriots referred to provincials who were against conflict with the British government as "tories," a derogatory term derived from the designation of the loyalist party in England (Tories).

S I X   *The Patriot Call to Arms*

1. "A Song on the Brave General Montgomery Who Fell within the Walls of Quebec Dec. 31, 1775, in Attempting To Storm That City"; included in a 1776 broadside issued at Danvers, Mass., Essex Institute, Salem, Mass. Reproduced in

Frank Moore, ed., *The Diary of the American Revolution, 1775–1781* (New York, 1968), 92–93.

2. Richard Montgomery to Robert R. Livingston, June 3, 1775, Bancroft Transcripts, Robert R. Livingston Papers, 1, 33, New York Public Library. Robert R. Livingston to Richard Montgomery, June 3, [1775], Bancroft Transcripts, Livingston Papers, 1, 31, New York Public Library. Philip John Schuyler (1733–1804) was born into one of the oldest and most affluent Dutch families in New York. After receiving an excellent education, he served as a logistical officer in the militia during the French and Indian War, rising to the rank of colonel. He became afflicted with hereditary rheumatic gout at the age of twenty-two. Elected to the Provincial Assembly in 1768, he proved to be an ardent patriot, although he opposed the Sons of Liberty and other radical activities. For Schuyler biographies, see Benson J. Lossing, *The Life and Times of Philip Schuyler*, 2 vols. (New York, 1873 [1860]); Martin H. Bush, *Revolutionary Enigma: A Re-appraisal of General Philip Schuyler of New York* (Port Washington, N.Y., 1969); Don R. Gerlach, *Proud Patriot: Philip Schuyler and the War of Independence, 1775–1783* (Syracuse, N.Y., 1987).

3. Janet Montgomery, "Reminiscences," 75.

4. *Journals of the Provincial Congress of the State of New York* 1:32, entry of June 7, 1775. Horatio Gates (1728–1806) retired on half pay as a major in the British army in 1765. Seven years later, he settled in Virginia with the help of George Washington, whom he had served with and befriended during the French and Indian Wars. As the Revolution approached, Gates sided with the colonists. Anticipated personal advancement in joining the Continental army, which desperately needed professionally trained officers, certainly played a part in Gates's decision for the patriot cause. His connections with Washington facilitated this ambition. After Congress selected Washington as the commander in chief, he nominated Gates to be his adjutant general with the rank of brigadier general. Charles Lee (1758–1815), a half-pay British lieutenant colonel who migrated to the colonies in 1773, recommended himself to the Congress for an appointment in the Continental army. Congress offered him a major-general's commission. Acceptance of this position would lead to the loss of his British army retirement pay and confiscation of his property in England, so Lee waited until Congress agreed to compensate him for these losses before accepting the commission.

5. Richard Montgomery to Robert R. Livingston, June 7, 1775, Robert R. Livingston Papers, New York Public Library. Richard Montgomery to Robert R. Livingston, June 28, 1775, Emmet Collection, New York Public Library.

6. Richard Montgomery to Capt. Perkins Magra, July 2, 1775, Richard Montgomery MSS, Clements Library. Also published in Clements Library Associates, *Major General Richard Montgomery*, 16–17. The British government deployed five regiments to Boston in August 1775, including the 17th Foot. The 17th Regiment remained in America until 1782. However, it did not see action in the Canadian campaign and thus never opposed Montgomery.

7. Janet Montgomery, "Reminiscences," 69–70.

8. Ford, *Journals of the Continental Congress* 2:97, 99, 103. The four major-general selections included: Artemas Ward (Massachusetts), Charles Lee (Vir-

ginia), Philip Schuyler (New York), and Israel Putnam (Connecticut), respectively. The initial brigadier-general appointments comprised: Seth Pomeroy (Massachusetts), Richard Montgomery (New York), David Wooster (Connecticut), William Heath (Massachusetts), Joseph Spencer (Connecticut), John Thomas (Massachusetts), John Sullivan (New Hampshire), and Nathanael Greene (Rhode Island), respectively. In addition, Congress named Horatio Gates (Virginia) as Continental army adjutant general with brigadier rank.

9. Congress did not fill the vacant eighth brigadier position. Therefore, the amended brigadier general order of rank was: Thomas, Montgomery, Wooster, Heath, Spencer, Sullivan, and Greene. For a discussion of the general officer selection process, see Allen French, *The First Year of the American Revolution* (Cambridge, Mass., 1934), 295, 752–54; Jonathan Gregory Rossie, *The Politics of Command in the American Revolution* (Syracuse, N.Y., 1975), 14–24; Robert K. Wright, Jr., *The Continental Army* (Washington, D.C., 1986), 21–29.

10. James Duane to Richard Montgomery, July 21, 1775, in Edmund C. Burnett, ed., *Letters of Members of the Continental Congress*, 8 vols. (Washington, D.C., 1921–36), 1:171; Paul H. Smith, *Letters of Delegates to Congress* 1:641–42. James Duane (1733–1797) was the son of a prosperous New York City merchant. He practiced law after being admitted to the bar in August 1754. After his election to the Continental Congress on July 4, 1774, he became a leader in the moderate faction toward independence. He served on a large number of committees, and his most significant work was done in the fields of finance and Indian affairs.

11. Janet Montgomery, "Reminiscences," 74–75.

12. Philip Schuyler to Peter Van Brugh Livingston, June 24, 1775, in *Journals of the Provincial Congress of the State of New York* 2:10–11. Peter Van Brugh Livingston (1710–1792), a wealthy distant cousin of the Clermont Livingstons, had profited greatly from military contracts during the colonial wars. He was elected president of the New York Provincial Congress when it was founded on May 23, 1775, and became its treasurer on July 8. He held both positions until August 28, 1775, when he withdrew from all public affairs due to poor health.

13. *Journals of the Provincial Congress of the State of New York* 1:54, entry of June 25, 1775.

14. Bruce Bliven, Jr., *Under the Guns: New York 1775–1776* (New York, 1972), 1–12.

15. George Washington to Philip Schuyler, June 25, 1775, in W. W. Abbot, ed., *The Papers of George Washington*, 7 vols., Colonial Series (Charlottesville, Va., 1983–90), 1:37. Col. Guy Johnson (1740–1788) commanded a ranger company during the French and Indian War. After the conflict, he became superintendent of Indian affairs for the British and built a good reputation with the Indians. During 1773 to 1775, he was a member of the New York Assembly, and he developed into an effective loyalist leader in the province. At this time, he was actively engaged in inciting the Indians against the patriot cause.

16. David Wooster (1711–1777), son of a Connecticut mason, graduated from Yale University in 1738. He became a militia officer in 1741 and participated in the French and Indian War. In 1746, Wooster married the daughter of Thomas

Clap, president of Yale. In 1750, he organized at New Haven one of the first lodges of Free Masons in Connecticut. In 1763, he served as customs collector in New Haven. He was also commissioned as a captain in the British army, retiring on half pay in 1774. He received appointment as a major general of six Connecticut regiments in April 1775 and was ordered to New York the next month. When Congress started commissioning Continental generals, it named him brigadier general on June 22, 1775.

17. Richard Montgomery to Robert R. Livingston, July 1, 1775, Robert R. Livingston Papers, New York Public Library. Richard Montgomery to Robert R. Livingston, August 6, 1775, Robert R. Livingston Papers, New York Public Library. Bliven, *Under the Guns*, 25–29. Tryon was not able to regain his governmental authority in New York. Increasing patriot activities, including the threat of kidnapping, forced him into seclusion, further alienating him from civic affairs. In October 1775, he took refuge aboard a British ship in New York City Harbor and remained there until British forces arrived in June 1776 for the New York campaign. Tryon's governorship was one of exile during this time. In this regard, Tryon followed the example set by three of his fellow royal governors of Virginia, North Carolina, and South Carolina, who had all retreated to British warships stationed in their respective province. Isaac Sears (1730–1786) was New York's most active and notorious patriot agitator. As a radical leader in the Sons of Liberty, he participated in nearly every mob action in New York City for ten years. However, his sometimes bizarre and unsanctioned activities were a frequent source of embarrassment to more moderate patriots.

18. Ford, *Journals of the Continental Congress* 2:75.

19. Gen. Thomas Gage to Lord Dartmouth, June 12, 1775, in Carter, *The Correspondence of General Thomas Gage* 1:403–4. The Second Massachusetts Provincial Congress enlisted the Stockbridge Indians in its fight against British authority and also attempted to include the Mohawk and Eastern Indians in their cause. William Lincoln, ed., *The Journals of Each Provincial Congress of Massachusetts in 1774 and 1775, and of the Committee of Safety* (Boston, 1838), 114–16, 118–20, 225–26).

20. John Adams to James Warren, June 7, 1775, in Robert J. Taylor, ed., *Papers of John Adams*, 4 vols. (Cambridge, Mass., 1977–79), 3:17–18. By sending many of his regular troops to fight at the siege of Boston, Guy Carleton depleted the British forces in Canada to about eight hundred regulars, a third of whom were stationed in the Great Lakes region far to the west. In an attempt to consolidate English authority in Quebec, he declared martial law on June 9, 1775.

21. *Papers of the Continental Congress*, National Archives, microfilm, 172. Return of July 14, 1775 reflected the following troop disposition and strength: Gen. Wooster's and Col. David Waterbury's Connecticut regiments at New York City numbered 576 and 929, respectively; Col. Benjamin Hinman's Connecticut regiment was dispersed among Ticonderoga (478), Crown Point (293), Lake George landing (98), and Fort George (104); Massachusetts troops scattered at various locations amounted to 174; and New York volunteers at Fort George added another 205 men—for a total force of 2,857. Two weeks later, troop returns

reported a rank-and-file strength of 2,958, of whom 2,419 were considered fit for duty.

22. Charles Havens Hunt, *Life of Edward Livingston* (New York, 1864), 32. By *blush*, Montgomery meant *feel ashamed*.

SEVEN *The March to Canada*

1. "A Fragment," a ballad by Robert Burns, reproduced in Frank Moore, ed., *Songs and Ballads of the American Revolution* (Port Washington, N.Y., 1964), 381.

2. William Smith, *An Oration in Memory of General Montgomery*, 28.

3. Philip Schuyler to George Washington, July 15, 1775, Philip Schuyler Papers, New York Public Library.

4. Philip Schuyler to George Washington, July 18, 1775, Philip Schuyler Papers, New York Public Library.

5. James Duane to Robert R. Livingston, June 7, 1775, Livingston-Redmond MSS, New York Public Library. The "young Mr. Livingston" was Robert R. Livingston's youngest brother, Henry Beekman Livingston, who raised a company and was commissioned a captain in the 4th New York Regiment on June 28, 1775. He went with his brother-in-law, Richard Montgomery, to Quebec and served as his aide-de-camp from July to December 1775.

6. Janet Montgomery in Hunt, *Biographical Notes Concerning General Richard Montgomery*, 7. The term "mechanics" refers to the unfranchised residents: leasehold tenants and those who worked for others—distinguished from the landowner and merchant segments of society.

7. Fred Anderson Berg, *Encyclopedia of Continental Army Units* (Harrisburg, Pa., 1972), 83–85; Eric I. Manders, "Notes on Troop Units in the New York Garrison, 1775–1776," *Military Collector and Historian: Journal of the Company of Military Historians* 25, no. 1 (Spring 1973): 18–21.

8. Alan C. Aimone and Barbara A. Aimone, "Organizing and Equipping Montgomery's Yorkers in 1775," *Military Collector and Historian: Journal of the Company of Military Historians* 28, no. 2 (Summer 1976): 53–54. Also see Alan C. Aimone and Barbara A. Aimone, "Brave Bostonians: New Yorkers' Roles in the Winter Invasion of Canada," *Military Collector and Historian: Journal of the Company of Military Historians* 36, no. 4 (Winter 1984): 134–50, for an excellent overview of the Canadian campaign; Asa Bird Gardner, "The New York Continental Line of the Army of the Revolution," *Magazine of American History* 7 (December 1881): 403; William L. MacDougall, *American Revolutionary: A Biography of General Alexander McDougall* (Westport, Conn., 1977), 66.

9. O'Callaghan and Fernow, *Documents Relative to the Colonial History of the State of New York* 15:11.

10. Ibid., 17.

11. Ibid., 22.

12. Aimone and Aimone, "Organizing and Equipping Montgomery's Yorkers in 1775," 54.

13. Richard Montgomery General Orders, July 19, 1775, Richard Montgomery MSS, New-York Historical Society.

14. New York Committee of Safety to Philip Schuyler, July 15, 1775, in Force, *American Archives*, 4th ser., 2:1730.

15. Rudolphus Ritzema, "Journal of Col. Rudolphus Ritzema of the First New York Regiment, August 8, 1775 to March 30, 1776," *Magazine of American History with Notes and Queries* 1 (1877): 98.

16. Philip Schuyler to New York Congress, August 19, 1775, in Force, *American Archives*, 4th ser., 3:177.

17. Richard Montgomery to Col. Goose Van Schaick, August 10, 1775, Richard Montgomery MSS, New-York Historical Society.

18. Ford, *Journals of the Continental Congress* 2:186; Force, *American Archives*, 4th ser., 3:177, 433–34.

19. Force, *American Archives*, 4th ser., 2:1702–4, 1734–35, 1762–63; 3:17, 242–43.

20. George Washington to Philip Schuyler, August 20, 1775, in Abbot, *The Papers of George Washington* 1:331–33.

21. John Brown to Richard Montgomery, August 23, 1775, in Force, *American Archives*, 4th ser., 3:468.

22. Richard Montgomery to Philip Schuyler, August 25, 1775, Philip Schuyler Papers, New York Public Library.

23. Capt. William Douglas to Hannah Douglas, August 28–29, 1775, William Douglas Papers, New-York Historical Society.

24. Richard Montgomery, Last Will and Testament, August 30, 1775, Richard Montgomery MSS, New-York Historical Society.

25. Philip Schuyler to George Washington, August 31, 1775, Philip Schuyler Papers, New York Public Library; Philip Schuyler to Turbutt Francis and Volckert Douw, August 31, 1775, Philip Schuyler Papers, New York Public Library.

26. Urieh Cross, "Narrative of Urieh Cross in the Revolutionary War," *Vermont Quarterly*, new ser., 15 (July 1947): 180.

27. Philip Schuyler to the Inhabitants of Canada, September 5, 1775, Philip Schuyler Papers, New York Public Library. About a week later, George Washington sent a similar appeal to the Canadians: see George Washington, "Address to the Inhabitants of Canada [c. September 14, 1775]," in Abbot, *The Papers of George Washington* 1:461–63. Ethan Allen (1738–1789) commanded the Green Mountain Boys when they seized Ticonderoga from the British in May 1775 but lost his position as commander in July 1775 and was at this time serving under Schuyler and Montgomery as a civilian scout. Seth Warner (1743–1784), whom the Green Mountain Boys elected as lieutenant colonel commander on July 26, 1775, was still attempting to mobilize his battalion in the aftermath of organizational turmoil so it could join the campaign as a coherent unit. James Livingston (1747–1832), a distant relative of the New York Livingstons and an in-law of Montgomery, was a merchant living in Chambly at this time who supported the patriots' campaign in Canada.

28. Philip Schuyler to John Hancock, September 8, 1775, Philip Schuyler Papers, New York Public Library; Philip Schuyler to George Washington, Sep-

tember 20, 1775, Philip Schuyler Papers, New York Public Library; Ritzema, "Journal," 99. Gilbert Tice was a former captain in the New York militia who became a loyalist, serving the British throughout the war by recruiting and leading various bands of Indians against the Americans.

29. Philip Schuyler to John Hancock, September 8, 1775, Philip Schuyler Papers, New York Public Library; Philip Schuyler to George Washington, September 20, 1775, Philip Schuyler Papers, New York Public Library; Ritzema, "Journal," 99.

30. Philip Schuyler to John Hancock, September 8, 1775, Philip Schuyler Papers, New York Public Library; Philip Schuyler to George Washington, September 20, 1775, Philip Schuyler Papers, New York Public Library. Schuyler wished to maintain the confidentiality of his informant, so he did not disclose his name in the letter to Hancock (Continental Congress). In the letter to Washington, he included the agent's name but requested that the commander in chief obliterate it after reading. Washington complied with the request. However, historical research revealed that the subject individual was Moses Hazen (1733–1803), a native of Massachusetts who had lived at St. Johns since 1763. Although Hazen had retired as an officer from the British army, authorities in Canada suspected him of being sympathetic to the American cause. They had earlier imprisoned him for a time and confiscated his considerable property holdings in the area. See Abbot, *The Papers of George Washington* 1:222 n. 4.

31. Philip Schuyler to John Hancock, September 8, 1775, Philip Schuyler Papers, New York Public Library; Philip Schuyler to George Washington, September 20, 1775, Philip Schuyler Papers, New York Public Library.

32. Rudolphus Ritzema to Alexander McDougall, September 8, 1775, Alexander McDougall Papers, New-York Historical Society; Philip Schuyler to John Hancock, September 8, 1775, Philip Schuyler Papers, New York Public Library; Philip Schuyler to George Washington, September 20, 1775, Philip Schuyler Papers, New York Public Library.

33. Philip Schuyler to Continental Congress, September 19, 1775, Philip Schuyler Papers, New York Public Library.

34. Force, *American Archives*, 4th ser., 3:741–42.

35. Ibid.

36. Ibid.

37. Richard Montgomery to Janet Montgomery, September 12, 1775, Janet Montgomery Papers, Edward Livingston Collection, Princeton University Library.

38. Philip Schuyler Letterbook 2:121, New York Public Library.

39. Richard Montgomery to Janet Montgomery, September 5, 1775, Janet Montgomery Papers, Edward Livingston Collection, Princeton University Library; Philip Schuyler to Continental Congress, September 19, 1775, Philip Schuyler Papers, New York Public Library.

40. "Extract of a Letter to a Gentleman in New-York from an Officer at Isle aux Noix, September 17, 1775," in Force, *American Archives*, 4th ser., 3:726.

41. Philip Schuyler to Continental Congress, September 19, 1775, Philip Schuyler Papers, New York Public Library.

EIGHT   *Struggle and Success against St. Johns*

1. "A Song on the Brave General Montgomery," in Moore, *The Diary of the American Revolution*, 92–93.

2. Philip Schuyler to Continental Congress, September 19, 1775, Philip Schuyler Papers, New York Public Library.

3. Janet Montgomery, in Hunt, *Biographical Notes Concerning General Richard Montgomery*, 7–8; Howard Thomas, *Marinus Willett: Soldier, Patriot, 1740–1830* (New York, 1954), 36.

4. Philip Schuyler to Continental Congress, September 19, 1775, Philip Schuyler Papers, New York Public Library.

5. Janet Montgomery, in Hunt, *Biographical Notes Concerning General Richard Montgomery*, 8. Major Charles Preston was a member of the 26th Regiment of Scottish Rifles at this time. He later received the title of Fifth Baronet of Valleyfield, Fife.

6. Fortescue, *A History of the British Army* 3:155; Justin H. Smith, *Our Struggle for the Fourteenth Colony* 1:343–44.

7. Harry Parker Ward, ed., "Diary of Captain John Fassett, Jr.," *The Follett-Dewey Fassett-Safford Ancestry of Captain Martin Dewey Follett* (Columbus, Oh., 1896), 217; Richard Montgomery to Philip Schuyler, September 19, 1775, Philip Schuyler Papers, New York Public Library. For a British version of the skirmish, see Lt. Gov. Hector Cramahé to Secretary of State, Earl of Dartmouth (William Legge), September 24, 1775, British Public Records Office, Colonial Correspondence (CO 5).

8. Maj. Timothy Bedel to New Hampshire Committee of Safety, September 23, 1775, in Force, *American Archives*, 4th ser., 3:779.

9. M. James, Return of Brass and Iron Ordnance and Mortars in the North and South Forts at St. John's, November 3, 1775, in Force, *American Archives*, 4th ser., 3:1395; Willett, *Narrative*, 37; George F. G. Stanley, *Canada Invaded, 1775–1776* (Toronto, 1973), 51.

10. Willett, *Narrative*, 37; Leake, *Memoir of the Life and Times of General John Lamb*, 112.

11. Diary of Col. Aaron Barlow extracted in Charles Burr Todd, "The March to Montreal and Quebec, 1775," *American Historical Register* 2 (1895): 646; "Military Pension Deposition of Justus Bellamy," in John C. Dann, ed., *The Revolution Remembered: Eyewitness Accounts of the War for Independence* (Chicago, 1980), 384.

12. Richard Montgomery to Col. [Maj.] Timothy Bedel, October 13, 1775, in W. T. R. Saffell, *Records of the Revolutionary War: Containing the Military and Financial Correspondence of Distinguished Officers* (Baltimore, 1969 [1894]), 25. Richard Montgomery to Philip Schuyler, September 24, 1775, Philip Schuyler Papers, New York Public Library. Capt. Gershom Mott had been one of the most active agitators in New York before the Revolution and his entry into the army. Capt. John Lamb and fellow officers, who had been associated with Mott in the Sons of Liberty, petitioned Montgomery to restore him to his company command. It appears that the general yielded to the request for mitigation, as Mott

led his company on subsequent expedition operations: the march to Montreal and the attack on Quebec (Leake, *Memoir of the Life and Times of General John Lamb*, 117).

13. Richard Montgomery to Philip Schuyler, August 1, 1775, Philip Schuyler Papers, New York Public Library.

14. Ethan Allen to Richard Montgomery, September 20, 1775, in Force, *American Archives*, 4th ser., 3:754.

15. Maj. John Brown had served under Allen with the Massachusetts contingent at the capture of Ticonderoga in May 1775. The reason he failed to join Allen before Montreal remains obscure. In his later account of the affair, Allen made no recriminations against Brown. He matter-of-factly told of Brown's failure to appear and let the matter drop. Since no one accused Brown of dereliction of duty in this regard, he felt no compunction to defend himself and left no explanation of the incident before he died in action in October 1780. For further analysis, see Charles A. Jellison, *Ethan Allen: Frontier Rebel* (Syracuse, N.Y., 1983 [1969]), 152–57; French, *The First Year of the American Revolution*, 422–23; Justin H. Smith, *Our Struggle for the Fourteenth Colony* 1:384–90.

16. The only detailed primary source of Allen's attempt on Montreal is his own account: Ethan Allen, *The Narrative of Colonel Ethan Allen* (New York, 1961, reprint), 16–24. His British captors sent Allen in irons to England. He returned to New York City under parole in October 1776.

17. Seth Warner to Richard Montgomery, September 27, 1775, in Force, *American Archives*, 4th ser., 3:953; James Livingston to Richard Montgomery, September 27, 1775, in Force, *American Archives*, 4th ser., 3:952–53; Timothy Bedel to Richard Montgomery, September 28, 1775, in Force, *American Archives*, 4th ser., 3:954.

18. Richard Montgomery to Philip Schuyler, September 28, 1775, Philip Schuyler Papers, New York Public Library; Richard Montgomery to Philip Schuyler, September 28, 1775, Philip Schuyler Papers, New York Public Library.

19. Philip Schuyler to President of the Congress, October 5, 1775, Philip Schuyler Papers, New York Public Library.

20. George Washington to Philip Schuyler, October 26, 1775, in John C. Fitzpatrick, ed., *The Writings of George Washington*, 39 vols. (Washington, D.C., 1931–44), 4:46.

21. *New England Chronicle*, November 2, 1775. For a British version of the incident, see Guy Carleton to the Earl of Dartmouth, October 25, 1775, in K. G. Davies, ed., *Documents of the American Revolution, 1770–1783*, Colonial Office Series, no. 11 (London, 1976), 165–66; Lieutenant Governor Cramahé to the Earl of Dartmouth, September 30, 1775, British Public Records Office, Colonial Correspondence (CO 5); Guy Johnson to the Earl of Dartmouth, October 12, 1775, in Davies, *Documents of the American Revolution*, 142–44; "Letters from Quebec," in Force, *American Archives*, 4th ser., 3:845, 924; *Quebec Gazette*, October 5, 19, 1775; *London Gazette*, November 4, 1775.

22. Richard Montgomery to Janet Montgomery, October 6, 1775, Janet

Montgomery Papers, Edward Livingston Collection, Princeton University Library; Samuel Mott to Jonathan Trumbull, October 6, 1775, in Force, *American Archives*, 4th ser., 3:973.

23. George Washington to Philip Schuyler, October 26, 1775, in Fitzpatrick, *The Writings of George Washington* 4:47. Schuyler endorsed Montgomery's plan of operations and later outlined the strategy in detail to Washington. Philip Schuyler to George Washington, November 6, 1775, Philip Schuyler Papers, New York Public Library.

24. Benjamin Trumbull, "A Concise Journal or Minutes of the Principal Movements towards St. John's of the Siege and Surrender of the Forts There in 1775," *Collections of the Connecticut Historical Society* 7 (1899): 159, entry of November 6, 1775; Richard Montgomery to Janet Montgomery, October 6, 1775, Janet Montgomery Papers, Edward Livingston Collection, Princeton University Library; Samuel Mott to Gov. Jonathan Trumbull, October 20, 1775, in Force, *American Archives*, 4th ser., 3:1124.

25. Ritzema, "Journal," 100, entry of September 11, 1775; Maj. John Brown to Gov. Jonathan Trumbull, August 14, 1775, in Force, *American Archives*, 4th ser., 3:136.

26. Col. Benjamin Hinman to Gov. Jonathan Trumbull, August 14, 1775, in Force, *American Archives*, 4th ser., 3:135; Col. Samuel Mott to Gov. Jonathan Trumbull, October 6, 1775, in Force, *American Archives*, 4th ser., 3:974.

27. Richard Montgomery to Janet Montgomery, October 9, 1775, Janet Montgomery Papers, Edward Livingston Collection, Princeton University Library. Henry Beekman Livingston (1750–1831) became the most distinguished of the fourteen Livingstons who served as commissioned officers in the Revolution. He continued as an aide to Montgomery until the general's death. Afterward, he became aide-de-camp to General Schuyler. He received his majority on February 28, 1776. Congress also presented him a sword in honor of his gallant service in Canada. He eventually rose to the rank of brigadier general by the close of the Revolution.

28. Ibid.; Richard Montgomery to Robert R. Livingston, October 5, 1775, Robert R. Livingston Papers, New York Public Library.

29. Richard Montgomery to Timothy Bedel, September 20, 1775, in Saffell, *Records of the Revolutionary War*, 19; Philip Schuyler to George Washington, September 20, 1775, Philip Schuyler Papers, New York Public Library; Aaron Barlow diary, entry of October 6, 1775, in Todd, "The March to Montreal and Quebec," 647; Benjamin Trumbull, *Bulletin of the Fort Ticonderoga Museum* (January 1928): 16, entry of October 6, 1775; Charles Preston journal, entry of October 6, 1775, in Canadian Public Archives, *Report of the Public Archives for 1914 and 1915*, Appendix B (Ottawa, 1916), 21.

30. Richard Montgomery to Philip Schuyler, October 13, 1775, Philip Schuyler Papers, New York Public Library; Frederick von Steuben to Baron de Gaudy [1787], in Friedrich Kapp, *The Life of Frederick William von Steuben* (New York, 1859), 699. (Baron) Frederick von Steuben (1730–1794), a former Prussian army officer, joined the Continental army in 1778 and became its inspector general with the rank of major general. His fame stemmed from his adroit military training of

Washington's ragtag troops at Valley Forge that year. He served with the Continental army until the end of the war, when he became an American citizen; he lived in New York until his death.

31. Richard Montgomery to Philip Schuyler, October 13, 1775, Philip Schuyler Papers, New York Public Library.

32. Ibid.

33. Henry Brockholst Livingston, "Journal of Major Henry Livingston of the Third New York Continental Line, August To December 1775," ed. Gaillard Hunt, *Pennsylvania Magazine of History and Biography* 22 (April 1898): 17–18; Oscar E. Bredenberg, "The American Champlain Fleet, 1775–77," *Bulletin of the Fort Ticonderoga Museum* 12, no. 4 (September 1968): 255–58. The *Royal Savage* came to rest in shallow water. After their capture of St. Johns, the Americans raised the vessel and put it to their own use. In October 1776, Benedict Arnold employed the *Savage* as part of his flotilla in the naval battle he conducted on Lake Champlain (Valcour Island). During this engagement, the ship was destroyed when it caught fire and her magazine exploded. Janet Montgomery was a great-aunt to Henry Brockholst Livingston (1757–1823), who should not be confused with Janet's brother, Henry (Harry) Beekman Livingston.

34. Philip Schuyler to David Wooster, October 19, 1775, Philip Schuyler Papers, New York Public Library; David Wooster to Philip Schuyler, October 19, 1775, Philip Schuyler Papers, New York Public Library. David Wooster (1711–1777) became a militia lieutenant in 1741. He continued to serve in the militia throughout the French and Indian War. He was a major general in the Connecticut militia at the beginning of the revolutionary war. When the Continental Congress started commissioning general officers, it offered Wooster a brigadier-general commission. He was the only major general of militia not given the corresponding rank in the Continental army. His familiarity with the rank and file made him well liked but also promoted lax discipline among the men in his command. His undisciplined troops and his lack of respect for authority formed a basis for the ill will between him and Schuyler.

35. Philip Schuyler to President of Congress, October 18, 1775, Philip Schuyler Papers, New York Public Library.

36. Richard Montgomery to Philip Schuyler, October 20, 1775, Philip Schuyler Papers, New York Public Library.

37. Philip Schuyler to George Washington, October 26, 1775, Philip Schuyler Papers, New York Public Library; Richard Montgomery to Philip Schuyler, October 20, 1775, Philip Schuyler Papers, New York Public Library.

38. "An Account of Stores Taken at Chambly," in Force, *American Archives*, 4th ser., 3:1133–34; George Washington to Philip Schuyler, November 5, 1775, Philip Schuyler Papers, New York Public Library.

39. Richard Montgomery to Joseph Stopford, October 20, 1775, in Force, *American Archives*, 4th ser., 3:1134; Richard Montgomery to Guy Carleton, October 22, 1775, in Ernest Cruikshank, ed., *A History of the Organization, Development, and Services of the Military and Naval Forces of Canada from the Peace of Paris in 1763, to the Present Time*, 3 vols. (Ottawa, 1919–20), 2:106–7. For Allen's account of his captivity, see his *Narrative*.

40. Guy Carleton to Lord Dartmouth, October 25, 1775, in Cruikshank, *A History of the Organization, Development, and Services of the Military and Naval Forces of Canada* 2:112–13.

41. Philip Schuyler to John Hancock, October 21, 1775, Philip Schuyler Papers, New York Public Library.

42. "Military Pension Deposition of Justus Bellamy," in Dann, *The Revolution Remembered*, 382.

43. Aaron Barlow diary, in Todd, "The March to Montreal and Quebec," 647–48; Trumbull, "Diary" (January 1928): 29–30.

44. "Extract of a Letter from Quebec, October 25, 1775," in Force, *American Archives*, 4th ser., 3:1185.

45. Ward, "Diary of Captain John Fassett, Jr.," 225–29.

46. Ritzema, "Journal," 102, entry of November 1, 1775.

47. Richard Montgomery to Charles Preston, November 1, 1775, in Cruikshank, *A History of the Organization, Development, and Services of the Military and Naval Forces of Canada* 2:114.

48. "Military Pension Deposition of Justus Bellamy," in Dann, *The Revolution Remembered*, 385.

49. Charles Preston journal, entry of November 3, 1775, in Canadian Public Archives, *Report of the Public Archives*, 24–25; Charles Preston to Richard Montgomery, November 1, 1775, in Force, *American Archives*, 4th ser., 3:1393; Richard Montgomery to Charles Preston, November 1, 1775, in Cruikshank, *A History of the Organization, Development, and Services of the Military and Naval Forces of Canada* 2:114.

50. "Extract of Another Letter from Fort St. Johns, November 3, 1775," in Force, *American Archives*, 4th ser., 3:1344. "Articles of Capitulation, St. Johns, November 2, 1775," in Cruikshank, *A History of the Organization, Development, and Services of the Military and Naval Forces of Canada* 2:115; Force, *American Archives*, 4th ser., 3:1394. Lt. John André (1751–1780) of the 7th Regiment was among the prisoners taken by the Americans when they captured St. Johns. He was exchanged a year later after serving parole in the interior of Pennsylvania. He returned to duty as a captain and aide-de-camp to Gen. Charles Grey with the British occupation force in Philadelphia. There, he befriended Benedict Arnold's wife, Peggy Shippen. Later, he became involved in Arnold's treason. André's second capture by the Americans resulted in his execution as a spy.

51. Stanley, *Canada Invaded*, 62; Justin H. Smith, *Our Struggle for the Fourteenth Colony* 1:459; Charles Preston, "Troop Return, November 1, 1775," in Cruikshank, *A History of the Organization, Development, and Services of the Military and Naval Forces of Canada* 2:115; "Extract of a Letter from an Officer of the New York Forces [Capt. John Lamb], November 3, 1775," in Force, *American Archives*, 4th ser., 3:1343–44.

52. William Douglas to Hannah Douglas, November 12, 1775, in Douglas, "Letters Written during the Revolutionary War by Colonel William Douglas to His Wife," 153–54.

NINE *On to Quebec*

1. William Smith, *An Oration in Memory of General Montgomery*, 29–30.
2. "A Song on the Brave General Montgomery," in Moore, *The Diary of the American Revolution*, 93.
3. Richard Montgomery to Philip Schuyler, November 13, 1775, Philip Schuyler Papers, New York Public Library.
4. Ibid. Richard Montgomery to Janet Montgomery, October 5, 1775, Janet Montgomery Papers, Edward Livingston Collection, Princeton University Library.
5. Trumbull, "A Concise Journal," 161, 163; Trumbull, "Diary" (July 1928): 26, 28; Timothy Bedel to the New Hampshire Committee of Safety, October 27/November 2, 1775, in Force, *American Archives*, 4th ser., 3:1207–8.
6. Richard Montgomery to Philip Schuyler, November 3, 1775, Philip Schuyler Papers, New York Public Library; John Brown to Richard Montgomery, November 8, 1775, in Force, *American Archives*, 4th ser., 3:1401.
7. Richard Montgomery to the Inhabitants of Montreal, November 12, 1775, in Force, *American Archives*, 4th ser., 3:1596–97.
8. Cruikshank, *A History of the Organization, Development, and Services of the Military and Naval Forces of Canada* 2:12; Stanley, *Canada Invaded*, 66–67.
9. "Articles of Capitulation, Montreal, November 12, 1775," in Force, *American Archives*, 4th ser., 3:1597–98; Richard Montgomery to Philip Schuyler, November 17, 1775, Philip Schuyler Papers, New York Public Library.
10. James Easton to Guy Carleton, November 15, 1775, in Justin H. Smith, *Our Struggle for the Fourteenth Colony* 1:487.
11. Harrison Bird, *Attack on Quebec: The American Invasion of Canada, 1775* (New York, 1968), 142–45; Robert M. Hatch, *Thrust for Canada: The American Attempt on Quebec in 1775–1776* (Boston, 1979), 94–95; Stanley, *Canada Invaded*, 68–69.
12. Justin H. Smith, *Our Struggle for the Fourteenth Colony* 1:488–90; Hatch, *Thrust For Canada*, 95–96.
13. Richard Montgomery to Janet Montgomery, November 24, 1775, Janet Montgomery Papers, Edward Livingston Collection, Princeton University Library. Montgomery sent Prescott with the other captives to Ticonderoga, and Schuyler further evacuated them to Pennsylvania. Philip Schuyler to Continental Congress, November 27, 1775, Philip Schuyler Papers, New York Public Library. Prescott remained detained there as a prisoner of war until September 1776, when he was exchanged for Gen. John Sullivan, who had been captured in the Battle of Long Island the previous month.
14. James Clinton, John Nicholson, and Lewis Dubois to Richard Montgomery, November 23, 1775, in Force, *American Archives*, 4th ser., 3:1695; Richard Montgomery to Philip Schuyler, November 24, 1775, in Force, *American Archives*, 4th ser., 3:1695.
15. John Lamb to the Continental Congress Committee of Safety, August 28, 1775, in Force, *American Archives*, 4th ser., 3:445; Richard Montgomery to Philip Schuyler, November 20, 1775, Philip Schuyler Papers, New York Public Li-

brary; Richard Montgomery to Philip Schuyler, November 24, 1775, Philip Schuyler Papers, New York Public Library. Capt. John Lamb (1735–1800), former Sons of Liberty leader, was one of the few Continental army officers who had acquired expertise in artillery techniques. Even by August 1776, only about five hundred American artillerymen were present for duty, compared to four times that number of British cannoneers. George Otto Trevelyan, *The American Revolution*, 6 vols. (New York, 1898–1914), 6:205. Vital to the army as a scarce artillerist, Lamb enjoyed special military status.

16. Richard Montgomery to Philip Schuyler, October 9, 1775, Philip Schuyler Papers, New York Public Library. Richard Montgomery to Philip Schuyler, November 20, 1775, Philip Schuyler Papers, New York Public Library. Initially, a captain of artillery received $26.66 per month in paper money, compared to a regular captain's pay of $20. Ford, *Journals of the Continental Congress* 2:220, entry of July 29, 1775. Later, Congress increased the pay of a captain in a "marching regiment" to $26.66 without a corresponding raise in the rate for an artillery captain. Ford, *Journals of the Continental Congress* 3:322, entry of November 4, 1775. This latest officer pay scale angered Lamb, who viewed it as a slight.

17. "Return of Military Stores on Board the Vessels under the Command of Brigadier-General Prescott, Bound to Quebec, November 19, 1775," in Force, *American Archives*, 4th ser., 3:1693; Richard Montgomery to Philip Schuyler, November 24, 1775, Philip Schuyler Papers, New York Public Library.

18. Ritzema, "Journal," 103, entry of November 14, 1775.

19. Richard Montgomery, Proclamation to Troops, November 15, 1775, Richard Montgomery MSS, New-York Historical Society; Trumbull, "A Concise Journal," 166, entry of November 15, 1775.

20. Philip Schuyler to Continental Congress, November 27, 1775, Philip Schuyler Papers, New York Public Library.

21. Richard Montgomery to Philip Schuyler, November 13, 1775, Philip Schuyler Papers, New York Public Library; Richard Montgomery to Philip Schuyler, November 24, 1775, Philip Schuyler Papers, New York Public Library. Some members of Congress were considering Maj. Gen. Charles Lee (1731–1782) at this time as a replacement for the infirm Schuyler, should one have been needed. George Washington expressed the widely held opinion of Wooster when he wrote: "General Wooster, I am informed, is not of such Activity as to press through Difficulties, with which that Service is environed." George Washington to Philip Schuyler, October 6, 1775, in Fitzpatrick, *The Writings of George Washington* 4:18–19.

22. Philip Schuyler to George Washington, November 22, 1775, Philip Schuyler Papers, New York Public Library; Philip Schuyler to the President of Congress, November 18, 1775, Philip Schuyler Papers, New York Public Library.

23. John Hancock to Philip Schuyler, November 30, 1775, in Paul H. Smith, *Letters of Delegates to Congress* 2:415–16; John Hancock to Richard Montgomery, November 30, 1775, in Paul H. Smith, *Letters of Delegates to Congress* 2:414–15.

24. George Washington to the President of Congress, November 28, 1775, in Fitzpatrick, *The Writings of George Washington* 4:120–23. For a comprehensive study of the unique nature of the Continental army, see James Kirby Martin and

Mark Edward Lender, *A Respectable Army: The Military Origins of the Republic, 1763–1789* (Arlington Heights, Ill., 1982). A different perspective is provided by Charles Royster, *A Revolutionary People at War: The Continental Army and the American Character, 1775–1783* (Chapel Hill, N.C, 1979).

25. George Washington to Philip Schuyler, December 5, 24, 1775, in Fitzpatrick, *The Writings of George Washington* 4:147–48, 178–80.

26. Philip Schuyler to George Washington, December [8], 1775, in Abbot, *The Papers of George Washington* 2:518–19.

27. Lossing, *The Life and Times of Philip Schuyler* 1:471–72.

28. Richard Montgomery to Robert R. Livingston, November 1775, in Force, *American Archives*, 4th ser., 3:1638–39.

29. Richard Montgomery to Janet Montgomery, November 24, 1775, Janet Montgomery Papers, Edward Livingston Collection, Princeton University Library; Richard Montgomery to Robert R. Livingston, November 1775, in Force, *American Archives*, 4th ser., 3:1638–39.

30. Ritzema, "Journal," 103–4, entry of November 28, 1775; Richard Montgomery to Philip Schuyler, December 5, 1775, Philip Schuyler Papers, New York Public Library.

31. Lt. William Humphrey, Capt. John Topham, Capt. Simeon Thayer, and Priv. George Morison journals, in Kenneth Roberts, ed., *March to Quebec: Journals of the Members of Arnold's Expedition* (New York, 1940 [1938]), 270, 534; [Priv.] John Joseph Henry, *Account of Arnold's Campaign against Quebec* (New York, 1968 [1877]), 94.

32. "Extract of Letter Received in England, Quebec, November 9, 1775," in Force, *American Archives*, 4th ser., 3:1420; Richard Montgomery to Philip Schuyler, December 5, 1775, Philip Schuyler Papers, New York Public Library. In the parlance of the time, "pretty" men connoted fine, stout persons.

33. Richard Montgomery to Philip Schuyler, September 23, 1775, Philip Schuyler Papers, New York Public Library; Richard Montgomery to Philip Schuyler, December 5, 1775, Philip Schuyler Papers, New York Public Library.

34. "Return of Men for the Defense, November 16, 1775," in Cruikshank, *A History of the Organization, Development, and Services of the Military and Naval Forces of Canada* 2:131; Henry Caldwell to Gen. James Murray, June 15, 1776, in Cruikshank, *A History of the Organization, Development, and Services of the Military and Naval Forces of Canada* 2:168.

35. Guy Carleton, "Proclamation, November 22, 1775," in Cruikshank, *A History of the Organization, Development, and Services of the Military and Naval Forces of Canada* 2:134–35; Henry Caldwell to Gen. James Murray, June 15, 1776, in Cruikshank, *A History of the Organization, Development, and Services of the Military and Naval Forces of Canada* 2:168. Edward Antill was one of the Quebec residents who chose to leave after Carleton's proclamation and performed "considerable service" for the Americans when Montgomery appointed him his chief engineer to replace the former one who had returned home. Richard Montgomery to Philip Schuyler, December 5, 1775, Philip Schuyler Papers, New York Public Library.

36. Richard Montgomery to Robert R. Livingston, November 1775, in Force, *American Archives*, 4th ser., 3:1638–39.

37. Richard Montgomery to Guy Carleton, December 6, 1775, in Cruikshank, *A History of the Organization, Development, and Services of the Military and Naval Forces of Canada* 2:138.

38. William Lindsay, "Narrative of the Invasion of Canada by the American Provincials under Montgomery and Arnold," *Canadian Review and Magazine* 3 (September 1826): 94–95.

39. Richard Montgomery to the Merchants of Quebec, December 6, 1775, in Cruikshank, *A History of the Organization, Development, and Services of the Military and Naval Forces of Canada* 2:136–37.

T E N *Attack on Quebec*

1. William Smith, *An Oration in Memory of General Montgomery*, 32.

2. Robert Burns, "A Fragment," in Moore, *Songs and Ballads of the American Revolution*, 381.

3. Rudolphus Ritzema to Pierre Van Cortlandt, January 3, 1776, quoted in William Hall, "Colonel Rudolphus Ritzema," *Magazine of American History* 2 (1878): 165.

4. Capt. Thomas Ainslie, "Journal of the Most Remarkable Occurrences in the Province of Quebec," in Frederic C. Wurtele, ed., *Blockade of Quebec in 1775–1776 by the American Revolutionists* (Quebec, 1906), 22, 23.

5. Ainslie, "Journal," in Wurtele, *Blockade of Quebec*, 21, 97; Capt. Henry Dearborn journal, in Lloyd A. Brown and Howard H. Peckham, eds., *Revolutionary War Journals of Henry Dearborn, 1775–1783* (Chicago, 1939), 64; Justin H. Smith, *Our Struggle for the Fourteenth Colony* 2:106.

6. "Extract of a Letter from a Gentleman in the Continental Service, Dated before Quebec, December 16, 1775," in Force, *American Archives*, 4th ser., 4:290; Justin H. Smith, *Our Struggle for the Fourteenth Colony* 2:103–4.

7. Leake, *Memoir of the Life and Times of General John Lamb*, 125; Justin H. Smith, *Our Struggle for the Fourteenth Colony* 2:104.

8. Richard Montgomery to David Wooster, December 16, 1775, in Force, *American Archives*, 4th ser., 4:288–89.

9. Philip Schuyler to George Washington, December 9, 1775, in Force, *American Archives*, 4th ser., 4:226; George Washington to Philip Schuyler, December 18, 1775, in Fitzpatrick, *The Writings of George Washington* 4:174–76; Henry Knox to George Washington, December 17, 1775, in Abbot, *The Papers of George Washington* 2:563–65.

10. The committee comprised Robert R. Livingston, Robert Treat Paine of Boston, and John Langdon of New Hampshire; for their report, see Ford, *Journals of the Continental Congress* 3:446–52, entry of December 23, 1775. Benjamin Franklin to M. Dumas, December 19, 1775, in Force, *American Archives*, 4th ser., 4:352–54.

11. Richard Montgomery to Philip Schuyler, December 18, 1775, Philip Schuyler Papers, New York Public Library.

12. Richard Montgomery to David Wooster, December 16, 1775, in Force, *American Archives*, 4th ser., 4:288–89; Richard Montgomery, "General Order, December 15, 1775," in Cruikshank, *A History of the Organization, Development, and Services of the Military and Naval Forces of Canada* 2:137; "Extract of a Letter from a Gentleman in the Continental Service, Dated before Quebec, December 16, 1775," in Force, *American Archives*, 4th ser., 4:290.

13. John Joseph Henry journal, in Roberts, *March to Quebec*, 374.

14. George Morison and Abner Stocking journals, in Roberts, *March to Quebec*, 535, 561–62; Richard Montgomery to Philip Schuyler, December 26, 1775, Philip Schuyler Papers, New York Public Library.

15. Philip Schuyler to President of Congress, December 26, 1775, in Force, *American Archives*, 4th ser., 4:463–64.

16. Richard Montgomery to Philip Schuyler, December 26, 1775, Philip Schuyler Papers, New York Public Library. The principals involved in this episode are obscure because their names were erased from the original letters in an effort not to sensationalize the affair if made known for general consumption. When writing Schuyler of the incident, Montgomery said, "I wish you would not mention names; for I know not whether the situation of affairs will admit of doing the publick the justice I could wish." Most historians agree that Capt. Oliver Hanchet of Connecticut instigated the trouble, and that he was joined by Capt. William Goodrich and Capt. Jonas Hubbard of Massachusetts. Arnold's field-grade officers who could have been in the conspiracy were Lt. Col. Christopher Greene, Maj. Timothy Bigelow, and Maj. Return Jonathan Meigs. However, the consensus is that Maj. John Brown was the one. Roberts, *March to Quebec*, 429; Ward, *The War of Revolution*, 188; Leake, *Memoir of the Life and Times of General John Lamb*, 126; Lossing, *The Life and Times of Philip Schuyler*, 493–94; French, *The First Year of the American Revolution*, 612; J. Smith, *Our Struggle for the Fourteenth Colony* 2:121–22.

17. Richard Montgomery to David Wooster, December 16, 1775, in Force, *American Archives*, 4th ser., 4:288–89; Richard Montgomery to Philip Schuyler, December 5, 1775, Philip Schuyler Papers, New York Public Library; Capt. Simeon Thayer journal, in Roberts, *March to Quebec*, 273.

18. Maj. Return J. Meigs journal, in Roberts, *March to Quebec*, 187–88; Capt. Henry Dearborn journal, in Brown and Peckham, *Revolutionary War Journals of Henry Dearborn*, 65–66.

19. Henry Caldwell to Gen. James Murray, June 15, 1776, Henry Caldwell, *The Invasion of Canada in 1775: Letter Attributed to Major Henry Caldwell* (Quebec, 1927 [1887]), 9; Capt. Thomas Ainslie journal, in Sheldon Cohen, ed., *Canada Preserved*, 31; John Joseph Henry journal, in Roberts, *March to Quebec*, 373. The first name of Sergeant Singleton is questionable. Hatch, *Thrust for Canada*, 129, indicated Samuel; C. Ward, *The War of the Revolution*, 190, wrote Stephen. He was one of several deserters to the British during the siege of Quebec.

20. Capt. Thomas Ainslie journal, in Cohen, *Canada Preserved*, 31–32.

21. Dr. Isaac Senter and Capt. Simeon Thayer journals, in Roberts, *March to Quebec*, 230, 273–74. For a monograph concerning the medical aspects of the

command, see Philip Cash, "The Canadian Military Campaign of 1775–1776: Medical Problems and Effects of Disease," *Journal of the American Medical Association* 236, no. 1 (July 5, 1976): 52–56.

22. Dr. Isaac Senter and Capt. Simeon Thayer journals, in Roberts, *March to Quebec*, 232, 275; George Morison, "An Account of the Assault on Quebec, 1775," *Pennsylvania Magazine of History and Biography* 14 (1890): 435–36; Benedict Arnold to David Wooster, December 31, 1775, in Force, *American Archives*, 4th ser., 4:481–82.

23. Richard Montgomery to Robert R. Livingston, December 17, 1775, Robert R. Livingston Papers, New York Public Library.

24. John Macpherson to his father, December 30, 1775, in James M. Le-Moine, *Quebec Past and Present: A History of Quebec, 1608–1876* (Quebec, 1876), 210. Jacob Cheeseman to Thomas Cheeseman, December 23, 1775, in Lossing, *The Life and Times of Philip Schuyler* 1:499; "Extract of a Letter from Canada, February 9, 1776," in Force, *American Archives*, 4th ser., 4:706–7; Dennis P. Ryan, ed., *A Salute to Courage: The American Revolution as Seen through Wartime Writings of Officers of the Continental Army and Navy* (New York, 1979), 18–19.

25. Some participants and historians erroneously recorded the date of the American attack on Quebec as January 1, 1776. For a comprehensive assessment of this subject, see James M. LeMoine, "The Assault of Brigadier-General Richard Montgomery and Colonel Benedict Arnold on Quebec in 1775: A Red Letter Day in the Annals of Canada," *Proceedings and Transactions of the Royal Society of Canada* 5 (1899): 457–66.

26. Capt. Thomas Ainslie journal, in Cohen, *Canada Preserved*, 33–34; Dr. Isaac Senter journal, in Roberts, *March to Quebec*, 233.

27. Donald Campbell to Robert R. Livingston, March 28, 1776, Robert R. Livingston Papers, New York Public Library.

28. Donald Campbell's father, Capt. Lauchlin Campbell, came to New York from Scotland in 1738. He entered into an agreement with Gov. George Clarke to bring settlers from Scotland at his own expense in return for land that would be granted to him for each family he transported. The governor broke his promise and Captain Campbell received no land for his efforts of bringing eighty-three emigrant families to New York. Subsequently, he purchased a farmstead in New York, leaving to serve with distinction in the British army during the Scottish Rebellion of 1745. Donald Campbell was a youth when his father died after returning to New York. The younger Campbell served as a lieutenant and quartermaster in the Royal American Regiment during the French and Indian War. Upon the Treaty of Paris in 1763, he retired from the British army on half pay. He then went to England and requested compensation from the Crown for his late father's loyal military service and the unsettled New York land claim. The British government recommended and referred the matter to Gen. Robert Monckton, then governor of New York. Although he petitioned for one hundred thousand acres of land, he received only ten thousand acres. "Donald Campbell Memorial, May 1764," in O'Callaghan and Fernow, *Documents Relative to the Colonial History of the State of New-York* 7:629–30. Donald Campbell relinquished his half pay on July 17, 1775, to accept appointment by the Continental Congress

as deputy quartermaster general of the Northern Department with the rank of colonel. Ford, *Journals of the Continental Congress* 2:186.

29. John Joseph Henry journal, in Roberts, *March to Quebec*, 376.

30. Ibid., 377; Simeon Thayer, George Morison, and Abner Stocking journals, in Roberts, *March to Quebec*, 275, 536, 564–65; Charles Porterfield, "Memorable Attack on Quebec, December 21, 1775: Diary of Colonel Charles Porterfield," *Magazine of American History with Notes and Queries* 21 (1889): 319. Daniel Morgan (1736–1802), a first cousin of Daniel Boone, joined Braddock's expedition as a teamster at the age of seventeen. In 1756, while employed in hauling supplies by wagon to frontier forts, he had an altercation with a British officer. His trial for insubordination resulted in a sentence of five hundred lashes. In 1758, Morgan became an ensign; and during a scrape with the Indians, he lost all of his teeth on one side when a bullet passed through his neck and mouth. In 1762, he married and settled on a farmstead. While prospering as a farmer he served stints as a lieutenant in several colonial wars. In June 1775, the six-foot, two-hundred-pound "Old Wagoner" formed one of the two Virginia rifle companies and received a captain's commission as its commander. Then, Morgan marched his company to join the Continental army forming at Boston. When Arnold organized his Canadian expedition, Morgan and his men participated in his march to Quebec. For a comprehensive biography of Daniel Morgan, consult Don Higginbotham, *Daniel Morgan: Revolutionary Rifleman* (Chapel Hill, N.C., 1961).

31. Daniel Morgan to [Henry Lee?], n.d., in Daniel Morgan, "An Autobiography," *Historical Magazine of America*, 2nd ser., 9 (June 1877): 379–80. A few historians question portions of Morgan's testimony. See French, *The First Year of the American Revolution*, Appendix 47, 768–69.

32. John Joseph Henry journal, in Roberts, *March to Quebec*, 375, 377.

33. Henry Caldwell to Gen. James Murray, June 15, 1776, Caldwell, *The Invasion of Canada in 1775*, 10–11. Anderson was a lieutenant in the Royal Navy appointed as a captain of the Quebec garrison.

34. Lamb survived but was permanently disfigured, losing an eye. He was included in the prisoners captured by the British troops.

35. Henry Dearborn journal, in Roberts, *March to Quebec*, 150–51.

36. Capt. Thomas Ainslie journal, in Cohen, *Canada Preserved*, 36; Jacob Danford, "Quebec under Siege, 1775–1776: The 'Memorandums' of Jacob Danford," ed. John F. Roche, *Canadian Historical Review* 50 (March 1969): 72–73; Lindsay, "Narrative of the Invasion of Canada," 102–3.

37. James Graham, *The Life of General Daniel Morgan* (New York, 1856), 102–3.

38. Henry Dearborn journal, in Brown and Peckham, *Revolutionary War Journals of Henry Dearborn*, 72. There is no eyewitness account of Montgomery's death. In addition to Dearborn, American secondary sources include Return J. Meigs and Abner Stocking journals, in Roberts, *March to Quebec*, 189, 563–64; and Francis Nichols, "Diary of Lieutenant Francis Nichols of Colonel William Thompson's Battalion of Pennsylvania Riflemen, January to September, 1776," *Pennsylvania Magazine of History and Biography* 20 (1896): 505. British secondary sources are found in Henry Caldwell to Gen. James Murray, June 15, 1776,

Caldwell, *The Invasion of Canada in 1775*, 13; and Capt. Thomas Ainslie journal, in Cohen, *Canada Preserved*, 36. The American accounts claim that all the guards in the blockhouse fled in panic when they were attacked, and one drunken sailor fired a single cannon that killed Montgomery and his men, before running away with the rest. The British statements assert that the garrison mounted a deliberate, sustained defense of the blockhouse with repeated fire from cannons and muskets. Although the evidence suggests that some shrinking guardsmen had to be steadied by more stouthearted members of the blockhouse detachment, the British rendition seems the more plausible in this instance. For a discussion of the contradiction, consult French, *The First Year of the American Revolution*, Appendix 46, 767–68. Some accounts credit Burr with being beside Montgomery when the general received his fatal wound. Burr supposedly tried to rally the men to continue the attack to no avail. After the others had fled, Burr attempted unsuccessfully to evacuate Montgomery's body by himself. Other authorities have discounted these activities by Burr. Arnold indicated that Burr was with his force on the other side of the Lower Town during the attack. Benedict Arnold to David Wooster, December 31, 1775, in Jared Sparks, ed., *Correspondence of the American Revolution*, 4 vols. (Freeport, N.Y., 1970 [1853]), 1:499–500. Although Burr was in both camps before the action, acting as liaison between Montgomery and Arnold, his whereabouts and activities during the assault remain in dispute. For an examination of this controversy, see Justin H. Smith, *Our Struggle for the Fourteenth Colony* 2:584–85 n. 65 (6); Nathan Schachner, *Aaron Burr: A Biography* (New York 1961), 521 n. 15; Herbert S. Parmet and Marie B. Hecht, *Aaron Burr: Portrait of an Ambitious Man* (New York, 1967), 28–29.

39. Donald Campbell to David Wooster, December 31, 1775, in Force, *American Archives*, 4th ser., 4:480–81; Donald Campbell to Robert R. Livingston, March 28, 1776, Robert R. Livingston Papers, New York Public Library.

40. Philip Schuyler to President of Congress, December 26, 1775, in Force, *American Archives*, 4th ser., 4:463–64; Ford, *Journals of the Continental Congress* 3:418, entry of December 9, 1775.

ELEVEN   *Aftermath of Quebec*

1. James Duane to Robert R. Livingston, January 31, 1776, in Paul H. Smith, *Letters of Delegates to Congress* 3:173–74.

2. Thomas Lynch to Philip Schuyler, January 20, 1776, in ibid., 125–26.

3. Henry Caldwell to Gen. James Murray, June 15, 1776, Caldwell, *The Invasion of Canada in 1775*, 13–14.

4. Dr. Isaac Senter journal, in Roberts, *March to Quebec*, 234–35; Ainslie, "Journal," in Wurtele, *Blockade of Quebec*, 32.

5. Benedict Arnold to David Wooster, December 31, 1775, in Roberts, *March to Quebec*, 102–3; Benedict Arnold to David Wooster, January 2, 1776, in Roberts, *March to Quebec*, 103–6; Benedict Arnold to Hannah Arnold, December 6, 1776, in Roberts, *March to Quebec*, 108–9.

6. Ainslie, "Journal," in Wurtele, *Blockade of Quebec*, 30; W. T. P. Shortt, ed.,

Journal of the Principal Occurrences during the Siege of Quebec (London, 1824), 33; Henry Caldwell to Gen. James Murray, June 15, 1776, Caldwell, *The Invasion of Canada in 1775*, 15.

7. James Thompson account, August 16, 1828, in E. P. Quebec, "The Hundredth Anniversary of Montgomery's Death," *New Dominion Monthly* 17 (December 18, 1875): 402–3; Lindsay, "Narrative of the Invasion of Canada," 104.

8. Ainslie, "Journal," in Wurtele, *Blockade of Quebec*, 33.

9. John Joseph Henry and Return J. Meigs journals, in Roberts, *March to Quebec*, 389–90, 192; James Thompson account, August 16, 1828, in Quebec, "The Hundredth Anniversary of Montgomery's Death," 403–4; Lindsay, "Narrative of the Invasion of Canada," 104.

10. John Joseph Henry and Henry Dearborn journals, in Roberts, *March to Quebec*, 379, 154. Also see Joseph Ware journal, in Roberts, *March to Quebec*, 27–40; Guy Carleton to Gen. William Howe, January 12, 1776, in Cruikshank, *A History of the Organization, Development, and Services of the Military and Naval Forces of Canada* 2:140–41. Henry tried to justify his assessment by stating: "Neither the American account of this affair, as published by Congress, nor that of Sir Guy Carleton, admit the loss of either side to be so great as it really was, in my estimation. It seems to be a universal practice among belligerents of all nations to lessen the number of the slain of the side of the party which reports the event, and to increase it on the part of the enemy." John Joseph Henry journal, in Roberts, *March to Quebec*, 379–80.

11. John Joseph Henry journal, in Roberts, *March to Quebec*, 381, 389. The amicable relationship between the American prisoners and Carleton did not last. Bored by the tedium of captivity and despairing of being rescued, the Americans planned an escape in April 1776. The British thwarted this bid for freedom when a few men informed on their fellow prisoners, alerting the captors of the escape plan. The unrest prompted Carleton to initiate more stringent security of the captives, clapping many of them in irons. In August 1776, Carleton paroled the prisoners and transported them to America. Henry Dearborn, Simeon Thayer, John Joseph Henry, George Morison, Abner Stocking, and John Forbes journals, in Roberts, *March to Quebec*, 158, 280–82, 398–411, 538–39, 566–67, 593–98.

12. Col. Henry Caldwell to Gen. James Murray, June 15, 1776, Caldwell, *The Invasion of Canada in 1775*, 12; Ainslie, "Journal," in Wurtele, *Blockade of Quebec*, 31.

13. Benedict Arnold to David Wooster, January 2, 1776, in Sparks, *Correspondence of the American Revolution* 1:501–2.

14. Ibid. In the summer of 1776, Colonel Campbell received a court-martial for his conduct during the attack on Quebec. The court ordered him to be cashiered; but on February 13, 1777, Congress decided on his appeal that he could continue his service as a colonel in the army. Ford, *Journals of the Continental Congress* 7:1140. However, Campbell did not return to duty, and he spent the rest of the war disputing with Congress over the settlement of his quartermaster accounts and trying to redeem his reputation. Congress rewarded Arnold by advancing him to brigadier general on January 10, 1776, to fill the vacancy left by Montgomery's promotion.

15. Col. Henry Caldwell to Gen. James Murray, June 15, 1776, Caldwell, *The Invasion of Canada in 1775*, 14.

16. David Wooster to Seth Warner, January 6, 1776, in Force, *American Archives*, 4th ser., 4:588–89. By early March 1776, approximately four hundred Green Mountain Boys had reached Wooster. David Wooster to Philip Schuyler, January 5, 1776, Philip Schuyler Papers, New York Public Library. Moses Hazen (1733–1803) retired on half pay from the British army and settled at St. Johns. After Canadian authorities imprisoned him for a time and confiscated his property, he joined Montgomery's expedition for its operations around Montreal and Quebec. Col. James Clinton was the commander of the 3rd New York Regiment. James Price, a wealthy merchant and sympathizer in Montreal, loaned large sums of money to finance the American expedition in Canada. Montgomery wrote that Price "has been a faithful friend to the Cause. . . . His advice and assistance upon every ocasion I have much benefitted by. . . . I cant help wishing the Congress to give him an ample testimony of their Sense of his generous and Spirited exertions in the cause of freedom." Richard Montgomery to Philip Schuyler, December 26, 1775, Philip Schuyler Papers, New York Public Library. On March 29, 1776, Congress appointed Price as the deputy commissary general of stores and provisions for the American forces in Canada.

17. Philip Schuyler to President of Congress, January 13, 1776, Philip Schuyler Papers, New York Public Library; Philip Schuyler to George Washington, January 13, 1776, Philip Schuyler Papers, New York Public Library.

18. George Washington to Philip Schuyler, January 18, 1776, Philip Schuyler Papers, New York Public Library; "Council of War [January 18, 1776]," in Abbot, *The Papers of George Washington* 3:132–34.

19. Richard Smith diary, January 18, 1776, in Paul H. Smith, *Letters of Delegates to Congress* 3:112–13; Ford, *Journals of the Continental Congress* 4:39–40, 70–76.

20. Richard Smith diary, January 18, 1776, in Paul H. Smith, *Letters of Delegates to Congress* 3:112–13.

21. Rudolphus Ritzema to Pierre Van Cortlandt, January 3, 1776, in *Journals of the Provincial Congress of the State of New-York* 1:286–87. Rudolphus Ritzema (1710–1795) was sent by Wooster to brief Schuyler on the situation in Canada. Schuyler subsequently referred him to Congress. After discussing his views with the New York Committee of Safety on February 11, Ritzema continued on to Philadelphia to confer with Congress on February 16. Ritzema, "Journal," 105–6. On March 28, 1776, Congress appointed Ritzema commander of the reorganized 3d New York Regiment and promoted him to colonel. However, he again became disillusioned with the American civil-military establishment. In November 1776, he defected from the Continental army and joined the British army with the rank of lieutenant colonel. He served as a quartermaster officer in the West Indies. After the war, Ritzema retired from the British army on half pay as a lieutenant colonel.

22. John Sullivan to the New Hampshire Assembly, January 18, 1776, in Force, *American Archives*, 4th ser., 4:768–69.

23. Oliver Wolcott to Philip Schuyler, January 22, 1776, Philip Schuyler

Papers, New York Public Library; Robert Alexander to the Maryland Council of Safety, January 30, 1776, in Paul H. Smith, *Letters of Delegates to Congress* 3:167–68.

24. Samuel Chase to John Adams, January 12, 1775 [1776], in Taylor, *Papers of John Adams* 3:400–401; John Adams to James Warren, February 18, 1776, in Paul H. Smith, *Letters of Delegates to Congress* 3:275–76.

25. Robert R. Livingston to Thomas Lynch [January 1776], in Paul H. Smith, *Letters of Delegates to Congress* 3:178–81.

26. George Washington to David Wooster, January 27, 1776, in Abbot, *The Papers of George Washington* 3:204–5; George Washington to Joseph Reed, January 31, 1776, in Abbot, *The Papers of George Washington* 3:225, 228–29.

27. For a comprehensive study of the standing army concept in the Continental army, refer to John Todd White, "Standing Armies in Time of War: Republican Theory and Military Practice during the American Revolution" (Ph.D. diss., George Washington University, 1978).

28. George Washington to John Hancock, February 9, 1776, in Abbot, *The Papers of George Washington* 3:274–77.

29. Richard Smith diary, entry of January 19, 1776, in Paul H. Smith, *Letters of Delegates to Congress* 3:116–17; "James Duane Notes of Delegates [February 22, 1776]," in Paul H. Smith, *Letters of Delegates to Congress* 3:294–96; Commissioners to Canada to John Hancock, May 17, 1776, in Paul H. Smith, *Letters of Delegates to Congress* 4:22–25.

30. Ford, *Journals of the Continental Congress* 5:762, entry of September 16, 1776; John Hancock to the States, September 24, 1776, in Paul H. Smith, *Letters of Delegates to Congress* 5:228–30.

31. *Pennsylvania Gazette*, January 24, 1776.

32. Force, *American Archives*, 4th ser., 4:1654.

33. Josiah Bartlett to Mary Bartlett, February 19, 1776, in Paul H. Smith, *Letters of Delegates to Congress* 3:277–78; Theodore G. Tappert and John W. Doberstein, trans., *The Journals of Henry Melchior Muhlenberg*, 3 vols. (Philadelphia, 1942–58), 2:716, entry of February 19, 1776.

34. "William Smith Oration, February 19, 1776," in Force, *American Archives*, 4th ser., 4:1681.

35. "Richard Smith Diary, February 21, 1776," in Paul H. Smith, *Letters of Delegates to Congress* 3:294; John Adams to Abigail Adams, April 28, 1776, in Paul H. Smith, *Letters of Delegates to Congress* 3:592–95.

36. Charles Lee to George Washington, January 24, 1776, in Abbot, *The Papers of George Washington* 3:182–83.

37. Thomas Paine, *A Dialogue between the Ghost of General Montgomery Just Arrived from the Elysian Fields; And an American Delegate, in a Wood near Philadelphia*, in Philip S. Foner, ed., *The Complete Writings of Thomas Paine*, vol. 2 (New York, 1945), 88–93. Thomas Paine (1737–1809) became the most famous and prolific revolutionary author. He continued his writings after enlisting in the Continental army as a volunteer during 1776–1777 and serving the American government in various capacities until the end of the war. His words that stirred the patriot's soul enshrined him in the cause for independence.

224 • *Twelve: Epilogue*

38. Hugh Henry Brackenridge, *Death of General Montgomery*, in Philbrick, *Trumpets Sounding*, 253. Two years later, Brackenridge included Montgomery in a eulogy he delivered: "When they mean to dress the hero with the fairest praises, they will say he was . . . virtuous, and prudent, and intrepid, as Montgomery." Hugh M. [Henry] Brackenridge, *An Eulogium of the Brave Men Who Have Fallen in the Contest with Great Britain: Delivered on Monday, July 5, 1779* (Philadelphia, 1779), 131. Hugh Henry Brackenridge entered the College of New Jersey (later named Princeton) in 1768, receiving his bachelor's degree in 1771 and a master's degree in 1774. During his time at college, he became interested in liberal ideas, joining a fraternal literary club—the American Whig Society. He served as a chaplain in the Continental army from 1776 to 1778, while studying to be a Presbyterian minister. Later he turned to another career—that of playwright and drama teacher. He stands as an excellent example of revolutionary authors who sought to inflame passions against the British.

39. Nathanael Greene to John Adams, May 2, 1777, in Bernhard Knollenberg, "The Revolutionary Correspondence of Nathanael Greene and John Adams," *Rhode Island History* 1 (April 1942): 49–50. Joseph Warren was killed at Breeds (Bunker) Hill on June 17, 1775, and was posthumously made a major general. Hugh Mercer, a brigadier general, was fatally wounded at the Battle of Princeton on January 3, 1777, and died on January 11, 1777.

40. Sabine, *Historical Memoirs of William Smith* 2:35, entry of June 30, 1777. Force, *American Archives*, 5th ser., 1:588, 659, 958, 1330; 2:79, 82, 357, 702, 711, 1126, 1394; 3:459, 821.

41. Jonathan Williams Austin, *An Oration Delivered March 5th, 1778, at the Request of the Inhabitants of the Town of Boston to Commemorate the Bloody Tragedy of the Fifth of March, 1770* (Boston, March 9, 1778), 14.

42. "House of Commons, March 11, 1776," in Force, *American Archives*, 4th ser., 6:314–15.

43. *London Evening Post*, March 12, 1776; *Scot's Magazine*, May 1776; *London General Evening Post*, April 2, 1776, reference is to Gen. Charles Lee, who like Montgomery served as a British officer before joining the Continental army; *London Morning Post*, September 4, 1776. Also see Solomon Lutnick, *The American Revolution and the British Press, 1775–1783* (Columbia, Mo., 1967), 91–94; James C. Gaston, *London Poets and the American Revolution* (Troy, N.Y., 1979), 132.

44. James Murray, *An Impartial History of the Present War in America*, 2 vols. (Newcastle, England, 1780), 1:564.

TWELVE *Epilogue*

1. George Washington to Sir Edward Newenham, July 29, 1789, in Fitzpatrick, *The Writings of George Washington* 30:367–68.

2. Robert Morris to Charles Lee, February 17, 1776, in Paul H. Smith, *Letters of Delegates to Congress* 3:267–70.

3. Benedict Arnold to John Sullivan, June [13 ?], 1776, in Force, *American*

Archives, 4th ser., 6:1104–5; Sparks, *Correspondence of the American Revolution* 1:528–29.

4. John Adams to Samuel Cooper, June 9, 1776, in Paul H. Smith, *Letters of Delegates to Congress* 4:175–77.

5. Dr. Isaac Senter journal, in Roberts, *March to Quebec*, 241. The estimated loss sustained by the Americans in the Canadian invasion—including killed, wounded, prisoners, and dead from disease—was five thousand individuals.

6. Simeon Baldwin, oration, May 12, 1783, in Simeon E. Baldwin, ed., *Life and Letters of Simeon Baldwin* (New Haven, Conn., 1919), 147–50.

7. Timothy Pickering to Gov. George Clinton, October 22, 1784, Timothy Pickering Papers, New York Public Library; Thomas P. Robinson, "Some Notes On Major-General Richard Montgomery," *New York History* 37 (October 1956): 395; Cullum, "Major-General Richard Montgomery," 297; O'Reilly, "Major-General Richard Montgomery," 188–89.

8. Janet Montgomery to Aaron Burr, March 7, 1779, Aaron Burr Papers, New York Public Library.

9. Richard Montgomery to Janet Montgomery, September 1775, quoted in *Harper's New Monthly Magazine* 70, no. 417 (February 1885): 353.

10. Janet Montgomery to Mrs. John Jay, September 6, 1780, in Henry P. Johnston, ed., *The Correspondence and Public Papers of John Jay* (New York, 1890), 1:402–3.

11. Mercy Otis Warren to Janet Montgomery, January 20, 1776, Janet Montgomery Papers, Edward Livingston Collection, Princeton University Library.

12. Sabine, *Historical Memoirs of William Smith* 2:170, entry of July 1, 1777.

13. Janet Montgomery to Montgomery Tappen, Esq., April 1784, in Charles I. Bushnell, ed., "Women of the Revolution: A Series of Letters Written by Distinguished Women of That Period," *Historical Magazine* 5, no. 2 (February 1869): 111; Janet Montgomery to Mrs. Tappen, November 24, 1784, in Bushnell, "Women of the Revolution," 111.

14. Janet Montgomery to Horatio Gates, June 1784, Horatio Gates Papers, New-York Historical Society. Like Montgomery and Charles Lee, Gates was a former professional officer in the British army whom the Continental Congress appointed general during its initial commissioning. The correspondence record of the relationship between Janet Montgomery and Horatio Gates, spanning the period between summer 1784 to 1803, is contained in both the Gates Papers, New-York Historical Society, and the Horatio Gates–Janet Montgomery MSS, New York Public Library.

15. Babbitt, *Janet Montgomery*, 20–22; George Washington to Sir Edward Newenham, July 29, 1789, and January 15, 1790, in Fitzpatrick, *The Writings of George Washington* 30:367–68, 503–4; Sarah Ranelagh to Janet Montgomery, n.d., Janet Montgomery Papers, Edward Livingston Collection, Princeton University Library.

16. Babbitt, *Janet Montgomery*, 19.

17. John Ross Delafield, "Montgomery Place, Barrytown, New York," *American Architect* 132 (October 5, 1927): 421–26; John Ross Delafield, "Montgomery Place," *New York History* 20, no. 4 (October 1939): 445–46, 448; Peter De-

Labigarre, "Mr. DeLabigarre on Silk Worms," *Transactions of the Society for the Promotion of Agriculture, Arts, and Manufactures*, 1, pt. 2 (1794): 179. A British expedition under Gen. John Vaughn burned Clermont in October 1777. Janet's mother, Margaret Livingston, had it rebuilt to its original grandeur; upon her death, ownership of the house passed to the eldest son, Robert R. Livingston.

18. Janet Montgomery to Stephen Van Rensselaer, January 20, 1818, Emmet Collection, New York Public Library.

19. American Scenic and Historic Preservation Society, "General Richard Montgomery and His Monument at New York," *Annual Report to the Legislature of the State of New York* (1916): 648–49; James Thompson account, August 16, 1828, in Quebec, "The Hundredth Anniversary of Montgomery's Death," 404; Janet Montgomery, in Hunt, *Biographical Notes Concerning General Richard Montgomery*, 29.

20. *New York Daily Advertiser*, July 8, 1818; *Port Folio* 6 (August 1818): 75–80; 7 (February 1819): 134–41. The original manuscript of the poem resides in the David Library of the American Revolution. Babbitt, *Janet Montgomery*, 26; Janet Montgomery, in Hunt, *Biographical Notes Concerning General Richard Montgomery*, 30.

21. Andrew Jackson to Edward Livingston, August 2, 1828, in John Spencer Bassett, ed., *Correspondence of Andrew Jackson*, 7 vols. (Washington, D.C., 1926–35), 499–500; Janet Montgomery, in Hunt, *Biographical Notes Concerning General Richard Montgomery*, 14.

Bibliography

PRIMARY SOURCES

Manuscript Collections

Boston Public Library. Letter. Richard Montgomery to Janet Montgomery, November 3, 1775 (G.51.7.4.55).
———. Proposed Inscription for a Monument to General Montgomery. Charles Thomson. January 25, 1776 (Ch.C.4.4).
———. Letter. John Pierce to Tapping Reeve. January 27, 1776 (Ch.C.5.29).
Clements Library, University of Michigan. Montgomery MSS Collection.
David Library of the American Revolution. Jules Daverza[c]. Poem Eulogizing General Montgomery. July 1818.
Franklin Delano Roosevelt Library, Hyde Park, N.Y. Livingston-Redmond MSS. Microfilm Edition.
National Archives. *Papers of the Continental Congress*. Microfilm Collection.
New-York Historical Society. William Douglas Papers.
———. Alexander McDougall Papers.
———. Horatio Gates Papers.
———. Richard Montgomery MSS.
New York Public Library. Bancroft Transcripts.
———. Aaron Burr Papers.
———. Emmet Collection.
———. Horatio Gates–Janet Montgomery MSS.
———. Robert R. Livingston Papers.
———. Livingston-Redmond MSS.
———. Timothy Pickering Papers.
———. Philip Schuyler Papers.
———. Philip Schuyler Letterbooks.
New York State Archives. Provincial Congress MSS.

Princeton University Library. Edward Livingston Collection. Janet Montgomery Papers.

Newspapers and Magazines

London Evening Post.
London General Evening Post.
London Gazette.
London Morning Post.
New England Chronicle (Boston).
New York Daily Advertiser.
New York Journal.
New York Mercury.
Pennsylvania Gazette (Philadelphia).
Pennsylvania Journal (Philadelphia).
Port Folio (New York).
Quebec Gazette (Quebec, Canada).
Rivington's Gazetteer (New York).
Scot's Magazine (London).

Books

Abbot, W. W., ed. *The Papers of George Washington.* 7 vols. Colonial Series. Charlottesville: University Press of Virginia, 1983–90.

Allen, Ethan. *The Narrative of Colonel Ethan Allen.* New York: Corinth Books, 1961 (reprint).

Babbitt, Katherine M. *Janet Montgomery: Hudson River Squire.* Monroe, N.Y.: Library Research Associates, 1975.

Baldwin, Simeon E., ed. *Life and Letters of Simeon Baldwin.* New Haven, Conn.: Tuttle, Morehouse and Taylor, 1919.

Ballagh, James Curtis, ed. *The Letters of Richard Henry Lee.* 2 vols. New York: Macmillan, 1911–14.

Bassett, John Spencer, ed. *Correspondence of Andrew Jackson.* 7 vols. Washington, D.C.: Carnegie Institution of Washington, 1926–35.

Bray, Robert C., and Paul E. Bushnell, eds. *Diary of a Common Soldier in the American Revolution, 1775–1783: An Annotated Edition of the Military Journal of Jeremiah Greenman.* DeKalb: Northern Illinois University Press, 1978.

Brown, Lloyd A., and Howard H. Peckham, eds. *Revolutionary War Journals of Henry Dearborn, 1775–1783.* Chicago: Caxton Club, 1939.

Burnett, Edmund C., ed. *Letters of Members of the Continental Congress.* 8 vols. Washington, D.C.: Carnegie Institution of Washington, 1921–36.

Burtchaell, George Dames, and Thomas Ulick Sadleir, eds. *Alumni Dublinenses: A Register of the Students, Graduates, Professors, and Provosts of Trinity College in the University of Dublin, 1593–1860.* Dublin, Ireland: Alex, Thom, 1935.

Butterfield, L. H., ed. *The Adams Papers: Diary and Autobiography of John Adams.* 4 vols. New York: Atheneum, 1964.

Canadian Public Archives. *Report of the Public Archives for 1914 and 1915.* Ottawa, 1916.

Carter, Clarence Edwin, ed. *The Correspondence of General Thomas Gage with the Secretaries of State, 1763–1775.* 2 vols. New York: Archon Books, 1969 (1931–33).

Cohen, Sheldon, ed. *Canada Preserved: The Journal of Captain Thomas Ainslie.* New York: New York University Press, 1968.

Colden, Cadwallader. *The Letters and Papers of Cadwallader Colden.* 9 vols. New-York Historical Society Collections, no. 56. New York: New-York Historical Society, 1918–37.

———. *The Colden Letter Books, 1760–1775.* 2 vols. New-York Historical Society Collections, no. 10. New York: New-York Historical Society, 1877–78.

Cruikshank, Ernest, ed. *A History of the Organization, Development, and Services of the Military and Naval Forces of Canada from the Peace of Paris in 1763, to the Present Time.* 3 vols. Ottawa: Canadian Government, 1919–20.

Dann, John C., ed. "Military Pension Deposition of Justus Bellamy." In John C. Dann, ed. *The Revolution Remembered: Eyewitness Accounts of the War for Independence.* Chicago: University of Chicago Press, 1980.

Davies, K. G., ed. *Documents of the American Revolution 1770–1783.* Colonial Office Series, no. 11. London: Great Britain Colonial Office, 1976.

Delafield, Julia. *Biographies of Francis Lewis and Morgan Lewis.* 2 vols. New York: Anson D. F. Randolph, 1877.

Fitzpatrick, John C., ed. *The Writings of George Washington.* 39 vols. Washington, D.C.: U.S. Government Printing Office, 1931–44.

Foner, Philip S., ed. *The Complete Writings of Thomas Paine.* Vol. 2. New York: Citadel Press, 1945.

Forbes, John. *Writings of General John Forbes.* Ed. Alfred P. James. Menasha, Wisc.: Collegiate Press, 1938.

Force, Peter, ed. *American Archives: A Collection of Authentick Records, State Papers, Debates, and Letters and Other Notices of Publick Affairs.* 4th and 5th ser. 9 vols. Washington, D.C.: M. St. Clair & Peter Force, 1837–53.

Ford, Worthington Chauncey, ed. *Journals of the Continental Congress, 1774–1789.* 34 vols. Washington, D.C.: U.S. Government Printing Office, 1904–37.

Fortescue, John William. *A History of the British Army.* 13 vols. London: Macmillan, 1910–30.

Freeman, Douglas Southall. *George Washington: A Biography.* 7 vols. New York: Scribner, 1948–57.

French, Allen. *The Taking of Ticonderoga in 1775: The British Story; A Study of Captors and Captives.* Cambridge: Harvard University Press, 1928.

———. *The First Year of the American Revolution.* Cambridge, Mass.: Houghton Mifflin, 1934.

Gaston, James C. *London Poets and the American Revolution.* Troy, N.Y.: Whitston, 1979.

Graham, James. *The Life of General Daniel Morgan.* New York: Derby and Jackson, 1856.

Great Britain War Office. *Annual Army Lists.* London, 1756.

Halpenny, Francess G., ed. *Dictionary of Canadian Biography.* 11 vols. Toronto: University of Toronto Press, 1966–82.

Henry, John Joseph. *Account of Arnold's Campaign against Quebec.* New York: Arno Press, 1968 (1877).

Hunt, Charles Havens. *Life of Edward Livingston.* New York: D. Appleton, 1864.

Jellison, Charles A. *Ethan Allen: Frontier Rebel.* Syracuse, N.Y.: Syracuse University Press, 1983 (1969).

Johnston, Henry P. *The Correspondence and Public Papers of John Jay.* New York: G. P. Putnam's Sons, 1890.

Jones, Thomas. *History of New York during the Revolutionary War.* 2 vols. New York: Arno Press, 1968 (1879).

Journals of the Provincial Congress of the State of New York. 2 vols. Albany, N.Y.: Thurlow Weed, 1775–77.

Kapp, Friedrich. *The Life of Frederick William von Steuben.* New York: Mason Brothers, 1859.

Knox, John. *An Historical Journal of the Campaigns in North America for the Years 1757, 1758, 1759, and 1760 by Captain John Knox.* Ed. Arthur G. Doughty. 3 vols. Freeport, N.Y.: Books For Libraries Press, 1970 (1914–16).

Leake, Isaac Q., ed. *Memoir of the Life and Times of General John Lamb.* Albany, N.Y.: Benchmark, 1970 (1857).

Lincoln, William, ed. *The Journals of Each Provincial Congress of Massachusetts in 1774 and 1775, and of the Committee of Safety.* Boston: Dutton and Wentworth, 1838.

Lossing, Benson J. *The Pictorial Field Book of the Revolution.* 2 vols. New York: Harper and Brothers, 1851–52.

———. *The Life and Times of Philip Schuyler.* 2 vols. New York: Sheldon, 1873 (1860).

Lutnick, Solomon. *The American Revolution and the British Press, 1775–1783.* Columbia: University of Missouri Press, 1967.

MacDougall, William L. *American Revolutionary: A Biography of General Alexander McDougall.* Westport, Conn.: Greenwood Press, 1977.

Montresor, John. *The Montresor Journals.* Ed. G. D. Skull. Collections of the New-York Historical Society, no. 14. New York: New-York Historical Society, 1882.

Moore, Frank, ed. *Songs and Ballads of the American Revolution.* Port Washington, N.Y.: Kennikat Press, 1964.

———. *The Diary of the American Revolution, 1775–1781.* New York: Washington Square Press, 1968.

Murray, James. *An Impartial History of the Present War in America.* 2 vols. Newcastle, England: T. Robson, 1780.

New York Secretary of State. *Calendar of Historical Manuscripts Relating to the War of the Revolution.* 2 vols. Albany, N.Y.: Weed, Parsons, 1863–68.

O'Callaghan, Edmund B., and Berthold Fernow, eds. *Documents Relative to the Colonial History of the State of New York.* 15 vols. Albany, N.Y: Parsons, 1856–57.

Parmet, Herbert S., and Marie B. Hecht. *Aaron Burr: Portrait of an Ambitious Man*. New York: Macmillan, 1967.

Philbrick, Norman, ed. *Trumpets Sounding: Propaganda Plays of the American Revolution*. New York: Benjamin Blom, 1972.

Quincy, Josiah. *Memoir of the Life of Josiah Quincy, Jun.* New York: Da Capo Press, 1971 (1825).

Roberts, Kenneth, ed. *March to Quebec: Journals of the Members of Arnold's Expedition*. New York: Doubleday, Doran, 1940 (1938).

Ryan, Dennis P., ed. *A Salute to Courage: The American Revolution as Seen through Wartime Writings of Officers of the Continental Army and Navy*. New York: Columbia University Press, 1979.

Sabine, William H. W., ed. *Historical Memoirs from 16 March 1763 to 25 July 1778 of William Smith*. 2 vols. New York, 1969–71 (1956–58).

Saffell, W. T. R. *Records of the Revolutionary War: Containing the Military and Financial Correspondence of Distinguished Officers*. Baltimore: Genealogical, 1969 (1894).

Schachner, Nathan. *Aaron Burr: A Biography*. New York: A. S. Barnes, 1961.

Shortt, W. T. P., ed. *Journal of the Principal Occurrences during the Siege of Quebec by the Revolutionists under Generals Montgomery and Arnold in 1775–1776*. London: Simpkin, 1824.

Smith, Justin H. *Our Struggle for the Fourteenth Colony: Canada and the American Revolution*. 2 vols. New York: G. P. Putnam's Sons, 1907.

Smith, Paul H., ed. *Letters of Delegates to Congress, 1774–1789*. 17 vols. Washington, D.C.: U.S. Government Printing Office, 1976– .

Sparks, Jared, ed. *Correspondence of the American Revolution*. 4 vols. Freeport, N.Y.: Books for Libraries Press, 1970 (1853).

Tappert, Theodore G., and John W. Doberstein, trans. *The Journals of Henry Melchior Muhlenberg*. 3 vols. Philadelphia: Muhlenberg Press, 1942–58.

Taylor, Robert J., ed. *Papers of John Adams*. 4 vols. Cambridge: Belknap Press of Harvard University Press, 1977–79.

Thomas, Howard. *Marinus Willett: Soldier, Patriot, 1740–1830*. New York: Prospect Books, 1954.

Trevelyan, George Otto. *The American Revolution*. 6 vols. New York: Longmans, Green, 1909–14.

Ward, Harry Parker, ed. "Diary of Captain John Fassett, Jr.," by Capt. John Fassett, Jr. In Harry Parker Ward, ed., *The Follett-Dewey Fassett-Safford Ancestry of Captain Martin Dewey Follett*. Columbus, Oh.: Champlin Printing, 1896.

Wharton, Francis, ed. *The Revolutionary Diplomatic Correspondence of the United States*. 6 vols. Washington, D.C.: U.S. Government Printing Office, 1889.

Whitworth, Rex. *Field Marshall Lord Ligonier: A History of the British Army, 1702–1770*. New York: Oxford University Press, 1958.

Willett, William M., ed. *A Narrative of the Military Actions of Colonel Marinus Willett*. New York: Arno Press, 1969 (1831).

Wolfe, James. *General Orders in Wolfe's Army during the Expedition up the St. Lawrence, 1759*. Quebec: Dawson, 1875.

Pamphlets

Austin, Jonathan Williams. *An Oration Delivered March 5th, 1778, at the Request of the Inhabitants of the Town of Boston to Commemorate the Bloody Tragedy of the Fifth of March, 1770.* Boston, March 9, 1778.

Brackenridge, Hugh M. [Henry] *An Eulogium of the Brave Men Who Have Fallen in the Contest with Great Britain: Delivered on Monday, July 5, 1779, before A Numerous and Respectable Assembly of Citizens and Foreigners, in the German Calvinist Church, Philadelphia.* Philadelphia, 1779.

Caldwell, Henry. *The Invasion of Canada in 1775: Letter Attributed to Major Henry Caldwell.* Quebec: Literary and Historical Society of Quebec, 1927 (1887).

Clements Library Associates. *Major General Richard Montgomery: A Contribution toward a Biography.* Ann Arbor: University of Michigan, 1970.

Dawson, Henry B. *The Sons of Liberty in New York: A Paper Read before the New-York Historical Society, May 3, 1850.* New York, 1850.

Fraser, Malcolm. *Extract from a Manuscript Journal Relating to the Siege of Quebec in 1759 Kept by Colonel Malcolm Fraser Then Lieutenant of the 78th (Fraser's Highlanders) and Serving in That Campaign.* Literary and Historical Society of Quebec. Quebec, 1927 (1868).

Hunt, Louise L. *Biographical Notes Concerning General Richard Montgomery, Together with Hitherto Unpublished Letters.* Poughkeepsie, N.Y., 1876.

[Paine, Thomas]. *A Dialogue between the Ghost of General Montgomery and an American Delegate in a Wood Near Philadelphia.* New York, 1865 (1776).

Smith, William. *An Oration in Memory of General Montgomery and of the Officers and Soldiers Who Fell with Him, December 31, 1775, before Quebec; Drawn up (and Delivered February 19th, 1776) at the Desire of the Honourable Continental Congress.* Philadelphia, 1776.

Articles

Ainslie, Thomas. "Journal of the Most Remarkable Occurrences in Quebec from the 14th of November, 1775, to the 7th of May, 1776, by an Officer of the Garrison." *Collections of the New-York Historical Society* 13 (1880): 175–236.

———. "Journal of the Most Remarkable Occurrences in the Province of Quebec from the Appearance of the Rebels in September 1775 until Their Retreat on the Sixth of May." In Frederic C. Wurtele, ed., *Blockade of Quebec in 1775–1776 by the American Revolutionists* (Quebec, 1906), 11–265.

Bushnell, Charles I., ed. "Women of the Revolution: A Series of Letters Written by Distinguished Women of That Period." *Historical Magazine* 5, no. 2 (February 1869): 105–12.

Cross, Urieh. "Narrative of Urieh Cross in the Revolutionary War." *Vermont Quarterly.* New ser. 15 (July 1947): 177–87.

Cullum, George W. "Major-General Richard Montgomery." *Magazine of American History, with Notes and Queries* 11 (April 1884): 273–99.

Danford, Jacob. "Quebec under Siege, 1775–1776: The 'Memorandums' of Jacob

Danford." Ed. John F. Roche. *Canadian Historical Review* 50 (March 1969): 68–85.

DeLabigarre, Peter. "Mr. DeLabigarre on Silk Worms." *Transactions of the Society for the Promotion of Agriculture, Arts, and Manufactures* 1, pt. 2 (1794): 172–97.

Delafield, John Ross. "Montgomery Place, Barrytown, New York." *American Architect* 132 (October 5, 1927): 421–26.

———. "Montgomery Place." *New York History* 20, no. 4 (October 1939): 445–62.

Douglas, William. "Letters Written during the Revolutionary War by Colonel William Douglas to His Wife Covering the Period July 19, 1775, to December 5, 1776." *New-York Historical Society Quarterly Bulletin* 12 (1929): 149–54.

Hall, William. "Colonel Rudolphus Ritzema." *Magazine of American History* 2 (1878): 163–67.

Hunt, Louise L. "General Richard Montgomery." *Harper's New Monthly Magazine* 70 (February 1885): 350–59.

Knollenberg, Bernhard. "The Revolutionary Correspondence of Nathanael Greene and John Adams." *Rhode Island History* 1 (April 1942): 45–55.

Knox, Henry. "Knox's Diary during His Ticonderoga Expedition." *New England Historical and Genealogical Register* 30 (1976): 321–22.

LeMoine, James M. "General R. Montgomery and His Detractors." *New York Genealogical and Biographical Record* 22, no. 2 (April 1891): 65–66.

———. "The Assault of Brigadier-General Richard Montgomery and Colonel Benedict Arnold on Quebec in 1775: A Red Letter Day in the Annals of Canada." *Proceedings and Transactions of the Royal Society of Canada* 5 (1899): 457–66.

Lindsay, William. "Narrative of the Invasion of Canada by the American Provincials under Montgomery and Arnold." *Canadian Review and Magazine* 3 (September 1826): 89–104.

Livingston, Henry Brockholst. "Journal of Major Henry Livingston of the Third New York Continental Line, August to December, 1775." Ed. Gaillard Hunt. *Pennsylvania Magazine of History and Biography* 22 (April 1898): 9–33.

Montgomery, Janet. "Reminiscences." Ed. John Ross Delafield. *Dutchess County [N.Y.] Historical Society Year Book* 15 (1930): 45–76.

Montgomery, Thomas H. "Ancestry of General Richard Montgomery." *New-York Genealogical and Biographical Society Record* 2 (July 1871): 123–30.

Morgan, Daniel. "An Autobiography." *Historical Magazine of America.* 2d ser., 9 (June 1877): 370–80.

Morison, George. "An Account of the Assault on Quebec, 1775." *Pennsylvania Magazine of History and Biography* 14 (1890): 434–39.

Nichols, Francis. "Diary Of Lieutenant Francis Nichols of Colonel William Thompson's Battalion of Pennsylvania Riflemen, January to September, 1776." *Pennsylvania Magazine of History and Biography* 20 (1896): 504–14.

O'Reilly, Vincent F. "Major-General Richard Montgomery." *American-Irish Historical Society Journal* 25 (1926): 179–94.

Porterfield, Charles. "Memorable Attack on Quebec, December 21, 1775: Diary of Colonel Charles Porterfield." *Magazine of American History with Notes and Queries* 21 (1889): 318–19.

Ritzema, Rudolphus. "Journal of Col. Rudolphus Ritzema of the First New York Regiment, August 8, 1775 to March 30, 1776." *Magazine of American History with Notes and Queries* 1 (1877): 98–107.

Todd, Charles Burr. "The March to Montreal and Quebec, 1775." *American Historical Register* 2 (1895): 641–49. Includes extracts of the diary of Col. Aaron Barlow.

Trumbull, Benjamin. "A Concise Journal or Minutes of the Principal Movements towards St. Johns; Of the Siege and Surrender of the Forts There in 1775." *Collections of the Connecticut Historical Society* 7 (1899): 137–73.

———. "Benjamin Trumbull Diary." *Bulletin of the Fort Ticonderoga Museum* (January 1927): 11–18; (July 1927): 26–33; (January 1928): 14–30; (July 1928): 21–35.

SECONDARY SOURCES

Books

Axtell, James. *The European and the Indian: Essays in the Ethnohistory of Colonial North America.* New York: Oxford University Press, 1981.

Baird, Henry M. *History of the Rise of the Huguenots of France.* 2 vols. New York: AMS Press, 1970 (1879).

———. *The Huguenots and Henry of Navarre.* 2 vols. New York: AMS Press, 1970 (1903).

Becker, Carl L. *The History of Political Parties in the Province of New York, 1760–1776.* Madison: University of Wisconsin Press, 1968.

Berg, Fred Anderson. *Encyclopedia of Continental Army Units.* Harrisburg, Pa.: Stackpole Books, 1972.

Bird, Harrison. *Attack on Quebec: The American Invasion of Canada, 1775.* New York: Oxford University Press, 1968.

Blackmore, Howard L. *British Military Firearms, 1650–1850.* London: H. Jenkins, 1961.

Bliven, Bruce, Jr. *Under the Guns: New York 1775–1776.* New York: Harper and Row, 1972.

Boatner, Mark M., III. *Encyclopedia of the American Revolution.* New York: David McKay, 1976.

Bonomi, Patricia U. *A Factious People: Politics and Society in Colonial New York.* New York: Columbia University Press, 1971.

Browne, James A. *England's Artillerymen: A Historical Narrative of the Services of the Royal Artillery, from the Formation of the Regiment to 1862.* London: Hall, Smart and Allen, 1865.

Bush, Martin H. *Revolutionary Enigma: A Re-appraisal of General Philip Schuyler of New York.* Port Washington, N.Y: Ira Friedman, 1969.

Cannon, Richard. *Historical Record of the Seventeenth, or the Leicestershire Regiment of Foot.* London: Parker, Furnivall & Parker, 1848.

Castries, Duc de. *The Lives of the Kings and Queens of France.* New York: Alfred A. Knopf, 1979.

Champagne, Roger J. *Alexander McDougall and the American Revolution in New York.* New York: Union College Press, 1975.

Coudy, Julien, ed. *The Huguenot Wars.* New York: Chilton, 1969.

Countryman, Edward. *A People in Revolution: The American Revolution and Political Society in New York, 1760–1790.* Baltimore: Johns Hopkins University Press, 1981.

Decker, Malcolm (Peter). *Brink of Revolution: New York in Crisis, 1765–1776.* New York: Argosy Antiquarian, 1964.

Gerlach, Don R. *Proud Patriot: Philip Schuyler and the War of Independence, 1775–1783.* Syracuse, N.Y.: Syracuse University Press, 1987.

Gilje, Paul A. *The Road to Mobocracy: Popular Disorder in New York City, 1763–1834.* Chapel Hill: University of North Carolina Press, 1987.

Guizot, François Pierre Guillaume. *A Popular History of France, from the Earliest Times.* 8 vols. New York: AMS Press, 1969 (1869).

Hatch, Robert M. *Thrust for Canada: The American Attempt on Quebec in 1775–1776.* Boston: Houghton Mifflin, 1979.

Higginbotham, Don. *Daniel Morgan: Revolutionary Rifleman.* Chapel Hill: University of North Carolina Press, 1961.

Hitsman, J. Mackay. *Safeguarding Canada, 1763–1871.* Toronto: University of Toronto Press, 1968.

Kane, Joseph Nathan. *The American Counties.* Metuchen, N.J.: Scarecrow Press, 1972.

Kierner, Cynthia A. *Traders and Gentlefolk: The Livingstons of New York, 1675–1790.* Ithaca, N.Y.: Cornell University Press, 1992.

Kim, Sung Bok. *Landlord and Tenant in Colonial New York: Manorial Society, 1664–1775.* Chapel Hill: University of North Carolina Press, 1978.

Lamb, Martha J. *History of the City of New York.* 3 vols. New York: A. S. Barnes, 1877–96.

Launitz-Schurer, Leopold S., Jr. *Loyal Whigs and Revolutionaries: The Making of the Revolution in New York, 1763–1776.* New York: New York University Press, 1980.

LeMoine, James M. *Quebec Past and Present: A History of Quebec, 1608–1876.* Quebec: A. Coté, 1876.

Lenk, Torsten. *The Flintlock: Its Origin and Development.* Ed. John E. Hayward. London: Holland Press, 1965.

McLennan, J. S. *Louisbourg from Its Foundation to Its Fall, 1713–1758.* London: Macmillan, 1918.

Malone, Dumas, ed. *Dictionary of American Biography.* 26 vols. New York: Charles Scribner's Sons, 1928–58.

Manucy, Albert. *Artillery through the Ages: A Short Illustrated History of Cannon, Emphasizing Types Used in America.* Washington, D.C.: National Park Service, 1949.

Mark, Irving. *Agrarian Conflicts in Colonial New York, 1711–1775.* Port Washington, N.Y.: I. J. Friedman, 1965.

Martin, James Kirby, and Mark Edward Lender. *A Respectable Army: The Military Origins of the Republic, 1763–1789*. Arlington Heights, Ill.: Harlan Davidson, 1982.

Mason, Bernard. *The Road to Independence: The Revolutionary Movement in New York, 1773–1777*. Lexington: University of Kentucky Press, 1967.

National Cyclopedia of American Biography. 63 vols. New York: James T. White, 1898–1984.

Nelson, Paul David. *The Life of William Alexander, Lord Stirling*. Tuscaloosa: University of Alabama Press, 1987.

———. *William Tryon and the Course of Empire: A Life in British Imperial Service*. Chapel Hill: University of North Carolina Press, 1990.

New York State. *The American Revolution in New York: Its Political, Social, and Economic Significance*. Albany, N.Y., 1926.

Parkman, Francis. *The Battle for North America*. Comp. John Tebbel. Garden City, N.Y.: Doubleday, 1948 (1851–92; 1902–03).

Peckham, Howard H. *The Colonial Wars, 1689–1762*. Chicago: University of Chicago Press, 1964.

Peterson, Harold L. *Arms and Armor in Colonial America, 1526–1783*. Harrisburg, Pa.: Stackpole Books, 1956.

Roberts, Ellis H. *New York: The Planting and the Growth of the Empire State*. 2 vols. New York: Houghton, Mifflin, 1887.

Roche, O. I. A. *The Days of the Upright: The Story of the Huguenots*. New York: Clarkson N. Potter, 1965.

Rossie, Jonathan Gregory. *The Politics of Command in the American Revolution*. Syracuse, N.Y.: Syracuse University Press, 1975.

Royster, Charles. *A Revolutionary People at War: The Continental Army and the American Character, 1775–1783*, Chapel Hill: University of North Carolina Press, 1979.

Stanley, George F. G. *Canada Invaded, 1775–1776*. Toronto: Hakkert, 1973.

Stephen, Leslie, and Sidney Lee, eds. *The Dictionary of National Biography*. 24 vols. London: Oxford University Press, 1968 [1949–50].

Thompson, James Westfall. *The Wars of Religion in France, 1559–1576*. New York: Frederick Ungar, 1957.

Todd, A. L. *Richard Montgomery: Rebel of 1775*. New York: David McKay, 1966.

Trevelyan, George Otto. *The American Revolution*. 6 vols. New York: Longmans, Green, 1898–1914.

Van Dyke, Paul. *Catherine de Medicis*. 2 vols. New York: Charles Scribner's Sons, 1922.

Ward, Christopher. *The War of the Revolution*. Ed. John R. Alden. 2 vols. New York: Macmillan, 1952.

Webb, E. A. H. *A History of the Services of the 17th (the Leicestershire) Regiment*. London: Vacher & Sons, 1911.

Williamson, Hugh Ross. *Catherine de' Medici*. New York: Viking Press, 1973.

Wilson, James Grant, and John Fiske, eds. *Appleton's Cyclopaedia of American Biography*. 7 vols. New York: D. Appleton, 1886–1900.

Wright, Robert K., Jr. *The Continental Army*. Washington, D.C.: U.S. Government Printing Office, 1986.

Wurtele, Frederic C., ed. *Blockade of Quebec in 1775–1776 by the American Revolutionists*. Port Washington, N.Y.: Kennikat Press, 1970 (1906).

Articles

Aimone, Alan C., and Barbara A. Aimone. "Organizing and Equipping Montgomery's Yorkers in 1775." *Military Collector and Historian: Journal of the Company of Military Historians* 28, no. 2 (Summer 1976): 52–63.

———. "Brave Bostonians: New Yorkers' Roles in the Winter Invasion of Canada." *Military Collector and Historian: Journal of the Company of Military Historians* 36, no. 4 (Winter 1984): 134–50.

American Scenic and Historic Preservation Society. "General Richard Montgomery and His Monument at New York." *Annual Report to the Legislature of the State of New York* (1916): 643–51.

Anderson, William J. "Canadian History: The Siege and Blockade of Quebec by Generals Montgomery and Arnold in 1775–76." *Literary and Historical Society of Quebec Transactions*. New ser., pt. 9 (1871/72): 49–71.

Boyer, Lee R. "Lobster Backs, Liberty Boys, and Laborers in the Streets." *New-York Historical Society Quarterly* 57, no. 4 (October 1973): 281–308.

Bredenberg, Oscar E. "The American Champlain Fleet, 1775–77." *Bulletin of the Fort Ticonderoga Museum* 12, no. 4 (September 1968): 249–63.

Burton, Robert. "Siege and Capture of Havana in 1762." *Maryland Historical Magazine* 4 (1909): 321–35.

Callahan, North. "Henry Knox, General Washington's General." *New-York Historical Society Quarterly* 44 (1960): 150–65.

Cash, Philip. "The Canadian Military Campaign of 1775–1776: Medical Problems and Effects of Disease." *Journal of the American Medical Association* 236, no. 1 (July 5, 1976): 52–56.

Flick, Alexander C. "General Knox's Ticonderoga Expedition." *New York State Historical Association Quarterly Journal* 9 (1928): 119–35.

Gardner, Asa Bird. "The New York Continental Line of the Army of the Revolution." *Magazine of American History* 7 (December 1881): 401–19.

Hitsman, J. Mackay, and C. C. J. Bond. "The Assault Landing at Louisbourg, 1758." *Canadian Historical Review* 35 (December 1954): 314–30.

Manders, Eric I. "Notes on Troop Units in the New York Garrison, 1775–1776." *Military Collector and Historian: Journal of the Company of Military Historians* 25, no. 1 (Spring 1973): 18–21.

Olm, Lee E. "The Mutiny Act for America: New York's Noncompliance." *New-York Historical Society Quarterly* 58 (1974): 188–214.

Poucher, John Wilson. "Dutchess County Men of the Revolutionary Period: Judge Robert R. Livingston, His Sons, and Sons-in-Law." *Dutchess County [N.Y.] Historical Society Year Book* 30 (1945): 54–74.

Quebec, E. P. "The Hundredth Anniversary of Montgomery's Death." *New Dominion Monthly* 17 (December 18, 1875): 397–404.

Robinson, Thomas P. "Some Notes on Major-General Richard Montgomery." *New York History* 37 (October 1956): 388–98.

Robson, Eric. "Purchase and Promotion in the British Army in the Eighteenth Century." *History.* New ser., 36 (February–June 1951): 57–72.

Varga, Nicholas. "The New York Restraining Act: Its Passage and Some Effects, 1766–1768." *New York History* 37, no. 3 (July 1956): 233–58.

Dissertations

Leroy, Perry Eugene. "Sir Guy Carleton as a Military Leader during the American Invasion and Repulse in Canada, 1775–1776." 2 vols. (Ph.D. diss., Ohio State University, 1960).

White, John Todd. "Standing Armies in Time of War: Republican Theory and Military Practice during the American Revolution." (Ph.D. diss., George Washington University, 1978).

Index

Abercromby, Gen. James, 22, 25
Adams, Abigail (Mrs. John Adams), 201 n. 31
Adams, John, 45, 77, 161, 163, 166, 168, 173
Adams, Samuel, 168
Ainslie, Capt. Thomas, 133–34, 139, 152, 153, 155
Albany, N.Y., 25, 125, 158, 180
Alexander, William (Lord Stirling), 195 n. 12
Allen, Col. Ethan, 57–58, 59, 76–77, 89–90; attack of Montreal, 101–4, 110–11, 115, 120–21, 206 n. 27
Amherst, Gen. Jeffery, 22, 24, 25, 31
André, Lt. John, 114, 212 n. 50
Antill, Edward, 152, 158, 159, 215 n. 35
Arnold, Benedict, 4, 157, 170, 199–200 n. 17; advance on Quebec, 104, 116, 127–28; attack of Quebec, 130, 134, 136, 137–150; argument for Canadian invasion, 76–77; cabal against, 137–38, 217 n. 16; capture of Ticonderoga, 57–58, 59, 75; continued siege of Quebec, 151–52, 156, 157–58; disgust with Continental army system, 69; promoted to Brig. Gen. to fill Montgomery's vacancy, 221 n. 14; retired to Montreal, 172, 173; selected for Canadian campaign, 86–87; wounded, 144, 155
Artillery (British), 21, 23

Artillery companies: New York, 82, 85, 98, 106, 108, 115, 127, 140, 144; Connecticut, 85, 87
Asia, 61, 62, 71
Austin, Jonathan Williams, 168
Austria, 18

Baker, Capt. Remember, 89–90
Baldwin, Simeon, 175
Barbados, 28
Barré, Isaac, 33, 38, 64
Bartlett, Josiah, 165
Bedel, Col. Timothy, 85, 98, 99, 100, 101, 103, 117–18, 123
Boston, Mass., 25, 41; siege of, 58, 71, 73, 124, 125, 127, 158–59, 174–75
Boston Massacre, 41, 43, 166, 168
Boston Tea Party, 41, 44
Bouchette, Jean Baptiste, 120
Brackenridge, Hugh Henry, *The Death of General Montgomery*, 4, 167–68, 224 n. 38
Braddock, Gen. Edward, 18, 19, 22
Bradstreet, Col. John, 32
British army: attitude toward colonial military, 66; battlefield tactics, 20–21; colonial attitude toward, 37, 40, 47, 66; grenadiers, 20, 23; light-infantry troops, 20, 28; ranger troops, 20; senior officer appointments, 193 n. 20
British (Royal) Navy, 22, 23–24, 28, 30
Brown, Capt. Jacob, 140, 141–42, 146

Brown, Maj. John, 57, 87, 90, 99, 100, 101, 102, 103, 105, 107, 118, 120, 127, 137–38, 209 n. 15
Bunker (Breeds) Hill, Battle of, 4, 49, 66, 73
Burgoyne, Gen. John, 173
Burke, Edmund, 3, 33, 38, 64, 169
Burr, Aaron, 175–76, 219–20 n. 38

Caldwell, Lt. Col. Henry, 129, 139, 142, 146, 152, 155
Calhoun, John C., 180
Campbell, Col. Donald, 143, 149–50, 152, 156, 157, 218–19 n. 28, 221 n. 14
Campbell, Maj. John, 103
Canada: American invasion of, 2, 19, 27–28, 59–60, 75, 77–78, 85–87; American withdrawal from, 172–74; strategic importance, 160–61
Canadians, 22, 27, 28, 75; militia in the British army, 112, 129–30, 146, 149; recruits for Montgomery's expedition, 109, 127, 138, 140, 141–42, 144; support for colonial resistance to Britain, 75–77, 85–86, 89, 90, 91, 92, 101–2, 129, 136, 173
Cape Diamond, 135, 138, 139, 140, 141–42, 146
Carillon, Fort, 25
Carleton, Gen. Guy, 3, 60, 76, 77, 85, 200 n. 22; attitude toward Indian allies, 86, 126; defense of Montreal, 102–3, 110–11, 112–13, 114, 118; defense of Quebec, 118–20, 126, 129–32, 134, 135–50, 157, 173; knighted, 174; preparation to defend Canada, 86, 99, 102, 204 n. 20; treatment of prisoners, 110–11, 154, 221 n. 11
Carroll, Charles, 163
Cavalry (British), 21
Chambly, 2, 28, 86, 91, 93, 99, 101, 109–10, 111, 112, 158, 173
Charles IX, King of France, 10, 11, 12, 13, 14
Chase, Samuel, 161, 163
Cheeseman, Capt. Jacob, 141, 148, 149, 154
Clermont, 36, 38, 39, 47, 177, 225–26 n. 17
Clinton, Gov. De Witt, 179, 180
Clinton, Col. James, 82, 108, 158, 222 n. 16

Coercive Acts, 41
Colden, Lt. Gov. Cadwallader, 52, 53–54, 55, 61, 197–98 n. 3
Coligny, Count Gaspard de, 10, 12
Committee of Correspondence, New York, 38
Condé, Prince de (Louis I de Bourbon), 10, 12
Connecticut militia, 60
Connecticut River, 26, 59
Continental army: adoption, 70, 73, 74; characteristics of soldiers, 81–82; egalitarian character, 81, 93, 107–8; makeup of leadership, 80–81; multisided character, 156–57; recruiting, 83, 158; sectionalism, 70, 105; senior officer ranking and promotion, 68–69; term of service, 83, 158–60, 162–63; training and discipline, 80, 81, 122–23, 124, 125; troop returns of Northern Department, 204–5 n. 21
Continental Association, 198–99 n. 9
Continental Congress, First, 41, 52, 76
Continental Congress, Second, 4–5, 6, 41, 53, 54, 55, 57, 59, 60, 61, 73, 74, 83, 103, 124, 173; directives for the invasion of Canada, 75, 76–77, 78, 136, 159; reaction to Montgomery's death, 159–64; selection of senior military commanders, 65–66, 68–70, 74, 202–3 nn. 8, 9
Cramahé, Lt. Gov. Hector, 129, 134
Crown Point, 22, 25, 26, 28, 75, 85, 88, 174

Dartmouth, Lord, 76, 111, 126
Dearborn, Capt. Henry, 147, 154
De Lancey family, 45–46, 48, 178
Despins, Jean Baptiste, 112, 114
Detroit, 32
Dinwiddie, Robert, 18, 27
Duane, James, 69, 80, 203 n. 10
Duquesne, Fort, 18, 22, 25
Dutchess County, N.Y., 38, 64, 68

East India Company, 43–44
Easton, Col. James, 57, 84, 98, 118, 119, 123, 127, 199–200 n. 17
Elizabeth I, Queen of England, 13
Enterprise, 87, 114

Fassett, Capt. John, 100
Forbes, John, 19, 22, 25, 26

Fort Royal, 28, 29
Fox, Charles James, 3, 33, 38, 64, 169, 194 n. 39
France, 17, 18, 19, 29, 31
Francis I, King of France, 9
Francis II, King of France, 11
Franklin, Benjamin, 5, 136, 163, 175
Fraser, Capt. Malcolm, 142
Fraser, Lt. Malcolm, 27
French and Indian Wars, 17, 36, 37, 47, 66, 77, 86
French army, 22, 23, 26, 28, 29
French navy, 22
French Wars of Religion, 11–15

Gage, Gen. Thomas, 76–77, 199–200 n. 17
Garretson, Catharine. *See* Livingston, Catharine
Gaspé, 110, 118, 119, 120, 127
Gates, Gen. Horatio, 66, 174; courted Janet Montgomery, 177–78, 202 n. 4
General Association, 198–99 n. 9
George I, King of England, 20
George III, King of England, 46, 59
"Glorious Revolution," 16
Golden Hill, Battle of, 42–43
"Grasmere," 176
Great Britain, 17, 18, 31–32
Green Mountain Boys, 57–58, 59, 75, 78, 85, 89, 98, 99, 101, 112, 123, 158
Greene, Nathanael, Gen., 168
Grenada, 29

Halifax, Nova Scotia, 21, 22
Hamilton, Maj. Isaac, 61
Hancock, John, 6, 73, 124, 163
Havana, Cuba, 29, 30
Hazen, Moses, 158, 159, 207 n. 30, 222 n. 16
Heath, Brig. Gen. William, 68–69
Henry, Priv. John Joseph, 144, 145–46, 153, 154, 157, 221 n. 10
Henry II, King of France, 9–10, 13
Henry III, King of France, 14
Henry IV, King of France, 15
Hinman, Col. Benjamin, 79, 84, 90, 92, 99, 105
Hobby, Maj. Thomas, 91
Holland House, 141
Holmes, Col. James, 125
Howe, Gen. George, 22, 25

Hudson Highlands strategy, 60, 78, 174, 200 n. 21
Hudson River, 25, 36, 60, 72, 77, 78, 168, 179, 180
Huguenots, military, 10–11, 12–13, 14, 15

"Ice battery," 134, 135
Indians, 22, 26, 27, 32, 60, 62, 74, 76, 77, 86, 87, 89, 91, 112, 126, 140, 144, 204 n. 19
Intolerable Acts. *See* Coercive Acts
Ireland, 8, 15, 16, 19, 21, 64, 67, 178
Isabella, Queen of Spain, 9
Isle aux Noix, 26, 28, 90, 92, 93, 95, 98
Isle La Motte, 90

Jackson, Andrew, 180
James II, King of England, 16
Jay, Sally Livingston (Mrs. John Jay), 176
John Street Riot. *See* Golden Hill, Battle of
Johnson, Col. Guy, 74, 76, 126, 203 n. 15
Johnson, John, 126
Jones, Thomas, 49–50

Keppel, Gen. George, (Earle of Albemarle), 29
Kingfisher, 71
King's Bridge, 36, 39, 60, 63, 74, 88
King's Swiss Guard, 12
Knox, Col. Henry, 125, 136

Lake Champlain, 26, 27–28, 60, 84, 85, 86, 87, 90, 92
Lake George, 25, 26, 60, 77, 84, 85
Lake Ontario, 27
Lamb, Capt. John, 53, 62, 81, 85, 98, 106, 108, 115, 121–22, 127, 134, 135, 140, 144, 146, 157, 213–14 nn. 15, 16, 219 n. 34
La Prairie, 100, 101, 103, 117, 118
Lasher, Col. John, 72–73
Laws, Capt. George, 147
Le Boeuf, Fort, 18
Lee, Gen. Charles, 66, 72, 123, 166, 202 n. 4
Lee, Richard Henry, 48
"Levelers." *See* New York, tenant riots
Lexington and Concord, 41, 53, 58
Liberty, 87
Liberty poles, 42–43
Lispenard, Leonard, 72, 73

242 · *Index*

Livingston, Catharine, 39–40, 78
Livingston-De Lancy political rivalry, 45–50
Livingston, Edward, 78, 180
Livingston Estate. *See* Clermont
Livingston family: marriages of sons and daughters, 194–95 n. 5; politics, 45–50; social attitudes, 39
Livingston, Capt. Henry (Harry) Beekman, 106, 205 n. 5, 210 n. 27
Livingston, Henry Brockholst, 211 n. 33
Livingston, Col. James, 90, 92, 103, 109, 118, 127, 140, 141, 142, 146, 206 n. 27
Livingston, Janet, 3, 36–37, 38, 39
Livingston, John, R., 49–50, 197 n. 30
Livingston, Lewis, 179–80
Livingston Manor, 38, 47
Livingston, Peter Van Brugh, 203 n. 12
Livingston, Philip, 38
Livingston, Robert, 38
Livingston, Robert Jr., 38, 197 n. 25; death, 49; support for independence, 49
Livingston, Robert R., 49, 67, 75, 80, 130, 141, 161, 164, 178, 197 n. 25; appointed to the Second Continental Congress, 53
Livingston, Judge Robert R., 3, 36, 48, 49, 78; attitude toward British soldiers, 37; background, 38; death, 49; during tenant riot, 47
Livingston, William, 48, 197 n. 28
London, 196 n. 20
Longueuil, 100, 103, 112, 113–14
Louisbourg, 25; siege of, 21, 22–24
Loyalists, 53, 57, 62, 64, 71, 74–75, 165, 166, 201 n. 33

MacLean, Col. Allan, 112, 118, 129, 146
Macpherson, Capt. John, 134, 141, 148, 149, 150, 154
Magra, Lt. Perkins, 40–41, 63, 67
Marlborough, Duke of, 16
Martinique, 28–29
Mary, 127
Mary, Queen of England, 13
Massachusetts Congress, 57, 58–59
Massachusetts militia, 57
McDougall, Alexander, 56, 62, 82, 84
Mead, Maj. Matthew, 91
Medici, Catherine de' (Catherine de Medicis), 9, 10, 11, 12, 13, 14
Meigs, Maj. Return J., 154

Mercer, Brig. Gen. Hugh, 224 n. 39
Michilimackinac (Michigan Territory), 36
"Mohawks." *See* New York Tea Party
Monckton, Gen. Robert, 26, 28, 29
Montcalm, Gen. Louis, 25, 27, 126
Montgomery, 168
Montgomery (Montgomerie), Col. Alexander, 8–9
Montgomery, Alexander John, 9, 16, 26–27, 193 n. 26
Montgomery, Count de (Gabriel de Lorges), 9–15
Montgomery, Hugh, 15
Montgomery, Janet, 32; as grande dame of Livingston and Montgomery families, 178–79; attended Washington's inauguration, 178; bade farewell to husband, 78; built Montgomery Place, 179; censure of Schuyler, 177; comments on grandfather, 49; comments on her husband's conversion to the whigs, 57; death, 180–81; embraced patriotism, 176–77; guardian of husband's memory, 175, 176, 177; included in husband's will, 88–89; instrumental in reinterrment of husband, 179, 180; personal philosophy, 40; reaction to husband's induction into the Continental army, 67–68; recalled husband's reaction to reluctance of social elite to serve in the Continental army, 81; relationship with Gates, 177–78; role as a woman, 40, 76; took charge of farmstead in husband's absence, 63, 176; visit to Ireland, 178
Montgomery, John (Richard's brother), 9
Montgomery, John (Richard's cousin), 35
Montgomery, Mary Franklin (Franklyn), 8, 9
Montgomery Place, 179, 180
Montgomery, Richard, 49; accompanied George Washington on visit to New York City, 72; adoration after death, 163–64; ancestry, 9–15; appointed Brig. Gen. in the Continental army, 65–68, 70–71; appointed Maj. Gen. in the Continental army, 150; appointed regimental adjutant in the British army, 27; as an American icon, 181; assumes command of Canadian expedition, 95–96; attack of Quebec, 1–3, 86–87, 122, 126–27, 128, 130–32, 133–50, 218 n. 25; attitude toward the social elite and military ser-

vice, 80; background, 2, 3; bade farewell to wife, 78; birth, 8, 191 n. 2; burial 3, 5, 153–54; capture of Montreal, 116–19; capture of St. Johns, 87–115; characteristic traits, 156–57; contribution to Canadian campaign, 173–75; courtship of Janet Livingston, 36–38; death, 2–3, 149, 219 n. 38; death used by Continental Congress, 6; disappointment with troop defections, 123; disgust with military service, 36; duty in the Seven Years' War, 19–32; education, 15; escaped death, 100–101, 134; estimation of Carleton, 126; eulogized in British Parliament, 3–4, 169; friendship with prominent Whigs, 33; heraldic armorial insignia, 15; impact on British perceptions of the Revolution 169–71; impression of Arnold's troops, 128; incorporated into patriotic propaganda, 167–69, 175; initial impression of Philip Schuyler, 66; involvement in the patriot cause, 45–50; joined British army, 15–16; lamented Ethan Allen's attack of Montreal, 103–4; leadership, 2, 100–101, 105, 107–8, 116–17, 121, 137, 143; life as a country squire, 41; marriage to Janet Livingston, 38–39; martyrdom, 4, 164; memorial service, 165–66; merged with Arnold's expedition, 128; migration to America, 35–36; monument, 5, 164–65, 175; naming of counties after, 6, 190 nn. 24, 25; nostalgia about former British army comrades, 40–41, 67; notion of honor, 68, 78; paucity of biographical studies of, 6; personal philosophy, 40; pragmatism, 108, 136–37; preparation for the invasion of Canada, 77–78, 83–85; promotion to lieutenant in the British army, 24; promotion to captain (company commander) in the British army, 29–30; reaction to death, 158, 159–60, 163; relationship with Arnold, 128, 137–38; relationship with Lamb, 121–22, 135; relationship with Schuyler, 87–88; relationship with Wooster, 111; remains reinterred, 179–80; resignation from British army, 34; sense of nationalism, 70; service in the N.Y. Provincial Congress, 51, 54, 55–64; stance on troop discipline, 84, 94–96, 98; suspicions of William Tryon, 75; tendered his resignation, 123–25 thoughts on eve of combat, 88, 141; troop description of, 127; unbiased standard of conduct for troops, 70, 105–6; uniqueness of service to the Revolution, 6–7, 174–75; view of recruits, 83; weary of field command, 123; whig sentiments, 56–57; wrote will, 88–89

Montgomery, Sarah (Lady Ranelagh), 9, 39, 88, 178

Montgomery, Thomas, 8–9, 194 n. 2

Montgomery's troops: attitude, 2; combat readiness, 2; New Englanders, 1; New Yorkers, 1; sectionalism, 2; short-term enlistments, 1

Montreal, 2, 22, 27, 28, 85, 86, 100, 102–3, 110, 112, 113, 115, 118, 122, 126, 128, 130, 133, 136, 158

Morgan, Capt. Daniel, 144–45, 146, 148, 155, 156, 157, 219 n. 30

Morris, Lt. Col. Arthur, 22

Morris, Gouverneur, 56

Mott, Capt. Gershom, 101, 208–9 n. 12

Mott, Capt. Samuel, 85, 87

Mott, Col. Samuel, 105

Muhlenberg, Henry, 165

Murray, Reverend James, 170

Musket, flintlock, 20–21

Mutiny Act. *See* Quartering Acts

Nairne, Capt. John, 146

Nancy, 196 n. 20

Nassau Street Riot. *See* Golden Hill, Battle of

Navigation Laws, 51

Necessity, Fort, 18

New Hampshire Grants, 59

New Hampshire Rangers, 85, 98, 99, 123

New York, 3, 25, 26, 28, 29, 31, 38; anti-British sentiment, 43; assembly, 47–48, 51; attitude toward rebellion, 41–42; committee development, 52–55; General Assembly, 52–55; General Association, 54–55; manorial tenancy system, 196–97 n. 23; militia, 63, 72–73; out ward, 194 n. 3; Provincial Congress, 51, 54–63, 65–67, 71–73, 74, 75, 77, 81, 82, 83–84; Provincial Convention, 53; recruitment of soldiers, 82; strategic location, 65; support of patriot cause, 60–61, 66, 83; tenant riots, 46–47

New York City, 5, 36, 42, 46, 60, 77, 78,
81, 82; British garrison, 61–62, 71;
crowd/mob activity, 53; George Wash-
ington's visit, 71–74
New York (Northern) Department, 73–74,
75, 77, 78
New York Restraining Act, 48
New York Tea Party, 43–45
Niagara, Fort, 26
Normandy, France, 8, 10, 12, 13, 15
North, Lord Frederick, 3, 169

Ohio Company of Virginia, 17–18
"Old sow," 106–7

Paine, Thomas, *The Ghost of General Montgo-
mery*, 4, 167, 223 n. 37
Parliament, 3, 42, 43, 44, 47, 51, 52, 76,
171
Patriots, 38, 41, 43–44, 53, 54, 55, 57, 64,
66, 71, 75, 76, 81, 164, 166, 201 n. 33
Philip II, King of Spain, 9
Phillips, Capt. Erasmus, 49–50
Pitt, William, 19, 25, 33
Pittsburgh, 25
Plains (Heights) of Abraham, 128, 134,
139, 141, 146, 167
Point aux Trembles, 127
Pomeroy, Seth, 68–70
Pontiac's Rebellion, 32
Prescott, Brig. Gen. Richard, 110, 120–21,
122, 127, 213 n. 13
Pres de Ville, 149, 152, 153, 156
Preston, Maj. Charles, 98–99, 100, 104,
106, 112, 113, 114–15, 208 n. 5
Price, James, 122, 158, 222 n. 16
Providence, 118
Prussia, 18

Quackenbush (Quackenbos), Capt. John,
98
Quartering Acts, 41, 47, 48
Quebec Act, 76, 85
Quebec City, 2, 5, 22, 24, 25, 26, 27, 86,
112, 118, 126; attack of, 1–3, 86–87,
122, 126–27, 128, 130–50, 173, 218 n.
25; Lower Town, 129, 138, 139, 140,
143, 144, 146, 147, 148, 150, 151, 155,
156; Palace Gate, 129, 130, 144, 147;
physical description of, 128–29; Prescott
Gate, 129, 140; St. John's Gate, 129,

134, 140, 146; St. Louis Gate, 129, 154;
strategic importance, 2, 126; Upper
Town, 129, 140, 145, 147, 155

Ranelagh, Charles, 9, 39
Reed, Lt. Col. Joseph, 161
Regiments, British Army, 19–20; 7th
(Royal Fusiliers), 99, 109; 17th, 16, 19,
22–24, 25, 26, 27, 28–31, 32, 41, 67,
192 n. 4, 202 n. 6; 26th (Cameronians),
99; 43d, 9, 27; 78th, 27; Royal Irish, 19,
21–22, 61, 67, 192 n. 5
Regiments, Continental Army: Connecticut, 60, 79–80, 84, 87, 90, 92; Massachusetts, 84, 98, 123, 140; New York, 77,
81, 82–83, 127, 138, 139, 141; 1st New
York (New York), 82, 84, 98; 2nd New
York (Albany), 82, 84, 87, 90, 92, 112;
3rd New York (Ulster), 82, 85, 108, 112;
4th New York (Dutchess), 82, 85, 111,
125; 5th Connecticut, 91, 108–9, 111,
114, 122 123, 126
Rhinebeck, N.Y., 39, 63, 64, 88, 176
Richbell, Gen. Edward, 19
Richelieu River, 60, 86, 90
Richmond, 180
Ritzema, Col. Rudolphus, 84, 92, 93, 105,
113, 122, 126, 159–60, 222 n. 21
Royal American Emigrants, 146
Royal Highland Emigrants, 99, 112, 118,
129, 142
Royal Savage, 92, 93, 94, 98, 108, 211 n. 33

St. Andrews School, 15
St. Bartholomew Massacre, 12–13
St. Joachim, 27
St. Johns, 2, 59, 86, 173; attack of, 87–115,
122, 135, 136, 141–42, 158
St. Lawrence River, 21, 25, 60, 77, 86, 87,
102, 112, 118, 122, 128, 130, 139, 142;
geographical directions, 193 n. 24
St. Lucia, 29
St. Paul's Church, 5, 175, 180
St. Roch, 128, 133, 134, 140, 141, 152
St. Vincent, 29
Scalping, 27
Schuyler, Maj. Gen. Philip, 4, 94, 95, 103,
110, 121, 123, 128, 136, 137, 158, 160,
165–66, 202 n. 2; accompanied George
Washington on visit to New York City,
71–74; commander of Northern Depart-

ment, 75; departed Canada, 95; deterioration of health, 92, 95, 125; maintained rear support for Montgomery, 100, 125–26; negotiations with Indians, 87, 89, 126; preparation for the invasion of Canada, 75, 77–78, 79–80, 83–87; problems with Wooster, 108–9; proclamation to the Canadians, 90, 92; reaction to Montgomery's death, 158; relationship with Montgomery, 87 88, 92; rejoined Montgomery, 90; selection as Maj. Gen., 66–67, 68, 70–71; tendered his resignation, 123–25

Scotch Royal Guard, 12
Scotland, 16
Sears, Isaac, 53, 62, 75, 204 n. 17
Senter, Dr. Isaac, 174
Seven Years' War, 3, 9, 17–32, 33, 126
Sherbrooke, John, 179
Sherman, Roger, 163
Smith, Michael, 43
Smith, William, 53–54
Smith, Reverend William, 165–66
Snow Fell, 118, 120
Sons of Liberty, New York, 43–44, 46, 53, 61, 81, 166
Sorel, 113, 119, 127
Spain, 18, 29, 31–32
Spanish army, 30
Spanish navy, 30
Stamp Act, 47, 51; Congress, 38, 46; crisis, 46
Staten Island, 28
Steuben, Maj. Gen. Frederick von, 107, 210–11 n. 30
Stopford, Maj. Joseph, 109–11
Strong, Capt. John, 99
Sugar Act, 51
Sullivan, Brig. Gen. John, 160, 173–74
Sweden, 18
Swiss mercenaries, 22

Tea Act, 43. *See also* Boston Tea Party and New York Tea Party
Tenant riots. *See* New York: Tenant riots
Thayer, Capt. Simeon, 139
Thomas, Gen. John, 68–70, 172–73
Thompson, James, 153, 179
Tice, Capt. Gilbert, 91, 206–7 n. 28
Ticonderoga, 22, 25, 26, 60, 62, 75, 77, 78, 84, 87, 109, 111, 136, 174; capture by Americans, 57, 59, 76–77, 78, 84, 85, 89, 90, 92, 98, 123, 125
Tories. *See* Loyalists
Treaty of Paris (1763), 31, 32
Trinity College, 5, 33
Trumbull, Benjamin, 122
Tryon, Gov. William, 52; return to New York City, 71–74, 204 n. 17

Valois-Hapsburg Wars, 11
Van Courtland, Pierre, 160
Vandeput, Capt. George, 61
Van Schaick, Col. Goose, 82, 84, 90

Wallace, Hugh, 73
Warner, Col. Seth, 59, 85, 89, 98, 101, 103, 112, 123, 158, 206 n. 27
War of the Spanish Succession, 16
Warren, James, 161
Warren, Maj. Gen. Joseph, 4, 168, 224 n. 39
Warren, Mercy Otis, 176, 180–81
Washington, George, 2, 18, 27, 79–80, 110; adopted Continental army, 70; appointed Commander in Chief, 65; assessment of importance of Canada, 161–62; denouncement of Ethan Allen, 103–4; directives concerning Canadian campaign, 86, 104, 136; inauguration as president, 178; persuaded Montgomery and Schuyler to remain in the army, 124–25; reaction to Montgomery's death, 158, 161–62; sense of nationalism, 70; visit to New York City, 71–74
Waterbury, Col. David, 84, 87
West Indies, 28, 29, 31
Wolf, Joshua, 139
Wolfe, Gen. James, 25, 26, 27, 126, 167, 169
Wolf's Cove, 141, 142
Whigs, 33, 167, 169, 201 n. 33. *See also* Patriots
Willett, Marinus, 53, 61–62, 81, 98
William III of Orange, 15, 16
Wool, Capt. Isaiah, 140, 152
Wooster, Gen. David, 74, 78, 108–9, 111–12, 114, 122–23, 126, 135, 152, 156, 157–58, 161, 172, 203–4 n. 16, 211 n. 34, 214 n. 21